Michigan
and the
Civil War
An Anthology

Michigan
and the
Civil War
An Anthology

A *Michigan History Magazine* Heritage Publication

Michigan Historical Center
Michigan Department of State
Lansing, Michigan
1999

Other Heritage Publications from
Michigan History Magazine

Father Marquette's Journal
When the Railroad Was King
Subject Guide to Michigan History Magazine, *1978-1994*
No Tears In Heaven
Michigan Soldiers in the Civil War
Roosevelt's Tree Army

Visit *Michigan History Magazine* and its growing family of
Heritage Publications on the World Wide Web:
www.sos.state.mi.us/history/mag/mag.html

Printed on recycled paper.
This product was not printed at Michigan taxpayer expense.
MHM-128 (7/1999)

Michigan Department of State
Candice S. Miller, Secretary of State

Table of Contents

Introduction

"Are they troops in which you can depend?"
"General, they are Michigan troops."
"But will they hold their ground?"
"Yes, General, they will hold against hell!"

This exchange between corps commander George Meade and division commander Charles Griffin occurred in the heat of battle at Chancellorsville on May 3, 1863. They were discussing the Fourth and Sixteenth Michigan infantries who Griffin handpicked to prevent a collapse in the Union line.

We discovered this anecdote, one of my favorites, as we produced "Thank God for Michigan," *Michigan History Magazine*'s 1998 collector's issue devoted to Michigan and the Civil War. The success of that 120-page magazine and the continued popularity of our book, *Michigan Soldiers in the Civil War*, by Dr. Frederick D. Williams, prompted us to publish *Michigan and the Civil War: An Anthology*.

Recognizing that Michigan's role in the Civil War has been underappreciated, we turned to back issues of *Michigan History Magazine* with one goal—to bring together, under one cover, stories that convey the experiences of the common soldier. As we gathered those articles, we added a few others that look at the state's contributions on the homefront or in the field of politics.

This first-ever anthology from the editors of *Michigan History Magazine* emphasizes the Michigan story through the diaries and letters of those men and women who witnessed the most pivotal event in American history. These articles will expand our understanding of Michigan's role in the Civil War and remind us that, as Lieutenant Samuel Hodgman of Climax recounted shortly after the bloody Battle of Antietam, war "is not very funny business."

Roger L. Rosentreter
July 1999

For the Glory of the Peninsular State

By Roger L. Rosentreter

*When their nation called, Michiganians left their jobs, homes and
loved ones to save the Union and, later, to emancipate four million
African American slaves. By the end of the Civil War, more than ninety thousand
Michigan men—and a few women—had put on the Union blue.*

On the evening of April 12, 1861, Sara and Carry Nelson had just finished their first musical piece when Detroit Theatre manager E. T. Sherlock rushed on stage with a telegram announcing that Confederate forces had fired upon Fort Sumter in Charleston Harbor, South Carolina. A momentary silence hung over the theatre and then the orchestra struck up "Yankee Doodle" and the audience rose as one and gave cheers for the Union.

Michiganians were not surprised that civil war had come to the nation. As early as January 1, 1861, Governor Austin Blair declared that South Carolina's secession two weeks earlier was "revolution, and revolution . . . is treason, and must be treated as such. It is not concession [to the South] that is needed now, it is patriotic firmness and decision." Blair offered "the whole military power of the State" to defend the Constitution. A month before the Fort Sumter firing, the Michigan legislature, observing that "a state of war actually exists," passed legislation allowing the governor to enlist two regiments for military service. But Michigan's response to the coming war was best characterized by U.S. Senator Zachariah Chandler, who boasted in February 1861, "Without a little bloodletting, this Union will not, in my estimation, be worth a rush."

Michigan responded quickly when war broke out. On April 15, 1861, Ann Arbor citizens gathered and adopted resolutions pledging support to Lincoln and appointed a committee to prepare for the inevitable call for troops. When news of Lincoln's call for troops reached farmers in Mecosta County, they stopped their threshers and headed for Big Rapids where a regiment was being formed. Less than a week after the surrender of Fort Sumter, George Woodruff, who died at the Battle of Gettysburg, informed Michigan's adjutant general, "Our

people are prepared for the most prompt and energetic action of the government, and are already becoming impatient of delay in forwarding volunteers." John Stephens, a Detroit merchant, offered three hundred dollars in gold to any member of Company A, First Michigan Volunteers, who would give up a position for his son. There were no takers. Sometimes, however, patriotism went too far. At one rally in Clinton, the newly appointed quartermaster general was injured when a cannon discharge shattered his railroad car window.

Michiganians flocked to join the army because, as Charles Woodruff of Niles noted, "Our country needs us." According to another Michiganian, "I enlisted because our rights, all that is dear to us as a nation, were in danger, and much as war is averse to my feelings, I do not wish to return until they are again rendered secure."

Besides a love of country, Michiganians responded eagerly to war because few thought it would last long or be bloody. A young Battle Creek woman told her brother who joined the army in August 1861, "I for one was glad when I heard of your decision to go . . . there seems but little fear of great loss of life from those craven, fear-stricken Southerners."

Initially, Michigan was asked to furnish a single one thousand-man regiment of infantry. Although the state treasury was empty, money from all across the state poured in to equip the unit. Michigan's most prominent antebellum politician, Lewis Cass, gave $3,000, but most contributors gave $25 to $50 each. In all, $81,000 was raised. Possibly short of cash, one Detroit man offered to contribute one ton of grapeshot, barreled and delivered to any city dock free of charge "for the express purpose of dealing death to all traitors."

On May 1 the First Michigan Infantry was mustered into federal service. Its companies, sent from nine different communities, included the Detroit Light Guard, the Jackson Greys and the Burr Oak Guard from St. Joseph County. The First camped at Detroit's Fort Wayne, where it began learning the rudiments of military discipline, the use of firearms and battle formations. On May 11 thousands of Michiganians gathered at Detroit's Campus Martius as the unit received its colors, which had been made by the ladies of Detroit. Two days later, the regiment left for Washington. According to tradition, President Lincoln greeted the First Michigan, the first unit to arrive in the capital from a western state, with, *"Thank God for Michigan."*

The federal government soon called for more troops, and each regiment went off to war in heroic fashion. A Niles company leaving to join the Second Michigan Infantry received a gala farewell. The city band played as a choral group sang "The First Gun is Fired; May God Protect the Right." The company received a flagstaff featuring an eagle clutching a scroll, which read, "At the Union's sacred call, Her patriotic sons will peril all." In accepting his regiment's colors at a camp near Adrian on June 21, Colonel Dwight A. Woodbury of the Fourth Michigan Infantry declared, "In whatever position we may be assigned, with our banner to cheer us, we will strive to do our duty as American soldiers." Woodbury, who died at the Battle of Malvern Hill, then turned to his men and added, "Let each man remember that he has the honor of Michigan in his keeping."

As Michigan units headed to the front they were well received. Perry Mayo noted, "We were nearly fed to death on the road through Ohio with pies, cakes, lemonade, and compliments. Flowers were showered on us at every station." His regiment's first casualty was a

Michigan's Civil War governor, Austin Blair was known for his staunch pro-Union views. At the outbreak of the war Blair accurately declared that it would be a long bloody conflict and offered the entire military might of the state to help defend the Constitution.

comrade who was so preoccupied with waving to the ladies on the platform that he failed to see an approaching post as his train pulled out of the station. Other unexpected pleasures occasionally greeted the Michiganians. Private Charles Robinson's regiment stopped at Jackson on its way to the nation's capital. The farm boy was approached by "a fine, sweet-looking girl" who grabbed him and planted four or five kisses right on his "trembling mouth." Momentarily stunned, the soldier regained his composure and "managed to get up enough to pay her back with the same kind of coin." The girl then released him. Robinson recalled, "I guess we both felt the better."

Michigan men made a positive impression as they traveled throughout the North. After the Fourth Michigan Infantry passed through Cleveland a local newspaper remarked, "When we see the splendidly armed and equipped regiments from Michigan pass through here . . . and compare their appearance with that of the regiments which recently left . . . Cleveland, it makes us ashamed of Ohio. . . . Why is it that Michigan in the same length of time, sends regiments to the field prepared for service, while Ohio, who boosts of her enterprise and patriotism, sends from her camps as regiments, mere mobs of men, half uniformed, unarmed, and wholly without drill." After passing through Cincinnati, a lieutenant in the Nineteenth Michigan overheard the women say Michigan boys were the "prettiest that ever passed through the city."

Although not yet soldiers, the Michiganians yearned for a fight. The state's earliest regiments were bivouacked around Washington during the early summer of 1861. There, the clamor of "On to Richmond" was exceeded only by the soldiers' self-confidence. After a visit from the army's commanding general, Winfield Scott, one Michigan private observed, "We can whip our weight in wild cats. . . . We stand open for any thing. *We fear nothing.*"

Soon the armies clashed and the war became horrible. After the Battle of First Bull Run, Philo H. Gallup, who "felt the wind" of a cannon ball fly past his face, noted the battlefield was "the awfuliest site that I ever sawe. . . . It is a site that nere can be for goten to see the men slatered some of them ded some of them with there legs off some with an arm off some with no hed some with their face off." From covering the retreat of a defeated Union army in the war's first battle, to capturing a fleeing Confederate president one month after Robert E. Lee's surrender at Appomattox Courthouse, Michiganians served courageously in all the war's campaigns.

Battlefield heroics captured headlines, but rebel bullets accounted for only a small portion of those Michiganians who gave their lives to save the Union. Measles, diarrhea, small pox, typhoid fever and pneumonia killed ten Michigan soldiers for every four who died on the battlefield. As early as December 1861 Ira Gillaspie of the Eleventh Michigan reported that "such coughing you never herd" made it impossible to hear drill commands. Diarrhea had a debilitating effect on the soldiers. As one Michiganian described, "There is but one kind of Sickness here, and that is the diarrhea, and everybody has it."

Michigan sent to war 50 percent of its military age male population. That included thirty-one regiments of infantry, eleven regiments of cavalry—more cavalry by proportion than any other Northern state—fourteen artillery batteries, and one regiment each of engineers and sharpshooters. Of the 92,220 Michiganians who served in blue, 14,855 died.

For all its discomfort and tragedy, the war was an exciting interruption in the comparatively humdrum lives of many young men. While stationed near Washington, Philo Gallup attended a dance in northern Virginia. Afterwards he wrote, there were "some of the pretys girls . . . I ever saw and good dancers they was to." Upon seeing the White House, another soldier noted "its splendor exceeds by far anything and all that I ever saw before." In December 1864 a Flint soldier who had just marched across Georgia with William Tecumseh Sherman thought Savannah was "a very nice place, the most so I think of any southern city that I have yet seen."

The war also led the soldiers to do things they never would have experienced back home—one of these was foraging. On their way to Gettysburg several soldiers of the Twenty-fourth Michigan stepped out of the ranks and confiscated a few geese. One of the drummers who placed two geese in his drum was soon reproached by Colonel Henry Morrow for not drumming. The boy drew his commander close and confessed, "Colonel, I have a couple of geese in here." Morrow straightened up and said with a glare, "If you're sick and can't play, you need not." That night both the colonel and the drummer had roast goose for dinner. As twenty-two-year-old Jan Wilterdink of the Twenty-fifth Michigan succinctly observed, "The war makes a decent person forget his Christian upbringing."

Campaigning in the South also gave many Michiganians their first personal exposure to slavery. From South Carolina, a Grand Rapids officer expressed shock at "the squalid Poverty & wretchedness of these helpless Beings, who are turned loose by the flight [of] their Masters." Describing slavery as "a profanity almost unpardonable," Captain John C. Buchanan wondered how slavery's "steady advance has been so long endured, countenanced & sustained."

In July 1863 Michigan was authorized to form a black regiment for federal service. Six months later, the First Colored Infantry toured southern Michigan cities where it was met by "enthusiastic crowds." The First (later the 102nd U.S. Colored Troops) saw only limited action, but one of its white officers claimed his men "fought with more determination than any troops I have seen or been in action with before." Another white Michiganian, who first believed blacks could not be good soldiers, grudgingly admitted not only do "they do nobly in battle," but they "vie with the Anglo-Saxon."

Michigan women also contributed to saving the Union. Thrust into leadership roles many had never experienced, they filled voids created by the men who went off to war. Shortly after the war started Michigan women organized relief societies to aid the soldiers. One of the largest and best state societies was the Michigan Soldiers Relief Association in Washington. Founded in 1861, it provided medical care and jellies, newspapers, books, canned fruit and comfort to Michigan men in hospitals in the Washington area. When U.S. Grant's 1864 campaign reached Petersburg, Virginia, in mid-1864 the Association maintained a depot and a soup house near the front, supplying Michigan men with fresh vegetables, tobacco, soft bread, clothing and a hot meal. Back home the relief societies raised money through dues, donations and sponsoring special events like ice cream socials. In late September 1864 a State Sanitary Fair (as they were known) in Kalamazoo netted over ninety-six hundred dollars for soldiers' aid.

Colonel Dwight A. Woodbury of Adrian was killed while rallying the Fourth Michigan Infantry during the Battle of Malvern Hill on July 1, 1862. One year later his successor, Colonel Harrison Jeffords of Ann Arbor, was killed during the Battle of Gettysburg while saving the flag that Woodbury swore to protect.

Some Michigan women took a more active role in the war. Dressed as a man and using the alias Frank Thompson, Sarah Emma Edmonds spent two years with the Second Michigan Infantry. She often acted as a spy, with her most effective disguise being that of a woman. Sarah deserted in 1863 when an injury would have led to hospital confinement and inevitable disclosure of her sex. In the 1880s she revealed her identity to her war comrades, had the desertion charge erased from her record, received a military pension and became the only female member of the postwar Grand Army of the Republic.

Elmira Brainard of Lapeer was the matron of the Seventh Michigan Infantry until orders prohibited women from serving with the regiments. Undaunted, she became an agent for the Michigan Soldiers Relief Association and visited hospitals in the Washington area distributing delicacies to wounded Michigan soldiers until the war's end. She accepted no pay for her services. Annie Etheridge, who went off to war with the Third Michigan Infantry, was the equivalent of a modern combat medic. Many times, she aided wounded soldiers back from the fighting. Annie, who received one of the war's few decorations for bravery, was mustered out of federal service in July 1865. As one historian later noted, "Few soldiers were in the war longer, or served with so slight intermissions, or had so little need of rest."

The closest thing to a rebel attack on Michigan occurred along the Canadian border near Detroit. In September 1864 Confederate agents planned to seize the fourteen-gun USS *Michigan* and free the three thousand Confederate officers imprisoned on Johnson Island near Sandusky, Ohio. On September 19, 1864, Charles H. Cole, a former rebel cavalryman disguised as a Pennsylvania oil speculator, was invited to dine aboard the *Michigan* where he planned to drug the dinner wine. On that same day, another vessel, the *Philo Parsons*, left Detroit for Cleveland. By the time the *Philo Parsons* reached Sandusky Cole's accomplices seized control of the sidewheeler. They awaited Cole's signal, which never came because an informant had talked and Cole was arrested. The mission was aborted and the *Philo Parsons* headed back to Detroit. It was scuttled near Sandwich (present-day Windsor) and the rebels escaped.

As the war dragged on, the earlier appeal of soldiering was lost amidst the miserable conditions, numerous battlefield setbacks and deaths of comrades. In December 1863 the Seventh Michigan Infantry returned home for a thirty-day furlough with only 160 of the original 1,000 men who went to war in August 1861. Captain Sam Hodgman was told by friends that he looked ten years older than when he had entered in 1861. The lingering effects of typhoid fever and the pain of leg wounds he had received at Antietam prompted the Climax native to admit he was "pretty well worn." He soon resigned his commission.

Many others refused to go home until the job was finished. One veteran admitted, "We don't think we can whip everybody as we used to, [but] we are willing to try anything which occasion requires." After over two years in the army, Henry Potter of Ovid declared, "We came down here to fight for the preservation of the Union, to put down the Rebellion which had broken out to destroy it. As long as the War was carried vigorously . . . we are satisfied." Another Michiganian noted in early 1865, "I think much of home but I wish to see what has caused me to run risk of my life through to a final end."

Understandably, the end of the war was greeted with relief. After hearing of Lee's surrender on April 9, 1865, Private David Lane of the Seventeenth Michigan recorded, "Everyone is wild with joy. As for myself, I cannot write! I cannot talk; only my glad heart cries "'Hosanna! Hosanna! in the Highest, the Highest!'" Charles Woodruff, who served with the Twenty-fifth Michigan, noted that after a courier brought the news of the surrender, "The men were wild with joy. Hats, haversacks, and knapsacks flew in the air in all directions. Officers were caught up by the men and carried upon their shoulders. . . . The greatest uproar imaginable took place. It seemed as if the men could not make noise enough."

The tragic assassination of Abraham Lincoln less than a week later placed a temporary pall over the end-of-the-war celebration. One Michiganian who had enlisted almost three years earlier claimed the assassination "caused each soldier's cheek to blanch, as if in the presence of some dire calamity." James Greenlach could scarcely think of the president's death without his eyes "being blinded with tears." The Flint corporal added that he would "cheerfully" stay in the service another year if it would somehow return this "great and good man."

Michigan paid special tribute to the slain leader. On April 19 funeral services were held in towns and cities all across the state. A week later, Detroit witnessed the largest demonstration in the city's 164-year history. A two-mile-long procession, described by the *Detroit Free Press* as a "moving panorama," was highlighted by a special, elaborate hearse built by craftsmen at the Detroit and Milwaukee Railroad. When the procession reached Campus Martius the Reverend George Duffield of the city's First Presbyterian Church led the assemblage in prayer. Then, the thirty thousand people who had gathered to pay their last respects sang the "Dirge," a specially composed piece sung to the tune of "Home Sweet Home."

The death of a beloved leader, however, could not stop Michigan's boys in blue from expressing joy over the war's end. Michiganians marched proudly at the grand reviews of Northern armies in Washington in late May 1865. As the veterans began arriving in Michigan they were joyously met by local citizens. From June 1865 until June 1866 over twenty-three thousand soldiers were fed and entertained at a Michigan Central Railroad warehouse in Detroit.

On June 10, 1866, the last Michigan volunteers were mustered out of federal service. On Independence Day

Annie Etheridge served as a nurse with the Third Michigan Infantry and the Fifth Michigan Infantry. During battle she was often risking her life at the front caring for wounded Michiganians.

the colors of the Michigan regiments were formally presented to Governor Henry Crapo at a ceremony in Detroit. The veterans than marched down to Campus Martius where General Orlando Willcox, who had commanded the First Michigan Infantry five years earlier, addressed them. He concluded, "I have seen the finger of providence through the thick smoke of battle, and now that the dark curtain is lifted, and the sun of victory breaks through in meridian splendor, I have more confidence than ever in our destiny. We have tried to do our duty, and we have done no more than that duty which every citizen owes to a free and fraternal government." Willcox symbolically surrendered the flags, adding, "We shall ever retain our pride in their glorious associations, as well as our love for the old peninsular state."

Profane, Hard Drinking & Eternally Grim

By Maria Quinlan Leiby

*Tall and bulky, with a voice to match, United States Senator
Zachariah Chandler refused to compromise his beliefs in the Constitution
and the Union. A Detroit businessman, Chandler helped establish
the Republican party and devoted the rest of his life to it.*

On March 12, 1858, Michigan's junior senator rose to present his maiden speech. Addressing the question of the admission of Kansas into the Union under the pro-slavery Lecompton Constitution, he began deferentially. He had

intended to leave the subject to older and abler and more experienced colleagues; but the occasion seems to me to be so great, and the consequences which may result from our decision so dangerous, that I cannot permit this bill to pass without, at least, entering my protest against it.

Quoting statutes, court cases and other documents, he argued the illegality of the Lecompton document in accepted senatorial fashion. But he also announced the arrival of a new breed of Northern legislator in tones more typical of his future speeches:

The race of Union-whiners, the old women of the North, who have been in the habit of crying out 'the Union is in danger,' have passed off the stage. . . . They were ready to compromise any principle; anything to save the Union. Sir, the men of the present day will compromise nothing. They are Union-loving men; . . . they will sacrifice anything but principle to save the Union.

The man who so boldly dismissed the generation of Daniel Webster and Henry Clay was Zachariah Chandler. A self-made Detroit businessman, Chandler helped establish the Republican party and would devote himself to its interests for twenty-five years.

Chandler was born in New Hampshire in 1813. Growing up in the staunchly Presbyterian community of Bedford, he was known as a good student, a champion hay mower and "the best wrestler in town." At the age of twenty, after trying his hand a little at school teaching and store clerking, he joined the settlers heading for Michigan.

Chandler's initial business venture in Detroit began as a partnership with his brother-in-law in a small general store. By 1836 he was the sole proprietor of a growing business. After weathering the panic and depression of the late 1830s, he shifted his enterprise to wholesaling and became "independently and permanently rich."

Despite his success in a growing city, he retained the unaffected common sense and good humor that had gained him popularity among the Bedford farm boys. A sociable man, he enjoyed a good party or a game of whist. He also was a major benefactor of the Fort Street Presbyterian Church.

As he prospered, Chandler began taking an interest in public affairs. He traveled about the state's more settled southern region, familiarizing himself with the major towns and making connections with their businessmen. A staunch Whig, Chandler did not seek public office until he defeated six-term incumbent Detroit mayor John R. Williams in 1851. Unable to overcome the state's strong Democratic loyalties, Chandler lost the governor's race the following year, but he outpolled the other Whigs on the ballot.

With the founding of the Republican party in 1854, Zachariah Chandler became a major figure in Michigan politics. He campaigned hard for the state ticket in both 1854 and 1856, building the support he needed to win nomination and election to the U.S. Senate in 1857. Chandler served three consecutive terms in the Senate (1857-75); he returned to begin a fourth term shortly before his death in 1879.

Both Chandler's physical size and forthright personality contributed to his impression as a speaker. He was a large man, tall and bulky, with a voice to match. His gestures were "ungainly" rather than "graceful." A contemporary evoked his speaking style in a memorial address after his death:

They [his audiences] understood what he said and knew what he meant. He threw himself into their modes of thought and habits of speech; he culled his illustrations mainly from common life. If he sacrificed anything, it was rhetorical elegance, never force; his one aim was to compel conviction.

The simplicity of his diction was a prime element and secret of his power. He did not speak as one who had to say something, but as one who had something to say and whose whole aim was to say it well, with clearness, plainness, force and effect. If he could not have both weight and luster, he would have weight.

Chandler's speeches reflect a simple but deeply held political faith. He believed in the Constitution and the Union. His conviction that the Republican party was the only one committed to supporting both was based, he believed, on common sense.

Chandler's political faith, unlike Abraham Lincoln's, was not expressed in religious terms. There was no divine being hovering in the background of his speeches. The Michigan senator spoke to and about men who worked out their own destinies.

Given this attitude, it is not surprising that religious images were rare in Chandler's speeches and were most commonly biblical allusions rather than controlling metaphors. In 1861 and again in 1879, he found "*Mene, mene, tekel, upharsin*" written, not on the wall of King Belshazzar's banquet hall, but all over the Democratic party. A digression on civil service reform in an 1874 speech argued that if the existing system—the spoils system—produced no more than one dishonest official in twelve, then it equaled Christ's record in selecting apostles and should be good enough. Images such as this, however, did nothing to alter Chandler's overall emphasis on self-reliance rather than divine intervention.

At the same time, the senator's speeches were shaped by a stark morality that may have been rooted in his Calvinist religious affiliation. Anything that was not right was unequivocally wrong. Chandler saw no middle ground, no room for compromise. Arguing against accepting the Lecompton Constitution, Chandler revealed his overall view of the U.S. Constitution:

Although I am not a lawyer, I wish to refer to two or three clauses of the Constitution of the United States; for I claim that it is so plain in language, and its intent so transparent, "that the wayfaring man, though a fool, need not err therein." I do not believe that it requires any hair-splitting of lawyers to comprehend that immortal instrument, the Constitution of the United States.

Chandler believed that simple common sense revealed the Supreme Court was standing the Constitution on its head in the Dred Scott decision: "It does not require a lawyer, in my estimation, to show that instrument is not what they [the Court] are attempting to make it, and what the framers of it abhorred, a pro-slavery instrument."

Prior to the outbreak of the Civil War, the Michigan senator spoke again of the need to uphold the Constitution. Negotiating with the seceding states—"traitors in thought, in heart and in act"—would reduce that document to meaninglessness: "Sir, I would rather join the Camanches [*sic*]; I will never live under a Government that has not the power to enforce its laws."

The principles of his political faith led Chandler to attack regularly both Democrats and white Southerners. He was characteristically blunt and emphatic in expressing his opinions. Before the outbreak of hostilities, Chandler was convinced that Southerners were engaged in a conspiracy to spread slavery throughout the nation. The Lecompton Constitution was "one of a series of aggressions on the part of the slave power." He argued that not merely the effect, but the actual intent, of the Dred Scott decision was to legalize slavery everywhere in the country. But that was not all:

After having established the property clause, and carried slavery all over these United States, there is something left yet to be done. The intention is then—it has ceased to be problematical—to open the African slave trade. Why not give us the whole dose at once—property clause, African slave trade, and all?

With the country on the brink of war, Chandler accused the Democrats of deliberately weakening the government's financial and strategic position in preparing for secession:

Sir, what is the history of the Democratic party for the last four years? When James Buchanan, four years ago, took possession of the Government, your Treasury was full. . . . How stands it now? Your Treasury is not only bankrupt, but your credit is destroyed. The very men who are preaching secession and disunion have been robbing you throughout the length and breadth of this land.

The passage of another decade did nothing to change his view of Southerners or Democrats. In 1872 he still blamed "the whole Democratic party of this nation" for the Civil War.

In 1872 Chandler spoke out vehemently against lifting the legal and political disabilities imposed on Southerners by the Fourteenth Amendment. Those Confederates who had shown "repentance" had already been pardoned; the rest "are as bitter rebels as they were when they wore the rebel gray with muskets pointed at the loyal heart of this nation." The Republicans, however, "not only stood by the Constitution, but . . . saved the Constitution." He lectured the Democrats:

Detroiter Zachariah Chandler helped found the Republican party in 1854 and three years later he was elected to the U.S. Senate. Chandler served three full terms as a U.S. senator.

swore before Almighty God that I would support the Constitution of the United States. . . . During four years I sat in this body with Mr. Jefferson Davis and saw the preparations going on from day to day for the overthrow of this Government. With treason in his heart and perjury upon his lips he took the oath to sustain the Government that he meant to overthrow.

After reminding his listeners of the Civil War's tragic human costs and expressing shock at hearing "a living rebel eulogized on the floor of the Senate," Chandler concluded that Davis was "a man whom every man, woman, and child in the North believes to have been a double-dyed traitor to his Government." Although a previous motion to eliminate benefits for all former Confederates had failed, the exclusion of Jefferson Davis passed.

In Chandler's plain, straightforward language one finds few of the literary devices employed by more self-consciously rhetorical speakers of the nineteenth century. Irony was his primary literary weapon, and he used it effectively. Sometimes it was a quick, sharp dig. He described at some length Michigan's wildcat banking law, which "authorized everybody everywhere to start a bank and furnish more money" and flooded the state with worthless currency. Chandler then commented, "Well, sir, you can see at a glance that the State of Michigan needed more money." After assailing the Democratic party's patriotism and fiscal management, he reassured its members, "I do not want our Democratic friends to be discouraged." Early in his Lecompton speech, he reviewed the history of the slavery issue in national debate. The Northwest Ordinance of 1787 was "a finality upon the slavery question. It settled that question

> You and your party would have overthrown the Government, and in so doing you would have overthrown the Constitution; and every shred of it that is left you owe to us, and you ought to get down on your knees and thank us for saving what we did.

Chandler's belief in the Southern conspiracy against the Constitution remained as strong as ever when he reentered the Senate in 1879. When Democrats argued against excluding former Confederacy president Jefferson Davis from his Mexican War pension benefits, Chandler countered with a short, extemporaneous outburst that became his best-known speech:

> Twenty-two years ago to-morrow . . . I, in company with Mr. Jefferson Davis, stood up and

forever." The Missouri Compromise of 1820 was "another finality."

On other occasions Chandler used repeated irony to emphasize his point. In 1862, when he attacked George McClellan's generalship of the North's Army of the Potomac, he noted the general's failure to follow up on gained advantages:

> What did we do? We found the worst swamp there was between Richmond and Williamsburg, and sat right down in the center of it and went to digging . . . digging in front of no intrenchments [*sic*] and before a whipped army of the enemy. We waited for them to recruit, we waited for them to get another army.

Following McClellan's victory at the Battle of Fair Oaks, Chandler queried: "And what did we do then? We found another big swamp, and we sat down in the center of it, and went to digging." He continued: "Fair Oaks was lost; that is to say we won a brilliant victory, but it did us no good; we did not take advantage of it. Of course it would have been very unfair to take advantage of a routed army; it would not have been according to our strategy. We magnanimously stopped, and commenced digging."

Although Chandler was not actively engaged in commerce during his Senate years, he remained a businessman to the core. He took as much interest in the financial side of the war as in the military and was justly proud of his role in establishing a national banking system:

> Then, again, the great national banking system, the best the world has ever seen, or perhaps ever will see, a system that, in my humble judgement, will be adopted by every commercial nation under heaven before ten years shall have rolled around . . . was a part of the mission of this Republican party.

As Chandler saw it, repaying the national debt was also part of that mission. The Democrats advocated repudiation, so it was up to the Republicans to "save the national honor." He was not loath "to boast a little" over the fact that his party had reduced the debt while cutting taxes.

Chandler's business background was also evident in his language. He was especially fond of the word "fraud." One basis for his opposition to the Lecompton Constitution was that "the whole matter was conceived and executed in fraud." The process by which it was voted upon was "a fraud from the beginning to the end." Popular sovereignty was a "great fraud upon the North" and the Missouri Compromise was "the greatest fraud ever perpetrated before the eyes of this nation." In 1861 he found the idea of continued compromise with the seceded South outrageous. He believed they had been planning to break up the Union all along. "But, sir, this is all a fraud; there is no sincerity in it." And again, in reference to the disputed presidential election of 1876:

> A great deal has been said about fraud; and I suppose you have all heard the word used. I had the honor of having a little something to do with the election of 1876. It was an election on one side of fraud and violence, and without any exception (and I say it deliberately after mature consideration) the greatest fraud, in my judgment, that ever was seen on earth was Samuel J. Tilden. I ran that campaign to a certain extent, as chairman of the national committee, and we heard the cry of "fraud, fraud, fraud." But the fraud was on the other side.

The validity of his accusations aside, Chandler clearly relished the word. Rarely, if ever, did he use synonyms such as deceit or trickery but remained with "fraud" and its connotations of dishonesty in business.

Zachariah Chandler maintained his political faith unshaken to the end of his life. In accepting nomination to the Senate in 1879 he said, "I am not here to apologize or explain anything that I have ever said or done in a public capacity. . . . Never during my political career in the senate of the United States have I uttered a sentiment or cast a vote that I would alter, explain, or change in any regard." He still believed that the Republican party was "devoted to freedom, to freemen, to free thought, free speech, and free exercise of republican institutions." And Chandler still vilified the South and the Democratic party. With both houses of Congress under Democratic control, he pledged himself ready to join with his fellow Republicans "to rescue from the grasp of rebels and rebel brigadiers the capitol of the nation."

Zachariah Chandler stood for laudable principles during his career. He refused to allow constitutional compromise to become capitulation. He advocated enlistment of blacks in the army and black suffrage before most politicians were ready to accept either. After the war Chandler condemned the intimidation and harassment of blacks by Southern whites. But his assumption that right was entirely on his (and his party's) side meant that those holding other views were not merely political adversaries but mortal enemies. His rigid partisanship led him to seek Southern humiliation rather than reconciliation.

It was in his approach to postwar reconstruction of the South that Chandler differed most markedly in both substance and style from the preeminent Republican of his day, Abraham Lincoln. Although the two had differed previously, they worked together in putting down the rebellion. In addition, Chandler helped unify the party to support the president's reelection. By early 1865, however, the government's attention was beginning to focus on policies for the postwar period that seemed at hand. The constitutional principles around which Republicans had earlier rallied appeared secure. What was now at issue was how the two sections of the country were to be reunited under one government.

Although Lincoln did not live to confront Chandler at his most virulent, the gulf between their approaches to reconstruction was already clear before the president's death. To say that Lincoln was more conciliatory than his Michigan colleague is an understatement. Lincoln associated morality with issues rather than

with any party and had thus always been less partisan than Chandler. Even in campaign speeches, he never attacked his opponents with the harshness that Chandler routinely used. Lincoln's recognition of ambiguity in politics and life and his balance of reason and emotion were alien to his colleague. Although Chandler pronounced Lincoln's second inauguration "brief and good," he was not truly in sympathy with the president's conciliatory tone. In contrast to most of his fellow Republicans, Chandler took Lincoln's assassination in stride, telling his wife, "I believe that the Almighty continued Mr. Lincoln in office as long as he was useful."

Zachariah Chandler died suddenly in late 1879. Future president James Garfield memorialized him as one of the "Cyclopean figures of history." This was meant as a compliment to the power of the Michiganian's oratory, but it was apt in another sense as well. The Cyclops viewed the world through a single eye in the center of his forehead. Zachariah Chandler was cyclopean not only in his forceful speaking, but in the narrow range of his vision as well.

Bound to See the President

Edited by Frank L. Byrne

*Few Civil War soldiers had the honor of meeting President Abraham Lincoln.
In a rare visit to the White House, Mount Clemens resident Julian Axtell
of the First Michigan Infantry not only met the president
but also caught a glimpse of the First Family.*

Abraham Lincoln's accessibility to the public is well known. His secretaries frequently complained of the amount of time he devoted to interviews with a stream of callers. His waiting room was often so crowded that men of prominence found it difficult to work their way into the presidential presence. Nevertheless, as the following letter indicates, it occasionally was possible for even the humblest soldier without the slightest excuse of business to drop in on his commander in chief. The lucky private's satisfaction is evident. Also implicit is the benefit Lincoln derived from his visit. While pleasing several constituents, the nation's master politician simultaneously continued his ceaseless probing of public opinion, both military and civilian.

The author of this letter, Julian H. Axtell, was born in Morristown, New Jersey; moved when young to Mount Clemens, Michigan; and was a medical student at the University of Michigan before the Civil War. In 1861, at the age of twenty-two, he joined the First Michigan Volunteer Infantry Regiment. During his military service, he worked at times in hospitals but more often was in or near the principal battles in the East. In 1862 he was promoted to corporal and a year later to first sergeant. During nearly four years in the army, he suffered only two slight wounds, but near the war's end he was seriously wounded and discharged a few months later as partially disabled.

In 1864 Axtell married Electa M. Whitney, the addressee of this letter and his former pupil. Returning to the University of Michigan, Axtell graduated in 1866 and practiced medicine. Increasingly crippled by his wound, Dr. Axtell died of its effects at Mount Clemens on October 16, 1872. Through the long years before her own death in 1926, his widow treasured relics of her soldier-suitor: his chevrons, bullet-torn scraps from his uniform and his portraits and letters, including the one printed here. Axtell had written this letter on a sheet patriotically headed with a picture of a knight standing on a rock labeled "Michigan" and pointing to the state's coat of arms superimposed on a flag and constellation of stars spelling the word "Union."

• • • • •

Kalorama heights
near Washington, D.C.
Sept 23rd 1861

Dear Lettie,

I wrote you one letter since I came down here, but through mistake directed it to Mt. Clemens so thinking perhaps you would not get it soon I take this opportunity to write again. I am sitting on a trunk with a drum in my lap writing on the head of it.

We are now encamped about 2 miles from the capital, on the Maryland side of the Potomac but expect soon to cross over into the sacred soil of Verginia as yet the regt. is without arms but will probably get them to day.

I wrote to you from Elmira and again on Saturday morning from Washington, the first letter no doubt you have recd. and possibly the last. On Saturday [September 21] I got permission to run around town a little.

I went to the capital, and all through it or at least as much of it as I had time to see which was a small part. I came to the conclusion that it was quite a house, from there we walked up Pennsylvania Ave. to the White House, and as some men were at work in the hall we got permission to go through part of the house. While we were there Mrs. Lincoln came home from a drive. She is a very pretty woman a good deal younger than Old Abe, and very agreeable to[o] I should think tho. I did not speak to her myself, but heard her conversing with some gentlemen. I also saw one of her children a little boy about 6 years old he had on a suit of compleat Zouave uniform & carried a little gun, but I was bound to see the president before I left. The servent said he was out at the war department and would be back in about 1/2 an hour if we would wait perhaps we might see him when he came, but the old rogue stole a march on us and came in the back way. The servent asked us what regt. we belonged to we told him the Mich. 1st he told us if that was so he thot we could see him for he liked the 1st when they were down before, and perhaps would put him self out so far as to see us. And bid us follow him [;] we did so, and entered a large room in the middle of which stood a large table covered over with papers, and the president sat beside it writing. The servent said "here are two boys of the Mich. first who wished to see you" he jumped up like a cat and came across the room to meet us, shook hands heartily and told us to sit down and make our selves at home upon our making some excuses for intruding, he shut us up with "its all right all right" I am glad you came, then he asked us a great many questions about our regt. and expressed himself very much pleased to think we were back again. Now I want you to write soon. I shant write to [you] again till [I] receive at least 2 letters as long as this.

Yours ever

Julian

Captured at Shiloh!

By Larry R. Houghton

*At dawn on April 6, 1862, members of Battery B, First Michigan Light
Artillery, who were camped around Shiloh Church in southwestern
Tennessee, awoke to the thunderous crash of musketry and
the roar of cannon. Ordered into action, the recruits of the battery
were soon engaged in the Civil War's first bloody battle.*

On a spring morning in April 1862 Battery B, First Michigan Light Artillery, fired on human targets for the first time. By day's end the exhausted Michiganians were on their way to rebel prisons.

In the tranquil green woodlands of southwestern Tennessee, at Shiloh National Military Park, a life-size granite soldier stands atop a twelve-foot-tall monument. He is dressed in Union uniform; his hands grasp the barrel of a musket standing before him. Below him an inscribed tablet singles out those Michiganians who fought at one of the Civil War's largest battles. It reads in part:

> Ross' Battery B, Michigan Light Artillery was conspicuous in the desperate struggle of the first day in the "Peach Orchard " and near the "Bloody Pond," fighting until ordered to retire. While preparing to execute this order it was charged and captured by Confederate Cavalry within a few feet of where this monument now stands, losing four of its six guns. Losses 5 wounded, 56 missing, total 61 men.

At the Battle of Shiloh, on April 6, 1862, the men of Battery B began the day as eager greenhorns and ended it as exhausted veterans.

Battery B (also called the Second Michigan Battery early in the war) was mustered into federal service in November 1861 in Grand Rapids. About half the volunteers were farmers, with a sprinkling of carpenters, tradesmen, lumberjacks, Great Lakes sailors, a cooper and even a couple of brewers. These Michiganians, although similar to most volunteers, were considerably older than their counterparts—their average age was twenty-seven years compared to twenty-three and a half years for the Union army as a whole.

Battery B first assembled at Camp Benton, Missouri, in January 1862 and then moved to Camp McClernand, Cairo, Illinois, in mid-February. There, at the confluence of the Ohio and Mississippi Rivers, they attended the "school of the piece," as one private described it.

Preparation for war and the nearness of battle crescendoed to a nervous excitement in the men. Private Elijah Shepard, a twenty-nine-year-old farmer from near Paw Paw, Van Buren County, wrote his wife Almeda about their arrival at Cairo, "The gunboats that was in the battle of Fort Henry and Fort Donelson are here now. They bear the marks of balls on them, but they only made dents in the side & glanced off. The smoke pipe suffered the worst. They are full of cannon ball holes which shows that the rebels shot too high."

The men had seen other boats arriving from downriver loaded with Confederate prisoners. Ever-present rumors promised the next Union victory at Columbus, Kentucky, or Nashville or Memphis, Tennessee. Camp talk of easy victories, the bravado of those who had not yet "seen the elephant" and thoughts of home conspired to raise the men's fighting spirit. Shepard boasted that "We expect marching orders from here every hour. How homesick some of the boys are & how they would fight, if they had a chance to end the war & be with their families. Let the men loose that is in & around Cairo & in less than a month they would stop every secession mouth on the Mississippi." The frustration, as Shepard noted in a March 17 letter, soon turned to concern as sickness took its toll. "How long we will stay here I don't know. I hope not long for out of the men there is not 50 that is well. Some have the diarrhea with an inward fever till they are so weak that they can scarcely crawl."

On March 21, 1862, Major General Henry W. Halleck ordered Battery B, "if ready," to join Brigadier General Ulysses S. Grant's army on the Tennessee River's Pittsburg Landing. Commanded by Captain William H. Ross from Detroit, Battery B, which consisted of 110 men and officers, six cannons and caissons (each pulled by six-horse teams), followed by horse-drawn supply wagons and two dozen spare horses, began its southern sojourn.

It was springtime and, except for sporadic rain showers, the weather was quite pleasant. Upon reaching Grant's army, Shepard wrote to his wife that "it is warm here as in summer & it makes the soldiers lay around like snakes in the spring sunning themselves. The peach trees, plum and cherries are in full bloom here now." Shepard attributed his "excellent health and spirits" to camping in tents, "which agreed with me."

Shepard described the Union camp as "full of life. The fife & drum bands of music are continually heard." More importantly, "none of the soldiers . . . want to go home on furlough now. They all think the war is very near over & they want to see the end of it . . . before they go to see their families." Although the rebels—estimated by Shepard at twice their actual strength—were camped ten miles away, "We feel just as confident of victory as tho it was already gained. You will hear of a great victory being gained in less than a month."

Despite his bravado, Shepard tried to ease his wife's fears for his safety while still acknowledging the possibility of death on the battlefield:

On March 21, 1862, General Henry Halleck (above) ordered Battery B, First Michigan Light Artillery, to join General Ulysses Grant's army near Pittsburg Landing, Tennessee. Two weeks later, the battery found itself in one of the war's most confusing and bloodiest battles.

Don't worry about me for I haven't got a very dangerous position. I am anxious to see this unholy rebellion crushed [so] that I can once more return to my family & enjoy the comforts of life, some of which I but little appreciated when I was there. Keep up your spirits for but two or three battles more will be fought. We have the rebels cowed down, they have lost all hope of conquering us.

Dear wife, if I am the one that falls in the battle

field don't think you have nothing to live for. Do not mourn my loss as tho you had no hope. Live for the little ones, live to guide their minds in the path of wisdom, teach them to love & fear God, to love good & shun evil.

On April 2 Battery B became a part of the Army of the Tennessee. Assigned to General Stephen A. Hurlbut's Fourth Division, the battery had joined other federal troops mostly from the Upper Midwest. Halleck also ordered Major General Don Carlos Buell's thirty thousand troops to join Grant's forces at Pittsburg Landing. The combined force would attack Corinth, Mississippi, twenty miles to the southwest. Taking Corinth, a strategic Confederate rail center, would be a major step in securing the entire Mississippi River Valley. The rebels, however, had other plans.

General Albert Sidney Johnston, commander of the Confederate forces located near Corinth, knew of Grant's presence at Pittsburg Landing and Buell's absence. To regain Tennessee, the rebels would have to defeat Grant before Buell joined forces with him. Johnston began moving his army into position for an attack on April 4. Muddy roads and the logistics of moving mostly green troops slowed their efforts. As a result, the rebels were not into position until late on Saturday, April 5.

Sunday morning dawned with a beautiful sunrise and warm temperatures. Recent rains had freshened the air. The camp of Battery B was located 125 yards northwest of the intersection of the Corinth and Hamburg-Savannah Roads, a mile southwest of the landing. The men had just finished breakfast when, according to First Sergeant Lucius "Lute" Mills, "The quiet of the camp was disturbed, the tired monotony broken by a volley of musketry continuous as the sound of the rolling drum, and so near to us as to be distinctly heard."

Captain Ross quickly gave orders to prepare for battle. Six teams of horses were speedily harnessed to pull the four ten-pound Parrotts and the two six-pound guns and caissons into position seven-eighths of a mile south of their camp. This location on the southern side of Sarah Bell's cotton field put them in the center of Colonel Nelson William's First Brigade line of battle, which anchored the Union army's left near the Tennessee River. From Hurlbut's division on the left, the Union line stretched nearly three miles, arcing westward to Brigadier General William T. Sherman's division near Owl Creek on the right. The general terrain varied from gently rolling hills with open woods to thick timber with dense undergrowth separated by steep open ravines and cultivated areas and all crisscrossed with roads and lanes.

In position at about 9:00 A.M., Battery B began firing for the first time at human targets. Sergeant Mills recalled:

We could see the enemy advancing at a rapid rate. We formed in battery, and poured upon them the deadly shell. Our position then being so near, it was responded to by a volley which fell like hail around and in our midst. We then retired a short distance [back to the Hamburg-Savannah Road] and ceased to fire. Here, for the first time, the dreadful havoc of war became a stern reality to us, and was no longer a picture of imagination.

While the battery was idle for about twenty minutes, Private Lowell Teed responded to Captain Ross's call for volunteers to go to the opposite side of the field fifty yards away to free some horses entangled in the brush. A shell from a rebel battery that was stationed in the abandoned Sixth Division camp of Brigadier General Benjamin M. Prentiss had struck, exploding a caisson loaded with ammunition belonging to Captain John B. Myer's Thirteenth Ohio Battery. The entire battery had stampeded, leaving guns and horses behind.

Teed, Mills and a few others dashed across open ground and tried freeing the horses as quickly as possible. Teed reported:

I saw six more farther back in the woods, and went to free them, while Mills went back to our men. I passed one dead man whose ghastly countenance was sickening to behold, but thought nothing of it at the time, and had got

the horses all loose but one, when I saw a man step [from] behind a tree about 25 rods off and in another instant a ball came within an inch of my face, and as I turned around another one passed so close to the back of my head that it almost touched my hair, and you can calculate that I got that horse loose and put out as soon as convenient.

At approximately 10:30 A.M. General Hurlbut ordered Captain Ross to move the battery to a level plain 150 yards west of the Peach Orchard, just northwest of the residence of William Manse George.

Repositioned, Battery B continued its fight by dueling with the same rebel batteries that had dislodged the Ohio battery. Shells burst around the Michiganians with dreadful rapidity and the air was alive with musket balls. Lieutenant Albert Arndt's horse was shot out from under him; a ball passed through Lieutenant William Bliss's shirt sleeve and his horse was wounded.

The Battle of Shiloh raged into the afternoon. With less-than-perfect communication between divisions—even between regiments—portions of the Union line surged back and forth as they first gained the advantage and then gave way to Confederate charges. Tens of thousands of men clashed in a fury never before witnessed on the North American continent. The roar of continuous firing sent clouds of blue smoke drifting over a hideous scene of death and suffering. Even nature's landscape of trees and brush seemed to scream from the hail of lead and steel. Thousands of wounded men cried for water in the sun's heat. Some crawled to a small pond for relief, their open wounds coloring the waters red and giving it a name to memorialize their sacrifice: Bloody Pond.

In this surreal scene Battery B held its midday position until 2:00 P.M., when it was forced to retire with the remainder of Hurlbut's division. The new location in the Wicker Field, just north of the old farm lane known as the "sunken road," was Battery B's last fighting position. The battery continued in heavy action backing up the furious fighting in front of them in the area dubbed the "Hornets' Nest." There, the intensity of the day's conflict reached its deadly apex. Numerous charges were repelled, leaving rows of dead rebels before the Union position.

At 4:00 P.M. General Hurlbut ordered a general retirement of his forces along the entire Federal left flank. Ross's battery fell back to the Hamburg-Savannah Road/Corinth Road intersection; there it was charged

Until April 6, 1862, the vast Union camps surrounding Shiloh Church, Tennessee, were as peaceful as the early war camp shown here. That morning, a Confederate attack caused mass confusion and sent Battery B, First Michigan Light Artillery, into action.

and surrounded by Colonel Andrew J. Lindsay's First Mississippi Cavalry, just in front of the battery's camp.

The battery's efforts to carry out Grant's orders to hold this "position at all hazards" had ended. Private Lute Mills later described the end of the day:

The enemy were still driving our lines back with unceasing vollies, both on our right and on our left. We retired and formed in battery on an elevation of ground, hoping thereby to gain a point where our shots would be effective, it now being late in the afternoon. I received an order from the captain [Ross] which called me away, but was afterward informed that he made an advance, and owing to the condition of the surrounding country, the enemy were obstructed from view. A squadron of cavalry approached, surrounded our little band that fought so bravely, demanded the sword, and officers, including Captain Ross, Lieut. Bliss, Lieut. Arndt and men became prisoners of war. Horses, guns and caissons became the property of the rebels. The number of the prisoners from Van Buren county, I will give: Sergeant L. C. Teed, Corporal R. W. Brown, Corporal Nelson Plumb, Bugler R. O.

Thayer, and Private Elijah L. Shepard. This occurred about five o'clock P.M.

Lieutenant Cuthbert W. Laing and his section of Battery B eluded capture. Earlier he had been ordered to move to a support position away from the other Michiganians. In the ensuing Union retreat, Laing's section was ordered to fall back; it was some distance from the rest of the battery at the moment of capture.

On the Confederate side of battle, Major General Benjamin F. Cheatham's report, which described the capture, recognized the Michiganians' determined resistance during the afternoon battle:

I directed Lieutenant-Colonel Miller, of the First Battalion of Mississippi Cavalry . . . to move forward rapidly in the direction of the retreating [infantry] column and fall upon him in his flight. This was well executed, and resulted in the capture of a number of prisoners, together with Captain Ross' (Michigan) battery of six guns [actually four] entire, including officers and men, which had acted vigorously in defending the position. As this position, with regard to my own command, was by far the most obstinately contested by the enemy during Sunday, so it was the last which he seriously contested during the day.

In all, the rebels captured approximately twenty-two hundred Yankees, including about one hundred men from the Twelfth Michigan Infantry. The excitement of taking such a large group of prisoners and the logistics of moving so many men back from the battlefront slowed the Confederate advance. The eventual arrival of most of General Buell's army and the artillery bombardment by two Union gunboats, the *Lexington* and the *Tyler*, halted any further advance. Darkness and exhaustion soon brought the day's horrendous battle to a close.

Battery B was now split in two. Forty-nine men and three officers were prisoners; five others had been wounded. Miraculously, none had been killed.

Eventually, the Battle of Shiloh—which resumed the following day—left 13,147 Union and 10,694 Confederate casualties. Late on the afternoon of the battle's second day the rebels began a retreat to Corinth. Preceding them were the men of Battery B, whose war experience took another unfamiliar turn as they settled into captivity.

According to Private Teed, after being captured the Michiganians were marched about six miles from the battlefield. "After we got to our resting place for the night," he recalled, "we received half of a hard cracker apiece for supper, which was quite acceptable, as we had eaten very little since morning. The men then took the covering for the guns, and lying down on the ground covered up with them, and although it rained hard did not get much wet."

Although near exhaustion from the daylong battle, the men slept little. The uncertainty of their fate and the shock of the day's events was on every man's mind. The distant "harrump" of the Union gunboats' cannons at ten-minute intervals throughout the night reminded them the fight was not over.

The prisoners were awakened early the next morning. Teed and the others started off on foot for Corinth, fifteen miles south; the guards rode horses. Rain during the night made the road nearly impassable in many places. When the prisoners attempted to cross these places on logs, the guards rode on them, yelling, "Close up, close up!" Several times during the day the rebels compelled their prisoners to wade through mud that reached their boot tops. Teed recalled:

It was night when we reached Corinth, and then we had the privilege of lying in an old box car that was very dirty, all night without any sup-

per. The rain fell almost in torrents the whole night, and came through the roof so bad that on the morning of the 8th of April, our clothes were completely soaked with mud, and a worse looking set of men I never saw.

The Battery B officers were separated from their men and eventually imprisoned at Montgomery, Alabama. While the men were removed for transport further south, Teed and another prisoner managed to escape. But their freedom was short-lived. Although getting as far as twenty-five miles from Memphis, they were apprehended and returned to their captors.

For several weeks various groups of prisoners were shuttled about in railcars and riverboats from Memphis to Huntsville, Alabama; Chattanooga, Tennessee; and Mobile, Alabama. Most of the Battery B captives finally reached the Confederate prison camp in Macon, Georgia.

Four members of Battery B died during their captivity. On May 1 Lieutenant Bliss was one. He had been escorted by a rebel guard to a nearby house to purchase milk for his fellow officers. While the woman of the house was filling Bliss's canteens the guard grew impatient and told Bliss to "hurry up." The lieutenant replied, "Yes, as soon as I can get my canteens." The guard then cocked his musket and put the muzzle against the lieutenant's chest. Bliss said, "I hope you will not shoot me." The sentinel replied, "Yes, I will, you damned Yankee" and then fired. Bliss died within the hour.

The other members of Battery B to die while imprisoned were two privates from Hillsdale: twenty-three-year-old George W. Baker in Cahawba, Alabama, on May 6, and twenty-eight-year-old Lyman P. Huff in Macon on May 22, both of disease. Twenty-three-year-old Carl Schwartz was reportedly shot by a rebel guard while held captive at Memphis.

The rest of the Michiganians were eventually paroled or exchanged for Confederate prisoners, though not as a single unit. The largest group (approximately twenty-five) was released after a total of fifty-three days at the Macon, Georgia, prison. Corporal James M. Chrouch of Dearborn described the situation at the time of his parole:

During the later part of the month of May about 1,000 prisoners were paroled and sent to Chattanooga and from Chattanooga they were sent down the Ten. river to Huntsville landing, Alabama—there were 2 boats—The 1st boat-load of prisoners was received by the U.S. Authorities, the 2nd boat were not so received and returned south and held prisoners.

It is unknown why the second boatload was not freed—possibly there were too many sick men on board. Private Teed reported that for some unknown reason they were not received and were taken back to Macon. At least two men from Battery B were on the second boat and were held for another four months: Elijah Shepard, who was ill, and Richard Doyle, the battery's nineteen-year-old trumpeter. They were exchanged along with six hundred other soldiers on October 19, 1862, at Aiken's Landing on the James River, downstream from Richmond, Virginia.

Returning Union soldiers called the exchange point at the landing "the gate into God's country." To these dirty, ill-fed and poorly clothed men, it meant a haven of freedom and proper care. Many, like Shepard, harbored maladies that resulted in premature death.

With their fellow cannoneers in captivity, the rest of Battery B helped occupy Corinth, Mississippi, following the town's capture by Union forces on May 30. Captain Ross reassembled the paroled men in Detroit and joined them at Corinth in January 1863. Ross then went to St. Louis to obtain new equipment for the battery. On March 9 the battery happily received orders to proceed to Bethel, Tennessee, for garrison duty and to guard the railroad. One correspondent's report undoubtedly reflected the group's feelings when he wrote that "the change is very much for the better, as Bethel is much pleasanter and healthier than Corinth, for the latter place is a vast charnel-house. Tens of thousands of friends and foes lie buried together in and around it, while the dead bodies of horses and mules cover the ground."

Battery B continued its dedicated service throughout the remainder of the war. Despite participation in a number of battles, its casualty list was surprisingly short. Only a dozen men were wounded in the last year of the war; none were killed in battle. After the war's conclusion, the Michigan artillery men participated in the grand review of Sherman's army on May 24, 1865, in Washington, DC. The battery was mustered out of federal service on June 14, 1865, in Detroit. These sons of Michigan returned to their homes justifiably proud of having given exemplary service to the Union and to their state. The Michigan monument at Shiloh had them in mind when it concluded, "More enduring than this granite will be the gratitude of Michigan, to her soldiers of Shiloh."

The Worst Colonel I Ever Saw

By Robert C. Myers

A politically appointed officer, Francis Quinn of Niles, almost single-handedly ruined the reputation of the Twelfth Michigan Infantry. Quinn's arrogance and incompetence so alienated the officers and men under his command that the regiment split into quarreling factions even before it left Michigan.

A few moments can define a person's life. For Colonel Francis Quinn of the Twelfth Michigan Volunteer Infantry, those moments came at the Battle of Shiloh in the early morning hours of Sunday, April 6, 1862. Like countless other officers in the Civil War, Quinn commanded his regiment by virtue of political influence, not military expertise. Quinn helped raise the Twelfth Michigan and Michigan governor Austin Blair commissioned him its colonel, but giving him that command proved disastrous, militarily and politically; Quinn's arrogance and incompetence so alienated the officers under his command that the Twelfth split into quarreling factions even before it left Michigan. Three weeks after leaving Michigan, the regiment was thrust into the war's first bloody battle, where its internal breakdown—not the enemy—caused it to fight as two separate groups instead of as a single unit.

Political appointees plagued both the Union and Confederate armies, particularly in the early stages of the Civil War, when such men assumed they could easily learn military skills. Many of Governor Blair's appointees turned into outstanding officers, especially Alpheus S. Williams, Michigan's first Civil War general, and Israel B. Richardson, a West Point graduate who won promotion to general and served with great distinction. Francis Quinn, however, may rank as Blair's worst military appointment. By Blair's own assessment, Quinn caused him more trouble than all his other Michigan colonels put together.

Quinn seemed an unlikely candidate for the lofty status of colonel. Born in Ireland in 1827, he emigrated to Niles, Michigan, sometime before 1850. His life thereafter resembled a Horatio Alger story: an Irish immigrant who, through ambition and hard work, attained modest fortune and fame. On June 26, 1851, he married Louise Babcock, the nineteen-year-old daughter of Deputy Sheriff George S. Babcock. The couple had three children: William, Mary and Isabelle, born in 1855, 1858 and 1860, respectively. As Quinn rose in prominence among Niles businessmen, he took a keen interest in politics and community affairs. He was a member of the city fire department and the Young Men's Republican Club. In 1858 he ran for state representative, narrowly losing the election to Democrat and fellow townsman William Beeson. The Republicans elected him president of the Wide-Awake Club, appointed him delegate to numerous party conventions and made him marshal for the city's 1860 Independence Day celebration. In March 1861 Michigan's new Republican governor, Austin Blair, handed Quinn the political plum of Niles postmastership.

When the Civil War erupted a month later, young men throughout Michigan rushed to volunteer for the army. The War Department expected a short conflict, but after the Union debacle at the First Battle of Bull Run in July 1861, President Abraham Lincoln called for more troops. During the fall and winter of 1861-62 Francis Quinn actively raised volunteers for the Twelfth Michigan Infantry, which would help fill Michigan's new quota. Companies were recruited from Niles, Cassopolis, St. Joseph, Buchanan, Albion, Lansing, Lawton and Berrien Springs.

Quinn's political connections and public service placed him in an ideal position to gain an officer's commission. He had no military qualifications, but in 1861 politics often outweighed experience and, like most Northern governors, Blair doled out commissions to his friends. Letters and petitions recommending Quinn for a colonelcy flowed into Blair's office from influential citizens, politicians and the Twelfth's officers. Quinn received his commission on November 18, 1861. Blair selected another prewar friend, William H. Graves of

Adrian, as the regiment's lieutenant colonel. Intelligent and ambitious, an ardent Republican and abolitionist, the twenty-six-year-old Graves had already distinguished himself at Bull Run, where he had been wounded while fighting as a captain in the First Michigan Infantry. The commission of major went to George Kimmel of Niles, who, despite being a Democrat, helped recruit local volunteers. Other Democratic officers included Captain Darius Brown and Chaplain Andrew J. Eldred of Niles. Captain Gustav Robert Bretschneider, another Republican friend of Quinn, served several years in the Prussian army and saw action at Bull Run as a captain in the Second Michigan Infantry.

Soon after recruiting started, a committee of prominent, politically connected Niles citizens traveled to Lansing and persuaded Governor Blair to designate their village as the rendezvous point and training camp for the Twelfth Michigan. The village fairgrounds were selected as a training camp site and grandiloquently renamed Camp Barker in honor of fellow citizen and former state representative Richard P. Barker.

As the Twelfth Michigan settled into Camp Barker, the political situation among its officers deteriorated. Colonel Quinn fought bitterly with Niles politicians over recommendations for officers' commissions. More important, the mutual dislike between Quinn and Lieutenant Colonel Graves soon blossomed into hatred. The two officers fussed over issuing rations, paying for laundresses and other details of the quartermaster's department. The appointment of regimental quartermaster grew into an open feud—Quinn promoted his business associate and neighbor George S. Bristol while Graves and his allies backed Fitz H. Stevens, a Niles grocer who had enlisted as a first lieutenant in Company E with the promise of appointment as regimental quartermaster.

On March 16 Quinn called his officers together to hand them their commissions. They unanimously supported Stevens' appointment, saying it would unite the regiment. Surprisingly, Quinn agreed. He and Graves had discussed the situation earlier and Stevens' appointment, Quinn assured Governor Blair, would be good for the regiment. However, he intimated darkly, "We will keep a close look after Stevens and if anything wrong happens it will be the last of him."

On Wednesday, March 19, 1862, the Twelfth Michigan marched out of Camp Barker, flags flying, regimental band playing and fixed bayonets glinting in the sun. The men crossed Niles to the Michigan Central depot, where a crowd of several thousand friends and family members had gathered to say good-bye. Amid the bustle of loading men and gear aboard the railcars, Quinn took a dig at his lieutenant colonel. Graves had appointed Captain Henry Gephart of Company E to serve as officer of the day until the regiment reached St. Louis. Quinn countermanded those orders at the last minute, telling Gephart to remain behind and tend to the regiment's sick and those under arrest for desertion. Although Gephart's men had already boarded the cars, they gathered around him with teary eyes, swearing they would never go into battle without him. Meanwhile, Governor Blair waged Quinn's political war from Lansing. The next day, while the regiment sped toward St. Louis and safely away from hometown politicians, Governor Blair discharged Stevens and appointed George Bristol as regimental quartermaster. Colonel Quinn had won his battle over the quartermaster appointment.

Quinn found a state of confusion in St. Louis. In the bustle of sending supplies and reinforcements forward, no one seemed quite sure what to do with the new regiment. After three days in St. Louis, the Twelfth Michigan proceeded down the Mississippi aboard the steamer *Meteor* to Cairo, Illinois. There, Brigadier General Benjamin M. Prentiss and his staff boarded the ship. Prentiss, a political appointee, was on his way to a little place called Pittsburg Landing, Tennessee, to take command of a new division, which included the Twelfth Michigan. The *Meteor* set off down the Ohio and Tennessee Rivers to Pittsburg Landing. There, the men disembarked, climbed the steep riverbank at the landing and marched a short distance to the middle of an open field, where Lieutenant Colonel Graves staked out their first camp. A few days later, the Twelfth Michigan moved its camp about three miles forward to join Colonel Everett Peabody's brigade of Prentiss's division. Besides the Michigan regiment, the brigade included the Twenty-first and Twenty-fifth Missouri and Sixteenth Wisconsin Infantries. Camp Prentiss, as the Michiganians christened their new campsite, lay in wooded terrain with a spring that afforded good water. Nearby stood a little log Southern Methodist meeting house called Shiloh. With the mixed impatience and apprehension common to green soldiers, the enlisted men expected a major battle. They were now part of General Ulysses S. Grant's army, which had recently captured Confederate Forts Henry and Donelson and were now preparing to attack the rebel army at Corinth, Mississippi. As Grant assembled his command at Pittsburg Landing, General Don Carlos Buell marched his fifty-five-thousand-man Northern army from Nashville to join him.

An important junction of the Mobile & Ohio and Memphis & Charleston Railroads, Corinth lay twenty-three miles from Pittsburg Landing. Confederate general Albert Sydney Johnston arrived in Corinth on March 23, uniting his thirteen thousand men with troops under Generals Pierre G. T. Beauregard and Braxton Bragg. Johnston planned to strike at Pittsburg Landing before Buell could join Grant. On April 2 he ordered his army to advance on Pittsburg Landing at 6:00 A.M. Due to delays in transmitting orders and confusion on the march, Johnston's army failed to fully deploy opposite the federal troops at the landing until the evening of April 5.

Amazingly, Johnston brought his army into position against the federals without alerting them. To the Union generals, minor skirmishing during the first days of April seemed nothing more than picket firing and reconnaissance probing. As Johnston moved his men into position, General William Tecumseh Sherman, whose division lay across the road to Corinth, reported everything quiet. He had noticed a couple of rebel infantry regiments about two miles in front of his lines but assured Grant, "I do not apprehend anything like an attack on our position." Grant agreed, wiring General Buell on April 5 that the Confederates were still in Corinth. Minor skirmishing and picket firing had been going on for several days, and some men in the Twelfth Michigan grew uneasy at the lack of preparation along their front. Chaplain Eldred observed that Prentiss had posted pickets no more than a half mile in front of his division, and that he had not bothered to have entrenchments or rifle pits dug.

However, the initiative of three officers in Prentiss's division—Major James Powell and Colonel Everett Peabody of the Twenty-fifth Missouri and Lieutenant Colonel William H. Graves of the Twelfth Michigan—prevented the Confederates from achieving complete surprise. Prentiss's division, placed to the left of Sherman, held part of the army perimeter that evening. Prentiss had established routine pickets and outposts, but he assumed that Sherman would detect any possible Confederate advance. On Saturday, April 5, as Prentiss conducted a review in a nearby clearing called Spain Field, Major Powell noticed about a dozen Confederate soldiers peering through the underbrush. He reported his observation to Graves, who was serving as officer of the day. Graves was concerned. "After my experience at Bull Run," he later reported, "I felt ill at ease." The two officers sought out Prentiss, who strengthened the outer pickets. Captain Gilbert Johnson and the Twelfth Michi-

gan's Company H reinforced the pickets, while Powell escorted Colonel David Moore, three companies of the Twenty-first Missouri and two companies of the Twenty-fifth Missouri on a reconnaissance patrol.

The Missourians returned to camp at about 7:00 P.M., reassuring Prentiss that they had made a thorough march of three miles but found nothing. Another account, however, claimed that Moore and his men had only trekked out about a mile to an old cotton field, where they found a group of slaves who told them of seeing a party of about two hundred rebel horsemen that afternoon. Actually, Moore probably lost his way and headed southwest, across the front of Sherman's division, and missed the gathering Confederates.

Captain Johnson came in from the picket lines at about 8:30 P.M. and told Graves that he had seen long lines of enemy campfires and heard drums and bugles. Graves immediately relayed Johnson's report to Prentiss. But Moore's reconnaissance had helped lull Prentiss into a false sense of security. The general decided that Johnson had simply detected a reconnaissance in force and feared that the green Michigan company would be captured if left in place. He ordered Graves to withdraw his men.

When Johnson arrived back in camp he again shared his concerns with Graves, who was so impressed with his subordinate's sincerity that the two went to see Prentiss. The general refused to worry, telling the two officers that everything was "all right." Despite Prentiss's reassurance, Graves remained anxious. Rounding up Powell and several other officers, he trotted off to see Colonel Everett Peabody of the Twenty-fifth Missouri. Peabody took the report seriously.

A hot-tempered but highly competent officer, Peabody had approached Prentiss earlier that evening to recommend putting the division in a ready condition to resist an attack. Prentiss had belittled the idea and refused to act. The report from Graves and Powell convinced Peabody that the Confederates had gathered a major force along the army's front. He pondered the situation, and at about midnight he took action. Without informing Prentiss, he ordered Powell to take three companies of the Twenty-fifth Missouri at 3:00 A.M. and go looking for the enemy. If Powell encountered rebels in force, he was to hold his ground as long as possible and then fall back. Besides the companies from the Twenty-fifth Missouri, Powell took along at least two companies of the Twelfth Michigan. Throughout this sequence of events, Graves apparently never consulted with Colonel Quinn. Their intense animosity kept

Graves from informing Quinn about his fear of an impending attack or making Quinn aware of the discussions on Powell's expedition. At about the same time Powell's expedition set off, a gun shot rang out in the Twelfth's camp. Quinn had somehow managed to shoot his left hand with his own revolver. He never explained how the accident occurred, nor any of his actions during those crucial predawn hours, but he probably spent the next hour or so tending to his wound.

While Quinn nursed his injured hand, Powell's reconnaissance team worked its way along an old wagon trail toward a little clearing known locally as Fraley's Field. Powell had divided his force into three segments when he reached the brigade's picket line. The men tramped through the woods in a southwesterly direction along the trail, once nearly firing into each other as they stumbled in the dark woods. The three prongs separated and just as dawn broke the men of the Twelfth reached the Pittsburg-Corinth Road, near the edge of Fraley Field. There they halted and waited for the Missourians.

As the sky lightened a few minutes before 5:00 A.M. Captain Phineas Graves of Albion ordered his squad to withdraw and link up with the rest of Powell's troops. As they pulled back, rebel pickets fired three shots at them. The Michiganians hastily retreated through the woods until they reached the Missourians. There, Powell established a skirmish line and moved forward.

The Twelfth Michigan had bumped into pickets of Major Aaron B. Hardcastle's Third Mississippi Battalion. As the federals advanced across Fraley Field, the Confederate pickets fired on them and then fell back. Powell's force reached the middle of the field, where some of the men could see a line of Confederates kneeling in the dense underbrush. At a range of about two hundred yards, Powell ordered his men to open fire. As the two sides traded volleys, the Michiganians and Missourians took cover behind some trees. When he heard the firing from Fraley Field, Confederate general Johnston ordered a general advance. As Hardcastle's rebel battalion moved into position across the field, Powell realized he faced a much stronger line of infantry than he had imagined. Rebel cavalry also appeared on his flank. Following Peabody's orders to withdraw if seriously threatened, the Missouri major ordered his men to retreat.

At about 6:00 A.M. casualties from Powell's expedition began returning to Prentiss's division. The wounded men informed Peabody of the fighting at Fraley Field. Peabody then ordered out five companies of the Twenty-first Missouri under Colonel David Moore to serve as a sustaining force. About halfway back Powell encountered Moore, who berated Powell's men as cowards for retreating. Moore refused to listen to Powell's warning that the Confederates were advancing in force. He told Powell that together they would beat back the Confederates. Moore then sent Lieutenant Henry Menn back to camp to bring up the rest of his regiment.

In camp, Menn found General Prentiss conferring with the Twenty-first's lieutenant colonel, Humphrey M. Woodyard. Although angry at Peabody for his unauthorized work in bringing on an engagement, Prentiss ordered Woodyard to reinforce Moore. The two units linked up about a half mile northeast of Fraley Field at about 7:00 A.M. and then continued along the road toward Fraley Field. On the way, Company A of the Sixteenth Wisconsin, out on picket duty, joined Moore's command.

Moore's men advanced in columns of fours. They had just reached the edge of a cotton field known as Seay's Field when a force of Arkansas infantry fired into them, shattering Moore's right leg, hitting Menn in the head and killing the captain of the Wisconsin company. Woodyard took command of the Twenty-first Missouri and drew back. Powell, apparently thinking the skirmish over, headed back to camp with his detachment. Woodyard led his men a short distance to a crest overlooking Seay Field, where he kept up a light fire at the enemy visible along a fencerow. At about 7:15 A.M. an advancing Confederate brigade poured out of the woods, laying down a heavy fire and forcing Woodyard to retreat to escape being flanked.

The commotion from Seay Field alerted Colonel Everett Peabody who, acting without orders, ordered the Twenty-fifth's drummer boy to sound the "long roll," calling the men to arms. The Twelfth Michigan's men had been awake for some time and were midway through breakfast when they heard the drums. They dropped their meals and grabbed their rifles and cartridge boxes. Suddenly, Colonel Quinn appeared, ordering the men into ranks and calling for Lieutenant Colonel Graves. Graves responded slowly, only after Quinn had called for him several times. The colonel, either not knowing or caring about Graves' work that night, later attributed his subordinate's lethargy to fear. As the men stood in ranks, the firing grew louder and more intense, although the rebels remained out of sight. General Prentiss appeared, berating Peabody for bringing on the engagement. Prentiss also ordered the colonel to move his two regiments forward.

At about 7:30 A.M. the Twelfth Michigan and Twenty-fifth Missouri advanced in a line of battle about a quarter mile. Along the way Peabody encountered Powell and his patrol and learned that the rebels held Seay Field. Peabody consolidated Powell's group with his two regiments and then deployed them along the crest of a hill, a ravine thick with undergrowth running immediately across his front. There, Peabody waited as the firing grew louder. Suddenly the rebels loomed up over the crest of the opposite ridge at a distance of only about seventy-five yards. "They were advancing in not only one but several lines of battle," Quinn later reported, and "every hilltop in the rear was covered with them."

The Union troops fired a volley. The Confederates— the Arkansans, Mississippians and Tennesseeans of Colonel Robert G. Shaver's brigade—returned the fire and for a short time the two sides traded volleys at close range. To Shaver, "The enemy's fire was terrific and told with terrible effect." Regiments disintegrated as Shaver's troops broke and ran, but the Confederates brought up artillery and started pounding the Union line. At about 8:15 A.M. Shaver ordered a charge that brought the rebels swarming across the ravine and flanking Peabody's line.

The rebel assault shattered the Twelfth Michigan line. As Graves saw the Union position collapse, he took command of his portion of the Twelfth Michigan and ordered the men to fall back and reform in front of their tents. Graves later claimed Quinn disappeared at that point, abandoning his regiment to its fate while he ran to the rear for safety. Graves, however, gave no indication that he spent much time looking for the man he despised and whom he had not treated as his commanding officer during the past few hours. When Graves ordered the regiment to fall back, the officers had to choose whether to follow

After the departure of adversary Francis Quinn, William H. Graves (seated at left) took over colonelcy of the Twelfth. One of his first actions as colonel was appointing a new regimental staff—all former opponents of Quinn.

Quinn or Graves. Most put their trust in Graves. By Quinn's own account, only two captains, including Bretschneider, and forty or fifty men remained under his command.

While he helped the surgeons treat the wounded, hospital steward Samuel H. Eells ducked in and out of the Twelfth's hospital tent to watch the Union retreat toward the camps. The Michiganians gave ground slowly, firing at the advancing rebels as they fell back. Eells later noted they did "splendidly for green troops."

As the Yankees continued to retreat, General Prentiss called his men to arms. But the confusion and Prentiss's neglect in preparing any defensive works rendered the effort futile. The division repulsed the first rebel assault, but casualties and great numbers of stragglers thinned the federal lines. Peabody was killed while riding near the Twenty-fifth Missouri's camp trying to rally the men who continued to fall back to the camps. Men streamed wildly through the Twelfth Michigan's camp, heading for the river bluffs at the landing.

Many men risked death to snatch personal possessions from their tents. Major George Kimmel jumped off his horse and ran into his tent to retrieve a purse of gold coins. As he did so his mount bolted, but the major caught another horse as it raced by and leaped into the saddle. Private Franklin Bailey escaped but regretted the loss of all his extra clothing and a letter he had planned to mail to his girlfriend. Surgeons George Brunschweiler and Robert C. Kedzie could have escaped but chose to remain behind in the hospital tent to treat the wounded. Eells stayed with them, despite being sprayed in the face with ammonia when a bullet shattered a nearby glass liniment bottle. Minutes later the rebels overran the hospital and took the staff prisoner.

As victorious rebels swept forward, Prentiss's retreat

turned into a rout. Only the timely arrival of two brigades under General Stephen A. Hurlbut averted a complete disaster by establishing a defensive line where Prentiss reassembled the remnants of his division. Prentiss put them into line along a road extending for about a half mile in a convex path facing the oncoming Confederates.

Throughout the morning and afternoon of April 6, the Confederates launched repeated assaults against the federal line. After Prentiss had repulsed an attack at about 10:00 A.M., General Grant inspected the position and ordered Prentiss to "maintain that position at all hazards." Prentiss obeyed the order, despite continual rebel attacks and such intense fighting that the place later was dubbed the Hornets' Nest.

Historians have noted the Twelfth Michigan as among the regiments defending the Hornets' Nest. Actually, there were two Twelfth Michigan regiments present: Graves' command and the handful of men under Quinn. The two groups appear to have fought independently, and neither may have even been aware of the other's presence. At about 4:00 P.M. Prentiss attempted to change front with five regiments under his command, including "part of the Twelfth Michigan." He did not specify whether Quinn or Graves commanded that segment.

Prentiss's maneuver occurred just as the Confederates launched a new assault on his position. The Union line had fallen back several times until it formed a *u*; the final Confederate attack broke that position and collapsed the Hornets' Nest defenses. When the regiments on Quinn's right and left surrendered at about 4:30 P.M., Prentiss ordered Quinn to find reinforcements and to bring up his own regiment. Quinn started off but found the enemy pouring in on the right, the firing there being more intense than in the front at the base of the *u*. Then, Quinn reported, came a "general giving way all over the Field. Artillery and all pell mell."

Quinn escaped, but at about 5:30 P.M. Prentiss and the remnants of his division surrendered. Prentiss's stand at the Hornets' Nest bought time for Grant. General Buell's reinforcements arrived Sunday evening and the next day Grant attacked and forced the rebels to retreat.

The Twelfth Michigan played only a minor role in Monday's fighting. Quinn located Graves that morning, and together they took the two hundred men still with the regiment and joined up with Colonel James M. Tuttle's brigade, fighting on the right of Colonel Marcellus M. Crocker's Thirteenth Iowa Infantry. Quinn technically commanded the brigade that day—in

addition to Peabody's death, the colonels of the Twenty-first Missouri and Sixteenth Wisconsin had been wounded, leaving Quinn as ranking officer. The battle also cost the regiment 22 killed, 24 mortally wounded, about 80 wounded and 106 taken prisoner.

The rebels may have retreated, but the political battle with the Twelfth Michigan renewed after Shiloh. Most of the regimental officers, including Quinn, Graves, Kimmel and Eldred, had escaped capture, and on April 12 the Confederates released Surgeons Brunschweiler and Kedzie and Steward Eells. Each faction believed the other guilty of cowardice and incompetence in battle, and their hatred spilled into the open. Charges filed by Major Kimmel against Quinn led to a hearing before a military commission. The commission apparently arrived at no definite conclusions and took no action. Quinn claimed that the enlisted men and noncommissioned officers all told the truth, while the officers lied. Graves felt that the commission did nothing because the Twelfth was being moved to another division.

With no immediate resolution in sight, Quinn and Graves fought their war with letters to Governor Blair and the press. Quinn complained to Blair that he commanded a regiment filled with cowards. He claimed he had dragged Graves from his tent on Sunday morning and forced him into the line, and when ordered to camp on Monday evening the lieutenant colonel had vanished until Tuesday afternoon. Major Kimmel had begged Quinn to be sent to the rear to bring up stragglers; then he, too, disappeared. Kimmel resigned on April 22 to avoid a court-martial. Quinn noted that Captain Phineas Graves was being court-martialed for cowardice and stealing; First Lieutenant Joseph McCloy of the same company had fled as soon as the firing started; and Captain Thomas Wallace and First Lieutenant Lewis Pearl of Company B were also cowards. The worst offender, Chaplain Eldred ("a bad bad man"), preached demoralizing sermons to the men and stirred up discord in the regiment. Despite the problems, a confident Quinn declared, "I have beat them all so far, doubled and twisted them because they lied, basely lied."

Graves offered Governor Blair his version of events. Only the efforts of Kimmel, Phineas Graves, himself and a few other officers had saved the regiment from ruin. Chaplain Eldred had "behaved nobly," helping the officers rally the men. Quinn lurked about the rear during the early stages of the battle but then ran for the river when the Hornets' Nest collapsed. That night, while Graves and the Twelfth Michigan lay in the rain, Quinn and Captains Bretschneider and Weston spent a comfortable night on a riverboat. According to Graves, when some of Sherman's men fired their rifles on Tuesday morning, Quinn thought the enemy had renewed their attack and again fled to the river. Major Kimmel, who had preferred charges against the colonel, told Graves he had resigned "rather than live in such a perfect Hell."

The affray soon broke in the hometown newspapers. The Republican, pro-Quinn *Niles Inquirer* printed a letter signed "B" that suggested cowardice on the part of Graves, Kimmel and Eldred and lauded Quinn's bravery. Graves got a copy of the May 14, 1862, article "Headquarters Regiment Michigan Infantry" and confronted Quinn, demanding to know who had written it. Quinn refused to speak to him, but when pressed he hinted Captain Weston was the author.

Graves had his own allies; the Democratic *Niles Republican* printed letters from Eldred, an anonymous "Witness" and Captain Darius Brown, all which praised Graves, Kimmel and Eldred but maligned Quinn. The *Detroit Free Press* picked up the story, spreading news of the regiment's political turmoil across Michigan.

Meanwhile, the discipline, morale and health of the Twelfth Michigan deteriorated as its officers waged political warfare. Whatever his personal courage, Quinn had no idea how to run a regiment. He gave impossible orders to company commanders as they drilled the regiment and then openly berated the officers when they failed to carry them out. Without proper leadership, the Twelfth acquired a reputation for stealing and outraged officers resigned rather than serve under Quinn. Brigade commanders had little use for an undisciplined, demoralized regiment and the Twelfth found itself shifting from one command to another, doing an extra share of hard labor and bringing up the rear while on the march. When ordered on June 30, 1862, to take his division to Washington, DC, Major General John A. McClernand asked "Had I better not leave the Twelfth Michigan and Sixty-first Illinois here? They are undisciplined, disorganized and deficient in numbers."

Sickness in the Twelfth and other nearby Michigan regiments prompted Governor Blair and Adjutant General John Robertson to visit to check on the troops' health. Shocked at the regiment's poor physical and mental health, Blair was convinced Quinn had to go.

Captain Weston and Surgeon Brunschweiler had both resigned, leaving Captain Bretschneider as Quinn's only firm ally in the regiment. Eells opined, "The Col. has hardly any friends left in the regiment either among the officers or the men." Even so, Quinn

hoped to salvage his personal and political reputation. He begged Blair, who had asked him to resign, to transfer him instead to the command of a new Michigan regiment, promising to help recruit men for the regiment and then resign. This course, he declared, "would satisfy my friends and should satisfy all concerned" and would allow him to leave the army with his honor intact. When this tack failed, he tendered his resignation on July 25, 1862, claiming ill health. So eager were the officers to have Quinn resign that regimental surgeon Robert C. Kedzie filed a false medical report to speed matters along, certifying that careful examination revealed that Quinn suffered from chronic diarrhea, jaundice and "other hepatic derangements" to such an extent that his life depended on a permanent change of climate.

As soon as he learned that his old political friend had tendered his resignation, a thankful Governor Blair urged General Grant to accept it immediately, assuring him that the Twelfth Michigan's success depended on Quinn's resignation. Quinn, however, had other ideas. On August 24 he applied for a thirty-day leave of absence, again citing ill health. Three days later he withdrew his resignation, citing greatly improved health and a desire by his regiment and his immediate superior that he remain in command. Blair, however, had no intention of allowing his erstwhile ally to remain in charge any longer than necessary. On August 30 he asked Secretary of War Edwin M. Stanton to accept Quinn's resignation, declaring that Quinn was "the worst colonel I ever saw and has made me more trouble than all the rest together. He keeps up a row in his regiment all the time."

Two days later the officers of the Twelfth Michigan formally filed eight separate charges against Quinn, including cowardice, neglect of duty, incompetence, inhumanity and disobedience of orders. They might have saved themselves the effort: Quinn had already resubmitted his resignation, which was accepted on August 31.

Characteristically, Quinn never informed his regiment he had resigned. He simply disappeared on September 11, taking along Captain Bretschneider, who had resigned the week before, and all the regimental papers. The Twelfth Michigan rejoiced at his departure. Captain Darius Brown succinctly expressed the general sentiment: "Col. Quinn skedaddled—no tears visible."

Graves was promoted to colonel of the Twelfth Michigan and proved an effective commander, rebuilding the regiment's morale and discipline and leading it ably through the war. From November 1862 to June 1863 the Twelfth headquartered at Middleburg, Tennessee, where it guarded the Mississippi Central Railroad. It participated in the siege of Vicksburg (Mississippi) in June and July 1863 and then moved to Helena and Little Rock, Arkansas. The regiment spent the rest of the war in northern Arkansas until mustered out of service on February 15, 1866. Francis Quinn returned to Niles a ruined man, unable to show his face on the street. After the war he secured testimonials from Generals Benjamin Prentiss and John A. Logan, making them public in the February 1, 1866, *Niles Inquirer*. With both officers' attestment of his integrity, Quinn hoped his status in the community might be redeemed. Veterans of the Twelfth Michigan, however, showed no inclination to make amends. At their first reunion in Niles on February 22, 1867, they voted unanimously to declare his statements "utterly void and destitute of truth," then published their denunciations in the local newspapers. His personal and political

career ruined, Quinn moved to Hyde Park, Illinois, near Chicago, where he resumed his career in livestock and produce-dealing. He and his wife had two more children, Lillian and Elizabeth, born in 1866 and 1869, but the marriage dissolved in 1874. Louise Quinn then took their children and moved to Jackson, Michigan, leaving Francis in Chicago.

Besides his reputation, the war cost Quinn his health and eventually his life. Physicians could provide no relief for the rheumatism he had contracted during the war. Quinn resorted to quack cure-alls and steam baths to ease the symptoms. On March 26, 1876, he stepped from the baths at the Grand Pacific Hotel in Chicago and fell dead. Doctors stated that the forty-nine-year-old died of "rheumatism of the heart." Quinn's body, returned to Michigan for burial, rests in the Niles Silverbrook Cemetery beneath a simple government-supplied tombstone. As a seemingly fitting epitaph for one of Michigan's worst officers, to this day there is no known image of Francis Quinn.

Skirmishing at Shiloh

By Joseph Ruff

In 1921 Albion resident Joseph Ruff completed a manuscript retracing his Civil War service with the Twelfth Michigan Infantry. In his discussion about the Battle of Shiloh he presents an interesting look at the unit's first encounter with the Confederates on the morning of April 6, 1862.

The Union army were sleeping in their tents, and yet in a portion of that army there was some stir for the Lieut. Col. of our regiment could not rest. He felt oppressed by some unseen impending danger and resolved to impress our division commander with the defenseless condition of our army. The upshot of it was that a force of 200 men, a portion of the Twenty-fifth Missouri Infantry and also the same from the Twelfth Michigan Infantry were told to reconnoiter our front. I am now speaking from my own experience—I was one of that number. We were roused a little after midnight to fall in line, the Captain counting us off. He allowed those to fall out who did not feel well. I would have been excused as I was cook that week for the squad I belonged to, but I decided to go. After waiting some time at headquarters we at last started out about 200 strong. The stars were shining, and as nearly as I could judge it must have been about three o'clock in the morning. We reached our picket line which was only a short distance. Here we were divided into three squads. Major Powell of the Twenty-fifth Missouri Infantry was commanding by order of Col. Peabody. I have a typewritten account of how Col. Peabody on his own responsibility ordered out this force saying to one of his officers before the move was made, that he would not live to see the result of it. He was right,—not more than four hours from that time he was shot from his horse, dead.

But to return to our scouting expedition. we started off in our three squads through the woods in what seemed to me as near as I could judge, a southwesterly direction. Once or twice we came to an opening and saw log cabins which were deserted though we heard the crowing of fowls. At one time in the darkness we came near opening fire on our own men of the party to our right who were coming toward us. Had one of our rifles been discharged there would have been a slaughter, and the

enemy would have been apprised of our coming. Again we separated when presently we came upon an open spot in the timber. When we halted, the first streak of daylight had appeared and we noticed at a short distance a rise of ground which seemed to be covered with thick underbrush. As we watched we noticed something while moving through the brush and in another moment we spied a horseman whose movements we made out to be those of an enemy. Our Captain at once ordered our counter march to the rear, but we had no sooner got well started than the crack of several muskets was heard and bullets were soon whizzing after us. I feel queer yet when I think what the result would have been had we walked unawares straight into the battle lines of 42,000 of the enemy! We soon were forming with the other squads in skirmish lines, advancing, firing, taking cover wherever we could. The enemy was as yet out of sight, hidden in the timber and brush and we could only direct our fire toward the flash from their guns. Several of our force were already wounded, one mortally. However we kept moving forward. As Dr. Kedzie has said, "Knowing nothing we feared nothing." We had now covered quite a space in advancing and as the rattling of musketry became thicker and faster it became evident that there must be quite a force in front of us. Here as I took cover behind a tree hardly large enough to cover me and kept busily firing, several enemy bullets were driven into the tree about at the line of my head. One just clipped by my right ear. Evidently someone took me for a good mark.

Daylight now came streaming through the woods. There was a short lull in the firing, and looking off to the left front I discovered a cavalry force moving to our left. I called the attention of Major Powell to them and suggested that perhaps they were endeavoring to flank us. He watched them a moment and decided that was what they were trying to do, whereupon he called his bugler and immediately sounded the retreat.

As soon as that movement began, the enemy followed, pouring a galling fire upon us. We were endeavoring to carry off our wounded, and so our progress was slow.

We had not retreated far when we met Col. Moore of the Twenty-first Missouri Infantry with five companies of his regiment. He rated us as cowards for retreating. We warned him not to be too bold or he would get into trouble. It was not twenty-five minutes after that before he was wounded twice and his force nearly annihilated or put to rout. Major Powell endeavored to hold back the enemy but could not stand against them. Our battle lines gave way and the Major himself was killed before we reached camp. As soon as the enemy got within sight of our camp they began to come on with renewed strength. Doubtless the commanders were satisfied that we were unprepared to meet them.

I have mentioned that I was cook for my squad during the week of the battle. After I reached camp carrying a wounded man, I picked up a pail and started for water at the Rhea Springs, not supposing even then that the enemy would drive us from our camp. About half a mile on my way to the spring, I stepped out to a clear field where there was a camp of the Fifty-third Ohio Infantry. A group of soldiers had gathered looking westward across a ravine from which continued fighting could be heard. In another instant the quartermasters came riding in from the south, and reported that the Confederate army were coming in force, that Col. Moore's men were routed and in retreat and that Col. Moore had been wounded twice. I looked across the ravine, saw the battle line of the Confederates, and started on a run toward the spring for my pail of water. Arriving there I found men in crowds from Sherman's division at the Shiloh Church, getting water and watering horses and mules. I dipped up my pail of water and started back towards our camp. I had gone but a short distance when on looking back I saw men, horses and mules on a run, a perfect rout. The Confederate line had already appeared and yet none of Sherman's men were in line.

In this late nineteenth-century photograph, Joseph Ruff wears a Twelfth Michigan Infantry badge bearing the names of the unit's battles, including Shiloh, where he helped discover the first Confederate attack.

As I came in sight of the camp of the Fifty-third up in the field, that regiment was forming in line of battle on the edge of the timber just east of their camp. I had not gone far before this regiment began firing and the bullets whistled by me. I held to my pail of water until I arrived at our tent. Our division was out in line of battle a little distance in advance on a rise of ground. The Confederate lines were pouring a withering fire into our army. Already men were leaving the lines. Many wounded were drifting through camp to the rear. I went into the tent, set down my pail, filled my canteen and got my gun and accoutrements for it did not look as though there would be any breakfast. Bullets were riddling the tent, and as I stepped out I saw our men wavering. The battle line was breaking. Both of Prentiss's lines gave way and broke for the rear,—also Sherman's division. Some distance to our rear we re-formed. Just as the new lines began to form, the artillery began work. I halted where the new lines were but many pushed on through to the rear and I did not see them come into the battle line that day.

The battle soon became general, and I need not speak any further on the progress of this terrible conflict, which lasted all that Sunday, April 6, 1862. Enough has been written so that anyone interested may easily be informed of all that went on.

The day closed with the Union army still holding sufficient ground to stand. I stayed in the line until I lost every comrade of my company. I was in the last effort we made to repel the Confederate army. Exhausted at length, I lay down on the bare ground that Sunday night under one of the large siege guns up on the bluff above the river and went to sleep. This cannon was covered with a canvas. I looked out and saw the stars shining. The battle had closed for that night and only an occasional shell from the gunboats came crashing through the timber. Sometime during the night I woke up and turned over. Something cold was on my shoulders,—it felt like water. Feeling around I discovered that it was a little rivulet and that it was running under my body down the bluff into a deep ravine. I sat up, resting my head on my knees and looked out from under the canvas. It was raining. What a godsend to both Blue and Gray, lying wounded out on the battlefields! It stopped the fire the shells had started at many points in the dry grass and also provided water for the parched throats of those who could move only a few inches.

With the light of another day, the battle again resumed and with three fresh divisions of Buell's army which had joined us and with Lew Wallace's division and the broken organization of Grant's army, the contest was resumed in full fury. Crawling out from under my shelter I moved down to where I could fill my canteen with dirty Tennessee water and a few hardtacks. I fell in with a portion of our regiment that our Lieut. Col. Graves had picked up, and we marched again to the battle line. We were attached as a reserve to a portion of Buell's men. By two o'clock, with occasional downpours of rain, the Confederates gave up the struggle and began their retreat back to Corinth. They showed themselves a wiser but a sadder army and left us master of the field of human slaughter. We followed up the retreating army and found among the fallen, Blue and Gray intermingled. Some were cold and stark in the embrace of death; some were breathing out their lives. Thousands of them had lain there all night torn and bleeding, with no hand to lend assistance.

One day not long ago when the armistice of the World War was being celebrated. I heard two ladies talking. One of them was saying what a terrible war this last one had been. The other answered that the Civil War was a terrible war too.

"Yes," said the first woman, "but that was only a picnic."

If that lady had walked with me on that Monday afternoon close upon the retreating Confederates, she would never have wanted to witness another such "picnic." There is one experience I would like to speak of in particular. I came upon three Confederate soldiers, two of them wounded so sorely that they were just breathing their last. One was a beardless boy, not more than fourteen or fifteen years old. He was sitting leaning up against a tree and as I approached him he called out in a clear voice:

"Well, if you are going to kill me,—kill me."

I said, "Why do you think I want to kill you?"

He answered, "Our folks say that you kill all the prisoners."

I replied, "Yes, your people have told you many things. They would make us out savages."

"But what are you going to do with me?" he asked.

"Why," said I, "the ambulances are out picking up all the wounded and they will come for you too."

A piece of shell had shattered his hip and he could not rise upon his feet. Just then an ambulance came near and I called their attention to this severely wounded boy. He continued saying like all the people did down there:

"What you'se come down to fight we-uns for? If you want the niggers I wisht you had all of them. I haven't got any."

When he asked again what would be done with him, I told him that when they came after him he would no doubt be taken aboard the hospital boat lying in the Tennessee River, where he would receive attention. He said he had a mother in Illinois and wanted to know if he would be allowed to see her. I told him I thought so, and that if ever he reached her I'd advise him to stay there. Again assuring him that he would certainly be cared for when the ambulance returned, I left him. I have wondered many a time whether he ever reached his mother.

My fellow comrade had now left me, so I plodded my way towards our camp, which the Confederates had captured and occupied the day before. There and everywhere the battle strife was evident. Of course our camps were rifled of everything that could be carried away. Some of our tents were burned, mine among them. Just on the right of our camp I saw the dead body of Colonel Peabody, commander of our brigade. He had evidently been shot from his horse for he lay with his legs across a log and his head and shoulders on the ground. All the buttons and shoulder straps had been cut from his clothes.

It was growing dark and but few of the regiment had arrived at the camp. Most of them started back to the river. Here I had another melancholy experience, for as I tramped over the battlefield, thick with darkness and occasional rain, I stumbled over something, and bending down to see more distinctly I found myself looking into the face of a dead soldier, I hurried on, reached the Landing, and there I found what was certainly a conglomerate host!—soldiers from every army of the service hunting and inquiring for their comrades. I found two or three of mine, and we proceeded to find a place to lie down and get some needed rest. We found some straw and spread it under a baggage wagon that would keep us up out of the mud. There we lay down and slept while the rain kept steadily on. Next morning we crawled out from under our partial shelter, filled our canteens with Tennessee water, muddy from the rains, and with a few hardtacks settled down to our "picnic" breakfast. These were the common experiences every soldier in the war met.

After breakfast we went again to the battlefield and to our camp, where we resumed our duties as a regiment organization. We buried our dead, cared for the wounded and numbered our total loss at 192. Our division being badly torn by this battle, we were assigned to John A. Logan's division and encamped with them.

It seemed to us that all the clouds in the universe had gathered over western Tennessee and were sending down a continual deluge, which at times we felt was cold enough to freeze. We lacked the most necessary things,—supplies, medical facilities and hospitals. Things began to tell on our way and as we moved toward Corinth, we had to leave the sick behind at every step.

The only thing to do with them was to send them north by steamboat, even though there was inadequate medical attention given to them on board so that many died before they arrived. Conditions in the army got worse every day. We were constantly moving, perhaps only a few miles at a time, and our supply and baggage trains were often mired so that they could not come up with us for days. Meanwhile, we were left without shelter, food or hospital care, and this soon caused nearly all to become sick. Stomach trouble, diarrhea, fever and chills soon brought a large share of our army to the point where they were in no shape for offensive service against any enemy. General H. W. Halleck then arrived from headquarters at St. Louis, Missouri, and took command in person, but I doubt whether any of the rank and file believed that conditions were bettered thereby. His commanders and army generally believe to this day that he could have captured Beauregard's army and not have allowed them to get away. No soldier who served in that campaign will ever forget it.

Our own regiment, the Twelfth Michigan Infantry, got so reduced by sickness and death on account of exposure and hardship that General Logan sent us back to the river to recruit. But alas! That was no place to recruit. Sick soldiers as we were, scores died and many were sent home. There was not a building for a hospital, nor physicians to care for us, nor the needed medical supplies. I myself was sick for three weeks and became so weak that I despaired of my life and felt I should never see home again. But He who cares for all His children must surely have been watching over me, for I recovered slowly. Many years later I offered up my thanks to Him as I knelt on that battlefield on the fifty-fourth anniversary of that terrible conflict.

Captured at Bull Run

By Tony L. Trimble

In April 1861, twenty-six-year-old William H. Withington of Jackson went off to war as captain of the Jackson Greys, a company in the First Michigan Infantry Regiment. At First Bull Run, Withington remained behind to care for his wounded colonel, Orlando B. Willcox. Willcox and Withington survived the war's first battle only to spend the next six months in a Southern prison.

Jackson, Michigan, resident William Herbert Withington experienced a short military career during the Civil War. However, the courage and leadership he displayed in two major battles earned him an honorary brigadier generalship and the congressional Medal of Honor.

Withington was born in Dorchester, Massachusetts, on February 1, 1835. His father, William, and his uncle Leonard, both noted scholars and clergymen, raised William in an academic atmosphere.

After attending public school in Boston, Withington enrolled at Phillips Academy in Andover, Massachusetts, excelling in mathematics and business. He first worked as a salesman for a Boston leather-goods store. Later, he kept books for the North Wayne Scythe Company, traveling to other eastern cities. On one journey Withington met representatives from Pinney & Lamson, agricultural-implement manufacturers in Jackson. The chance meeting eventually brought Withington to Michigan when in 1857 he received an offer from the company to help sort out its financial difficulties. Before he could do so, the business was further weakened by a national financial panic and Pinney's suicide. An employee group bought the firm and reorganized it under the name Sprague, Withington & Company. At about the same time, Withington met and married Julia Beebe, daughter of Joseph E. Beebe, a prominent Jackson citizen. Withington's new company and his marriage had just begun to flourish when the Civil War and President Abraham Lincoln's call for troops reached Michigan.

As a youth, Withington had been a member of Boston's Independent Cadets, a militia organization that traced its roots back to the American Revolution. Late in the spring of 1861, the Jackson Greys was organized, with Withington as captain. The Greys became Company B, First Michigan Infantry.

On May 16, 1861, Withington and his men were part of the first Michigan regiment to arrive in Washington, DC. On May 25 the First Michigan participated in the capture of Alexandria, Virginia; Withington's company was assigned to occupy city hall. "I did so," Withington wrote, "taking the colors, which I caused to be flung out of the window of the mayor's office."

On July 21, 1861, Colonel Orlando B. Willcox led the First Michigan into combat at the Battle of Bull Run. When the regiment regrouped following an attack on the enemy works, both Colonel Willcox and Captain Withington were missing. Major Alonzo F. Bidwell, who succeeded to command, reported that Withington, while attempting to bind Willcox's wound, was also injured and had fallen on the field.

For the next twenty days Bidwell's report was the only official word to reach Withington's wife. On August 7 Julia Withington received a telegram from H. L. Skinner, a member of Withington's regiment, who assured her that her husband was uninjured but had been taken prisoner and would soon be transported to Richmond. A few days later the War Department confirmed Withington's status.

Withington was imprisoned for the next six months. On July 29 he wrote in his diary he hoped he would soon leave the Lewis house near Manassas, Virginia, and be sent to Richmond. "The putrification about this house is horrible. The wounded men are covered with maggots."

In September, along with other Michigan officers, Withington was herded aboard a train bound for Castle Pinckney in Charleston, South Carolina. On January 30, after nearly a month of negotiations, Withington was exchanged. He arrived in Jackson and was greeted at the railroad station by "an immense concourse of people," including Governor Austin Blair and a few members of his company, who stood at attention awaiting his arrival. With the townspeople marching behind Withington, a band led him home to his wife.

Following his release from the Confederate prison, Withington discovered that the First Michigan had been reorganized without him. Since his term of service had expired during his imprisonment, he was formally mustered out of the army on January 31, 1862.

Withington was dissatisfied with the way his military service had ended. "I hate exceedingly the idea of ending my military career in [prison], yet I see no present prospect of re-entering the service," he noted. Early in 1862 Withington was appointed commander of the Twentieth Michigan. However, he soon was transferred to the Seventeenth Michigan, where he was commissioned a colonel.

On August 27, 1862, the Seventeenth Michigan departed for Washington, DC. On September 14 the newly formed regiment fought at South Mountain. The unit's determined charges under heavy fire across an open field to rout rebel troops from positions behind stone walls earned it the nickname Stonewall Regiment. A few days later the Seventeenth saw heavy fighting at the Battle of Antietam.

Withington remained in command until March 20, 1863, when he resigned. He was needed at home, where the death of his only child had affected his wife's health. On March 13, 1865, Withington was made brevet brigadier general for his "conspicuous gallantry" at South Mountain.

Once home in Jackson, Withington returned to his implement business. Julia recovered and five more children, three of whom survived childhood, were born. In 1873 Withington was elected to the state legislature, where he introduced a bill to organize a state militia. His efforts earned him the unofficial title "father of the Michigan state troops." His military expertise and leadership skills led to an offer of a colonelcy with the First Regiment. In 1879 the state militia was organized into a brigade and Withington was appointed brigadier general. As commanding officer, he held high expectations and maintained strict discipline.

By 1883 Withington determined that the state militia was well established and he resigned, dividing his time between his family and his business affairs. He also served as trustee of the State Insane Asylum in Kalamazoo and president of the Union Bank of Jackson. He was active in the Episcopal church, Jackson's Grand Army of the Republic chapter and the Masonic lodge.

Withington was a delegate to the 1876 national Republican convention, where Rutherford B. Hayes was nominated as presidential candidate.

While Withington busied himself with his many activities, his former subordinate, James O'Donnell, editor of the *Jackson Daily Citizen*, sought the highest recognition possible for Withington's service to his country—the congressional Medal of Honor—citing the general's performance at both Bull Run and South Mountain. On January 7, 1895, the War Department issued the medal to Withington for pushing forward at Bull Run with a small body of his regiment, in repeated charges, in one of which a lost battery was momentarily recovered, and for his gallant attempt under the hottest fire of the day to save the life of his colonel.

Withington received the honor with pride but was disappointed with the medal's appearance. He wrote the War Department, acknowledging the tribute paid him, but then he criticized the medal and its presentation case. "I would not have any other old soldier feel as I did on opening the package. They are a disgrace to the department and very near an insult to the recipients of the medals." The War Department marked Withington's letter, "File, no reply." However, a year later, a new ribbon and rosette were designated and offered to all Medal of Honor recipients. It is unknown if Withington requested the new medal.

Withington died on June 27, 1903, at age sixty-eight.

Known as the "father of Michigan state troops" for his role in organizing the state militia, Jackson businessman William H. Withington had an impressive war record, earning a general's star and the congressional Medal of Honor.

The Second Michigan Joins the Army of the Potomac

Edited and with an introduction by Chester McArthur Destler

On April 17, 1861, with the war just days old, Philo Gallup of Pokagon
strolled into an army recruiting station and joined the
Second Michigan Infantry. For the next seven months he fired off
many letters home vividly describing army camp life and drill.

The Second Michigan Volunteers was an important unit of the brigade that protected the rear of the Union army during the retreat from the First Battle of Bull Run. Recruited, initially, as three-months' volunteers following President Abraham Lincoln's proclamation of April 15, 1861, it was formed on April 25, 1861, in Detroit from uniformed militia companies, with the exception of the Kalamazoo and the Niles companies. After brief training at Detroit and being mustered into federal service as a three-year regiment, the Second entrained for Washington, DC, where it was among the first regiments to arrive for the relief of the capital. After having been complimented repeatedly by General Winfield Scott on its quality, the Second became part of the army of General Irvin McDowell. The regiment's excellence must be attributed to its fortune in having as its colonel Israel B. Richardson, who had served with distinction during the Mexican War.

Twenty-one-year-old Philo H. Gallup of Pokagon, Berrien County, joined Company E as a private under Captain Robert Brethschneider at Niles on April 17, 1861. Later the women of that town gave the company a silk flag that became the regimental colors when the Second Regiment was mustered into service in Detroit on May 25, 1861.

Gallup's letters home provide a contemporary record of the experiences and reactions to army life of a private in a crack regiment. Its strict discipline, the troops' pride in this and their assertion of the superiority of the Wolverines were important factors in their morale and the unit's superior performance during the early months of the Civil War. Its steadiness under fire at Blackburn's Ford, Virginia, and during the retreat from Bull Run; its loyalty to Richardson, who was quickly promoted to command of the Wolverine Brigade; and its discipline while on garrison duty at Washington endeared it to President Abraham Lincoln.

The letters reproduced here, with their original spelling and lack of capitalization and punctuation, extend from May 3, 1861, to January 23, 1862, by which time the regiment had become part of General George B. McClellan's Army of the Potomac. The remainder of the series is omitted because of lack of historical significance. Gallup was killed in action at Williamsburg during the Peninsular Campaign on May 5, 1862. His staunch Unionism, bravery, scorn for the faint hearted, humor, fun-loving nature, readiness to join other soldiers in direct action against civilian secessionists and pride in the regiment are patent, while the subsequent decline in his morale stems from illness and idleness. His accounts of that unit's brush with the Baltimore mob early in June 1861 while en route to Washington, supplement the remininiscences of Herman Petzold and the account in the *Record of Service of Michigan Volunteers in the Civil War, 1861-1865.*

●●●●●

Detroit
May 3d, 1861
Dear Father

i take my pen in hand to let ou no that i am well and i hope that i shal find you injoing the same helth i hav thought of home severl times the onley time that i think of it is when i gow too bead they are made of 1 blanked and 1 straw tick wee have to bunk at 9 o clock and get up at 6 wee hav got musket too drill with no suit but will get them soon wee hav receive no pay yet what ever i talk of leving for home if i dont get some money pretty soon there are 10 Co here now in drill some of tehm with miny rifels but wee will all have rifels so the Captin seys i Could right lots but i hav not time too sey much too night i was sadly disappointed when i came too the citty it dont campare with Niles as for beuty i nevers was in any place that is as lonesum as it is here but wee shal see niles next week or week after the captin says that wee will have to gow to caro Cairo 365 miles south of chigago well i must quit giv my respects too all i want you to right and right away Di rect your leters in car of Captin Bredsnider

• • • • •

Robert Bread snider
the captin of the Co E second regiment
Detroit
May 8th 1861
Dear sir

I take my pencil in my hand to let you now hat i am well and i hope that i shall find you enjoying the same helth i have simply to say that if anybody had cause to complain it would be our men camping as we did three days and three nights in Niles and marching the forth night to Detroit to be on duty by the time required by battalion order No. 1 we arrived at contonment Blair at 1-1/2 o clock in the morning and not finding the quarters fitted up like the aster [Astor] house we went to work to do what we were able it si the duty of a soldier or a citisan who stands up for his coutry not to Complain if he cannot hav the acommodation he lieves behind and if there should be any one who complains he had better pack his knapscak and gow home to his mother but i am certain there is no man in the whole regiment who woudl go or who has complained they evidently know more about our history; than citsan did the revolutionary patriots in valley forge complain they had to march in the snow with there bare feet and to stand the cold twenty degrees below zero without blankets and meny times without camp fires did the armey complain when our beloved washington crossed the delaware and fought the battle of trenton they had to march in snow and mud and fight the hessians besides and they did it in good stile too this patriotic feeling is yet in the men who form the second regiment and of wich our men are in fact there is no suffering here in any we are all soldiers and as such we will show our fathers and mothers wifes sisters brothers and sweethearts that we are contented if can but go where a fight is in prospect we are well provided with the fat of the land and if the rain of heaven falls on us and makes our grond a little mudy we will be the last to complain

Yours Please show this to father
Please right ameadiatly Direct your letters in Car of captain Robert Bretchsnider Co E second
Philo II Gallup
A Member of the
Coler Compney
E No 1 second regment

• • • • •

May 8th 1861
Dear Father

I am at a stand now to know what to Do we must do one thing or the other you requested me to consult with you be fore enlisting for more than three months all them that wants to volunteer for during the war has the privleg and the rest is not excepted there is the bigest part of the company is going for three years or during the war i for one wants to gow with the company if you sey no I shall be under the necessity of coming home this is all i hav to say . . . Dont sey No
Yours truly Right Amediately

• • • • •

Detroit
May 14 1861
Dear Sister

there is nothing that don me so much good as to here from you i began to think that ou dident think of me much i roughs fore letters three tow ou and one to stancel and i recieved one that . . . came yesterday i had just finished and maled a letter to ou but that makes no diferaces . . . i told you in the other that we was a going to the fort we will gow to day or to morrow we are all glad of that the Captin seys that we will be of for carlstian in a few day that suits the most of the boys some of them is a backing out they dont like eideah of going for three years or fore the turm of ware that just suits me i hav started now and i want to see it through if i ever felt discureg it was the other morning when I found that spider in my coffee and a little fus but chat dident amount to much they started to the yard house but the captin saw them it is not worth while to say mutch about it i was glad to here the nuse theis morning the Coucel sed that all them that goes for the war can hav a pass home if you request it i will come home you spoke about my degarotipe as soon as we get our uniforms i will send it to ou and i should like to hav yours very much there nothing that would suit me as well as to have it i would not bee much surprised if you would see me home in a few days i can have to days ican leve here at seven oClock in the evning and reach home in the mornning and if you want to hav me come i will i can com in cide of a week there is a good meny of the boys that left Niles that starts for home to day they left the company there spoted for ever i had rather die than leve the company now i hav no more time to right to da i giv mi respects to all right as soon as you get this

• • • • •

Fort Wayne, Detroit
May 23 1861
Dear sister

i take my pen in hand to let you now that I am well and i hope that i shal find you injoying the same helth there is a good eel of excitement here this morning the boys is all geting vaxenated there was one man broked out yesterday with the small pox the doctor was cared on ameadley. there is a conciterable in canidday to day as well as here this is the forth day the boats are under motion all the time caring pasengers back and forth the Captim sed that wee would get our pay this morning we got our uniforms Tuesday we hardley new one another it revive the boyes up a conciterable they all feel firstrate with the except some of them that court not gow home i spoke to the ordly this morning he snaped us of and sed dont talk to him about owing home our compny is ful now we hav a, 100, and i now all very good boys there was too marchd out by the point of baonet yesterday and there was once man caut for derserting the compny the offesers took him and cut his hair all of of his hed and march him out we are having good times now we hav too fiddles here there is dancing and dancing all the time soldiers must hav fun as well as some hard work it has been a long deaf so lonsome time here every thing look deaf there is nothing to be sene but the boats saling up and down the river i must quit they are calling out beetalian drill good by giving respects to all yours truley

I must ad a few lines more after i came in from drill i got your leter you spolk of my coming home i had giv up coming but i shall try it again if i don't succede this time i shal tri no more i had my picthure you shal have as soon as i can get it and for the lengh of the time that we will stay here i do not know but there is no prospects of leaving yet for a month we was musterd in to the united, states servis this after noon there was not one thrown out of this compny your degarotype i would like if i could get it myst git i hav not time to right eny more rite as soon as you can and as often as you can

• • • • •

Fort Wayn Detroit
June 4th 1861
Dear sister

i take my pen in my hand to let you now that i am still in joying the sams helth i hav not sene a sick day sence i enlisted you would think sow if you would see me now i hav gand 7 pd a ready times are lively by spells and then agane they are dull last week once of the boys of Co B ide the drumss was mufeld and the corps was cared to the cars and sent home at that time there was 22 sick in the hospital but there on the gane now we are a gowing to Camp to morrow on an island 10 miles below here it has been the report that we would march for western verginia next thurs but how tru it is i dont know there is so meny reports flying now days that now body mows what one to believe day before yesterday we had our fun on bertalion drill wee had blank catridges and if we didant rays a smoke then i wouldent sey sow there was to ramrods shot off i hav sen eny one that felt sow cheep when the Cornel sent then to find there rods Co I take the rag of the bus we hav the prase of being the best Co in the regment and wee calculated gane the prase and wee expect to ceap it the rules are very stricket if the boys dont tred rite up they are put in the gard and if that dont do they put them to wheeling stone for 12 hours the most of the fue commence about gow to meting evry soldier is ordered to gow to meting evry sonday and that is oneley time wee can get out without a pas form the captin and the Curnel's name sind to it i hant out sence we came to the fort i wanted to gow down to day to see the desstruction of the uper part of the town the fier broke out last night and burned down severl blocks and shortly after the fire was stopt another broked out in caniday and done a good eal of damge that and the death of dugles [Stephen A. Douglas] caused grate excitement here to day the flags all stands at haf mast they will probley bee histed to morrow well i must quit i have not time to right eny more this after noon i send my respects to all ou must answer this do son as you can yours truley right amediateiley giv my respects to all

O hant i glad
i coming out of the wilderness
out of the wilderness out of the welderness
O hant i glad i comemg out of the wilderness
out of the wilderness out of the wilderness
say down in tenniscsea. . . .

I had seulad this leter up be fore i had perfect nues but i thought i would rite few lines more this is the last leter that i shal hav a chance to rite to you from here there was a teligraph dispatch for us for to march for washington . . . that wee would march on Thursday that will be day after morrow you nead not rite to mo till you here from me agane i will right to yo as soon as i get to the landing place that will bee soon next week sirten let it rest as this

• • • • •

Washing
June, the, 10th, 1861
Lizzy Dear sister

i take my pen in my hand to let you now that i shal find you in joying the same helth i resieve yours Thursday nite just after starting for Clevland concequently i hav not had time to rite to you be four now but i hav to right all ishould like to i have viseted one of the greateis of senery emagnible we was treted in all the towns on the road to pitburg [Pittsburgh] we had all the cake and py all we wanted we cept the roud hot all the way we got to pitsburg in the night we stade there . . . and left for harisBorg we got there the next night about 5 o'clock in the afternoon we piched our tents and stade there over night Sunday morning we started for washington we reach Baltimore just at dark there we was not molested untill we got in the cars just after we started the sones flu one was throwed at the sentnel and hit him in the brest then the captin giv orders to shute the first man that threw the next he had not sut the dors before another one was throwed and hit the ordly and he put a ball threw him they did not troubled us eny more bit to have revenge they went down to the batry and Commenced on the sentnels there they kiled 6 of thim the Sentnels beng ood shot ganed the day the union men has got the upper-hand of then now we reached wasington a bout 11 o clock last night it is sed that we would go to harpers fery tere was 3000 men went there yesterday and there is 6000 more a going to day there is a bout 1700 soldiers here now there is a man sunstruck to day he can not liv i must quit i hav not time to right any more whin i get to a soping place will right to you agane and let you now where to direct your leter you will here from me agane and i will tell you more about it . . . Godd By Lizzy Giv my respects to all that Nose me

• • • • •

Washing June 17 1861
Dear sister

i take my pen in hand . . . to let you now that i wel and i hope that you are injiying the same helth i thought i would tell you where i am and i hope i shall here from you we ar Camping in gorgetown hights

[Georgetown Heights] near the potomac—river clost to the chane Brig [the chain bridge] it is a nise plas the river just devids us from the enyomy we and another one on the other the third Rigment of michigan is camping close to us and the forth will be here to morrow michigan agin the world General scot [Winfield Scott] sed that our rigiment was the best that had ben in washington we hev the prase of being the best where ever we got we can whip our weight in wild cats we stand open for eny thing we fear nothing we are the worst pille in the box we get the verginy cramps very frequently there is a nise lot of chicens in verginy and the prtist girls there i ever sea but the dos us but little good if the boys nowed as much be fore they jond they war there would not meny here i am sure that i would not but i am here now and i am bound to sea it throught it suits me firstrate i aam geting fat and lasey i though that we should hav a little brush the other nite bit it past over then the boys are eaching for a fite there is one secesionis lives here we got at him the oter nite and we was a goning to string him up onely for the Captin we would have hung p in the treas the oferser of the day made him taken the oth of leagence he took the oth and then sloped we had agood ell of fun with him but it is all over the worst of all is to of our men is to be cort marcheled and hav a ball and chane for 20 days it looks hard but the rules must be obade if we could get some money i would feal beter i want to send some money i would feal beter i want to send some to father but i cant send it till i can get it the 8 of next month we get our money and then i will send home about 25 dollars to fix up the little maters i hav not sene a sent sences i hav left home i am sorey to sa that i hav not sene to this be fore i must quit i am on poleas deuty . . . Good By Dear Lizzy Re Memeber Me Di rect your letters to Washington Second Rigment Compny E

• • • • •

Washington
June the 24, 1861
Dear sir

i take my pencil i my hand to let you know that i an well and i hope that is shal find you injiying the same helth i hav sene some hard times since i left Pohagon as well as some good we are at camp now on gorgetown hights near the potomac river in the deastrict of Columbia we are having fine times but it will not last long we expect to march ovr in verginig soon as soon as the forth Rigment gets here we are agowing over to take farfax [Fairfax, Virginia] ther is bout three thousand seseionis there we think we hav forse enough to take it now but we want all the michigan boys together we had the nane of the mich wolverreans at Baltimore they gif us the name of the mich Bull dogs the reason of that was the rebells thought to hav revenge of us they commenced througing stones at us to stop it the ordly shot one of them and kild him instley that spilt there fun we was not molested agane we reached washington at nite about 9 o clock we lade over there 2 days and 3 nites then we marcht up and sene uncal abe [President Abraham Lincoln] and jeneral sCot [General Scott] he giv us the name of his mich tigers and you would think we was tigars if you would sea us now we are the worst pills in the box we fear nothing care for the same who wouldant bee a soldier a man could not . . . me to come home to stay fur all there is noting like home i am bound to be a soldier some of the boys think that it is hard fare to sleap on the ground with nothing but there blankets over them but they must put up with it now there are here it will do them no good now i shall hav to quit it is time to mount gard . . . pleas rite to me and let now how the folks . . . to pokago [Pokagon, Michigan] i have not hurd from there yet dont forget me giv my respects to all.

• • • • •

Washington
July 6/61
Dear Friend

    it is with pleasure that i . . . wright to you i am happy to inform you that i am in the best of helth . . . i got a letter from home the third of July she sed that you would like to hear from me i was surprised i hav rote to you twiss before i had made up my mind that care much about me or yould hav rote to me i hav rote eight letters home and i hav received one sence i left Detroit . . . i should like to know what is a gowing on about Pokhagon i dare say that there is more a gowing on there than there was here it was as still the forth as it would bee with you on Sunday the war escitement is sow grate they dare not make much stur there was not a gun fired the whole day i thought i would hav a little fun so i began to proseed i dug a hole in the ground the boys stole some catrages and took the balls out of them and put the powder in the hole and put a flew [fuse] and placed the dirt all a round it and then set it on fire we had just time to get out of the way of it it blode the ground up for fore feet a round it that is all the forth we hed here they kept a duble gard over us all day and not a man loud to gow out at all it is the first forth that i spent with out five cts in my pocket and not bee aloud to gow eny were to see

Israel Richardson of Pontiac led the Second Michigan Infantry to war in 1861. A West Point graduate, Richardson was mortally wounded during the Battle of Antietam on September 17, 1862. The fifty-two-year-old general died on November 3, 1862.

eny body or eny thing just after the explosion i had aninvitation to adance at knite in verginaa they todde us that i wouldent cost no eny thing if we would come so we sed we would gow and a nice time we had to there was some of the pretys girls there that i ever saw and good dancers they was to i just giv my self a way they fell in love with me rite a way the old planter told me that if stay i should not loose eny thing well i must quit my nonces i should like to right more. . . Rite soon

• • • • •

Washington
July 6/61
Dear sister

    i receaved yours letter that you rote the 26 of June . . . i am glad to in form you that i am as tuff as a bare now . . . all the forth i had was to stay in here and study

45

devetry [deviltry] the boys had don all they could then H filips and i went to work and dug a hole in the ground and then put in some pouder and fild it up with dirt and fixt a flew and packed all around and set it a fire we had just time to get awa it bloud it up the ground for three feet a round the captins all ran down to se what was up but you may bet that philo was not to be sean they could not find out nothing about it all they could sea was the ground throught yp if we had some money we would feal better the Curnel sed we should not drill another step till we got our pay i is usless to sey eny thing a a bout it i should like to hav some to send home . . . Dont forget Me

• • • • •

Camp Windfiel scott
July 10 1861
Dear sister

I have a little time to rite this morning Co be fore leaving we are a gowing to verjinia for to hav a little fight they hav been at it for some ime the Curnell sed it was time fore us to hav a hand in sow we wholder our arms and three days provisions in our haversack and one blanket rold up tite and strapt a corss our shoulder that suits the boys it is just what they hav been wanting for a long time i think that they will get enough of it we have got to march rite in to the hotest of the battle the first charge of some of them will bee in ther britches i hav no time to right eny more this morning i am well and harty

• • • • •

Camp Arlington, Highis Washington July 28th 61
Dear sister

Being that i hav a few minits that i can call my one i will im prove it in wrighting to ou i suppose that you hav hurd more a bout the Fite than i told you Bee fore in the last letter i was in ahury when i rote to you bee fore Concequently i Could not tell you the pertickler but i will try to giv you them now when i rote to you Bee fore i had just Came to Campt from the Battle we marched from Camp on tues and commencet the Battle on thurs we fitt for 4 hours and killing some 3 or 400 of them we then silancet for the nite all was still till morning the first thing we saw was a flag of truse coming to the Curnell Beging Leaf and time of him tu Bery the ded and being that the Jenerl marched us in bee fore the time given him he gave them the time so that we Could get a few more men so Sunday the Battel be gun after fighting with Canons for 4 long hours and the muskets

about 3 hours then having to Retreat it didant feal first trate there was to meny lives lost there is a bout 1300 men ling on the field 6 or 8000 [sic] of them are seces it is a mear accident that i am left to rite to you againe there was a Canon Ball came so clostt to my face that i felt the wind of it as it past if that wasant a clost call i dont now but it is closter than i want them to come every day for fear they mint scorch the fethers a little did i think of it then and little do Care about if if they will onley keep there distance i wish that you could sea the feald then you could form some ideah of it but as it is you cannont onely pa can he has sene the like of it be fore if he has he can tell you somethig about it i dont now as i can tell you sow you would now eny more than to sey that a man can walk on the ded Bodys and Blood for 6 miles o it is an awful cite itell you the Battle was Faught at a place cald Buls Run it is the worst place that they hav got to take but Jenerl seys that if we take that place he will Bring us back to washington and keep us there for his Citty Gards the Balance of our time . . . dont for get me now

• • • • •

Camp Arlington Hights
Washington Citty D C
Aug 9th 1861
Dear sister

it with pleasure that i set down this evening . . . i am gat greasy and rosy you hav hurd all about the Battle at Buls Run i think it hardley Nessessery to give a history of the fight i think you havgot it Correct but little could you immagen the siet that i hav sene sence i left home the awfulist site that i ever sawe was at the Battle ground it is a site that nere can bee for goten to se the men slaterd some of them ded some of them with there legs off some with an arm off some with now hed some with there face off one in partickler with a Canon Ball through hs Boddy there was a hole throught him Big enough to stick your head in o libby it is awful but i fear it not all though it may bee my turn next if it is here gose i hav had the plesure of suting a man on picket guard there is not a man mising in the Co with the exceptions of 11 of them that Deserted sence the fight Ca if i never git home wthout desertg i will never see home i hav thought of home severl times sence i hav been Cooking if there was eny thing that was to bee cooked that i did no now at a moment notis i would stop and think how ma ust to cook them and then i could gow to work and do it i am yet a cooking there is know prospect of my geting out of it nether i hope that i could see you all come in to the Camp while i am in here owoudent i bee glad o come and see us you spoke a bout Charley Russy i hope that you and George Henry has not fel out o it cant be so if it is i hope that you wount let Charley come in now you now that he could not if i was there for i would rase a muse for i had rather fite than eat now you and him couldent agree before and i am sure you can not now if you do now it is a wonder you spoke about your trubbles you can rite to me and tell me what it is and if I can do you eny good By riditing i will do it for you ou need not be afraid to tell me what it is i am sure i should like to know . . . we are expect an attack we are setting here this evening a hearing the guns firing at fare fax there was about 1000 rops started for there this morning the Rebbels has got persesion of the town they sed they was a gowing to make a stand there and if they did they are having a little Brush we are wayting for a Call well i hav told ou all the nues this time

Giv my Respects to all speak a good Word to the girls For me

• • • • •

Aug 24th 1861
Head quarters Camp Arlington Hights
Washington DC

I Now take my pen in hand to Answer you letter I got it this after noon i was glad to here from you . . . o words Cannot expres my felings I looked for a answer from them packegs o I have got it I was pleas to my harts Contents . . . Libby you spoke of the pictures that I sent you I had one taken to send you with my uniform on and my gun I my hand and then I thougt that it is not enough we had got our Cook house done thinks that would bee nice to send so I had it taken you sed that I was standing by the side of the tabel with a fork in my hand and a knife in the other well it is so you spoke of the one or too Boys that was sitting by the fier one of them was harvy Dellano [James H. Delano] John Nose him he use to worke for mur in the shop the other was a Boy that we Call Big ingen you would now him eny way the one that had the Bottle in his hand was William DeLano [William H. Delano] he work for mury to and the one that wants it is I, shanahan pa nose him if you dont the one that had the ax in his hand was a man that lived to, Parmers and the one that is got the kittles in his hand is a duchman that I had to carie water for me to Cook with there is Bily Randel [William B. Randall] from Burtend and J B Richesen [J. B. Richardson, a corporal] from Burtrand and the Captin stands up be side the fort with his hand Resting on, it and C Morse [Charles Morse] standing be side table Cuting Bread it is not as I, wanted it but I had to hav it taken in the morning just after Brekfast and then there was to meny a round but how ever I though it would be nse the other one that is standing up with a revolver in my hand that was taken for the nonsance of it the young man that is with me is J. B. Ricken he spoke of it and he wanted to send one home to his folks and i thought I would do the same so up we went to the degeroing Room well libby you dont No how glad I was to get yours o I had thought of it severl times o how I should like to bee at home for a little while

• • • • •

Sept 1st 1861
Dear Sister,

As I am at leasure, for a few minutes, I will attempt to write you a few lines.

Your letter dated the 17th, was at hand a few days since. I was very much pleased to receive your likeness, it came through all safe and sound, and loks very natural. the rebils have been advancing upon us, our regiment has been in advance of our army for several days to keep them back until we are ready for them. I have been out on picket guard for the last three days and was close enough to them to hear them whisper among themselves. I shot one and wounded another. our boys have killed about twenty of them. We have only lost one and two wounded, so far. the same time our man was shot one of his comrads shot their Major, or some other field officer, for the Secession flag was lowered to a half amst, and has been so ever since.

When I was out Skouting, it put me in mind of father hunting Deer, but you better believe it is sharper hunting them than Deer, when we are hunting Deer, only one side does the shooting, but in this case, both sides has a hand in shooting.

We are in sight of them all of the time, and they can see our movements, as well as, we can theirs. each side works to the best Advantage, and try to kill all they can.

About two thousand men have been at work, for the last week, clearing the timber off of a large hill, and are preparing to build a large Fort, and by the time that is done, I expect you will hear of a very heavy battle somewhere near hear.

The news is to day that Gen. McDowel has taken 800 prisoners at Fortress Monrowoe, Lizzie how do you like your new Beau, it may be a mistry to you how I

A member of Philo Gallup's company, Berrien County resident John Noll wears the new dress uniform issued to the men of the Second Michigan Infantry while they were in winter quarters outside Washington, DC.

found out about it his friends told me I had a spirit, and I dont know which . . . perhaps I dreampt it.

Do you know where L'ze Ducket is, if you do please let me know in your next letter, I think it is time I had written her afew lines, . . . Give my love to all, Yours as ever,

• • • • •

[written approximately September 3]

Dear sister

we hav been ordered to Pack up our things and Put 2 days Provisions in our haver sacks and Bee redy for a fight with all expecttacions there will Be afight at Balls Cross roads that is 4 miles from here I have Been on Picket For th last week they hav shot at me time and agane I have shot 4 of them we hav kild all of 50 and they have kild 1 of ours we hav done very well so far you wind all the Placis that we hav fought on and all that we will hav to fight on here is a map that I send you so that you Can find all them your self . . . From your effection Brother Phlo H Gallup Here is a little Peace of telegraph wier that belonging to the secessionis I hav not time to rite much a bout it I will tell you all about it in the next

• • • • •

Sept 5th 1861
Campt as usul
Absent But still Presant

I rkeived your letter from the other day when i was on Picket gard . . . I had just come in from skouting I had fun I tell you although they came very near geing me they shot at me twice they hit me rite where they mist me before. I was within a few Rods of them near enough to count the butens on one of there coats I studied for a few monents Coming to the concluysion that there was but one way to get a way from there that was to get up ad Run take leg Ball for security so off I starts I hadent went But a few stepts before he shot at me he did not mis me more than 4 inches neither time i felt confident that he could not hit me it was luckey for me that he did not sea me before he did if he had I would hav been a goner they shot at me in the morning on Post they cut off the little twigs of off the Bushes that I stod in under it was not more than half a mild of I tell ou they made me wink eny now that is clost enough for me there is a man to bee shot to day at 10, O Clock he is to be shot for gowing to sleap on his post at night leaving the Rigiment in of their lifes just on the acount of one man not doing his douty deth is every mans Porthan that is ketched a sleat on his Post ther was a little Bit of a fight here the other day Privet stafford [Martin Stafford] and Corpel their the Corpel Cald stafford a damed lier stafford Broke his nose with a Pickax stafford is now under a rest wayting for arest acort marchel you speke about geting your ambertipe taken in your Riding suit that will be nice I should like one of themmyself . . . tell Father that I shal send a check to him Pretty soon there is a Prospects of geting a furlow home I am at a stand to now what to do we are aloud 20 days every 6 months which will be the Best to take it every 6 months or once a year what is your opinion on the subject it will be just as you sey I suppose you can Play eny thing amost on the malodion. . . . I have been aling for to or three days but i gues i will come out all rite.

• • • • •

Washington
october 5th 1861
Camp, Arlington

I received your letter last night it gave me much joy to here from you I hav not been well since I rote to you before i hav had the intermiting Feiver [malaria] but I am geting better now i was taken night before last with a cramp in the stomach i thought i was gon up for a while the ordeley went for docter Bernine he gave me some medison that feched me out all rite by morning you wanted me to tell you how i herd of your new bau well i will tell you if i though it would not cause a fus i was told by a friend from the side track that you had gon to keeping Co with, Mr. Rusye he sed it was hard for him but it could not bee helped now he sed Probley you thought he was to wild for you eny way i expected to here of your weden before i got home i am sure i would like to eny way if i dont i onley formed this opinion sence i spoke of being maried iw ill tell you a little Privicy if nothing hapens i shal come home this winter on a furlow if i do you may look for a weden for my intencion of coming home this winter is to get maried onley for that i think i should not come home till i come for good it is not work while to mencion eny names dont sey eny thing a bout this and dont tell G H C that i told you eny thing a bout the beau for he beged of men not to i dont want him to think that i tell you all he tells me that wouldent bee no good way you now this will do for today . . . we expect to march soon at the distance of about 25 miles down the river i think we will have an other Brush soon well we are redy for it . . . i am hardley able to set up or i could rite as much again o you wanted me to tell the young man that rote the other letter to you to sine his name so that you would now who two rite to well i will tell you it was J S gliton i got him to rite for me because i was not able to rite myself and if he was here i should hav him rite for me agane he is one of my best friends he spoke in fun when he saw your Picture for unequantence of you there is a chance fore a correspondences if you chus he is one of the best of us Boys he seams as near to me as a brother

• • • • •

Oct 13th 1861 Camp Near Alexandria
Dear sister

i went out to role Call this morning ofre the first time in a bout 5 weeks i am not able to doo duty yet yesterday we had orders to march me Pick up Bag and Bagage and stared we marched through Alexandria to Fort Sciano the expectacion of finishing the fort it is calculated to hold 160 guns so you can judg how Big it is it is a bout one third done i guess we will hav to finish it the re Ports is this morning that if we had not been in such a hurrah that we would not had to marcht at tall for three or four days and Probley we would hav got a chance to gow to Kentuckey i for one wishes that we had not started i wish we was a gowing there where it is some warmer than it is here it is so Cold that we

hav to keep our over Coats on all the time een to sleap in at night it was so cold handel a gun that i bought me a pare of gloves to ware and a good meny of the others did the same it is coldier here now thn it is in mich in the winter that is the most of the time i hav had enough of verginia the citizens ses that this was the warmest sumer that has been nown for several years a cording to all accounts it was a great eal warmer in mich deuring the last season wall we are within a bout 3, miles of the Rebbles again wall i guess we are a nough for them we have been enoug for every thing that we hav undertaken yet that whats the matter Leizzy what is the matter of the foks and you with the rest that you dont wright eny more i hav not herd from any of you fore three weeks . . . i sent one letter home with 20 Dollars in it if Pa got it i should like to know it iam sure if i dont here from it my money will stay here after this well i have nothing more now . . . Rite Soon

• • • • •

Sunday Novem 10th 61 Camp Leyon

Well lizzy here goes for an other letter . . . you are well are you not, if you bee, you are better off than I bee. I hav had a back Pull, I hav not gained much sense. I hardley know what to make of it, it has been all most three months sence I hav done any duty with exceptions, of twenty four hours gard What do you think of my coming home I could get a discharge if I want it the Cornel sed all that unfit for duty too months must be discharged but I hav not sed eny thing about it yet nor dont want to but I am a fraid that the dockketer will giv it to me eny how he has to make his re Ports to head quarters as well as the rest of us if he choses to send me home I shal hav to gow. I suppose what do you think of it speek to our folk and see what they think a bout it. if i should come home and should get better I should enlist again but the question is could I make as much there as I could here. see what our folks thin of it and tell me there opinion.

I hait the eyedea of coming home eny how for they will say there goes a coward he was a fraid to stay with his rigment had to come home hellow here is a fite I will gow and see what it is, well I hav seen the fite it was one of the Cooks and Ed lambert [Edwin H. S. Lambert] they got at it over the rations they got so far a loud that they cald one and enother lyors then at it they went thinks as i Old file would hav a hand in a man cant fite here without a cort marshal they are both in the guard house how long they will stay there I dont now and that ant the worst of it, I dont care, a good joke on Co E, to day 9 men in the guard house a better joke on the guard house I i here is a call for Poleace this the boys haits hah hah one of them ses I had rather bee a cat and cry mew.

hant i glad that i dont hav any of that to do it makes the offisers so mad to see me do nothing

well there is a little talk of our gowint to south Carolinie

I hope so eny how fore we will get where it is a little warmer . . . I will Close by gaving my best respects to all inquiring friends a good share of it for yourself . . . P H Gallup to his Dear sister Leizzy L

Give me an answer to this as soon as you get it dont forget . . . So rite soon

• • • • •

Camp Lyon November 21th 1861
Dear sister

I received you letter dated the 17th you Cant tell or imagin how glag I was to here from you I am gaining slowley at Presant. I hav had the Blues so bad that new hardly what to do I hav been fighting mad all day. the ordley and my self, had a fight be caus I would not gow on revew yesterday they went out a bout 9 miles I thought that I could not stant it he was a gowing to make me gow eny how you now that I was allways hard to bee made to do eny thing they dont Care no more for us than they do for a dog.

I dont think much of such Performance. you sed that Pa, had a chance to get leutenantship in the Rigment at Niles o how I hav much to do o tell him to except of it if he does I will have a chance to get out of this Cursed Rigment.

if there is now other way get out of it I shal disert.

Now lib I am telling you just as I fell you now that when I get mad I am bound to have re veng. lib dont borrow any trubble eny bout that affare of yours and georges. I think there is better men in the worled than he is I now how it is to be treated in that way, but never mind it there is a better time a coming. dont greav your Self away. O lib if you onely new how I filt you would think that you had good times words can not excpress my fealings wo be unto the head of the Co. if I ever get a chance with these few lines I will Close I am full to rite much to nite . . . your ever remembering Brother

• • • • •

Camp Leyon November 26th 61

I now take the opperetuneity to address you with a few lines to let you now that I am geting along fine now I sood on guard last night it snowed all night it was Cold enough to freas a dog hav you had eny snow out there

we hav got to stay in tents this winter I am a fraid. I got a man to . . . I got a stove and Put up in the tent I tell you it made a grate diferance it seams a little like old times to set a round the stove I dont know what we will do when cold wether sets in for good we feel the cold so now. well i got my Picture taken to, once for you and one fore my woman. i thought that I would sent it to you for i think you will never see me a gain . . . i thought it would get your ming on the subject my mind is fuley determing what to do there is one of to things will bee done. if Pa dont joine the rigment at niles or eny one that he had a mind to if not the consequences will be the result of my doings here af ter I mint dye for an old sheep as a lamb what do you think about has Pa made up his mind to goin with that rigment yet? if he has tell me in your next letter, I am very ancious to now, . . . you must tell sarah and keemy to send me there Picture rite a way. i have got your spoilt i carraid it in my Pocket on Picket till i got the varnish rubed of i had rather of lost a ten dolar Bill than hav it done, but it cant get eny of the rest. . . . i should like to have Pa and ma to they mint hav them taken and send them to me this Pickture that i am sending to you cant be beet . . . how is the watch is it all right hellow here comes one of the boys with a Package from home all the boys are eting Package from home with shirts colars socks and such things as necessary for the cold wether

• • • • •

Camp Leyon Dec 1st 1861

As I hav a few moments, I will improve it in addressing you a few lines to inform you that I am well at this Presant time, and hoping that you are injoing the same Blesing. how would you like to have a Correspondence I should like to hav some Correspondance with some of the youg ladys. I hav but one or there is but one Person that wrights to me that is from home. Otho Cam is here in the same Co that I am in, he ses he wishes that he was at home this winter well I wish I was to. how would you like to gow to another dance and hav some of them old times that we used to have over agane I am sure I should like it eny way is there as meny Boys and girles there as ever if there is there is no chance for me is there. I thoug I would come home and get me a woman if there was one to be found how is it with you do you want to get maried if you do just tell it and I am at your sister's now is your Chance if ever you a greed to hav me at salsbery tavern, one nit if you want me now is your time, for I am hard up now for the Presant time fur a woman

I suppose you hav not forgoten the nite that we had su a time at the tavran hav you the nite that I got fire wood enough to last me the winter well I hav got over that but I guess I am just as bad now . . .

• • • • •

Camp in the woods. Decem 13th 1861

I now take my Pen in hand to answer the letter, just received you cant imagin how glad I was to here from you and to see "kemy." I think it is very, natcheral, you sed he went a loan and got it taken, you dont mean to sey that hee ent from home dow you. well i suppose you would like to now whey I cald this Camp woods well we hav moved twice sence monday we first moved to "Doc. Chaces" grave. sleeing there one night Picked up and moved Back to "Macons and jancencs" there Piched our tents in a holar, woods on one side and a big feild on the other side we hav fixed up for winter but how long we will stay I am not Prepard to sey but there is one thing I do now we are a gowing to hav a little fight soon we are a gowing to open the blockade be low "mountvarnam" [Mount Vernon] near acquatinck they hav dared us to come down we hav Concluded to give them a call you spoke of a gowing to a[r?] with Pa, if he gowes "lib" take my advice and dont gow for there has been several, nice girles, ruend by coming into this Rigment there is only one woman in the rigment, and she is such that that now lady cares for here, not it is no Place for a women unless she is marraid and got a husband in the army or regment I should like to see Pa gow but not you you spoke of lerning to Play a Peace of mucsick did you get the Peace that I sent you it wass "McCland serrawait" [sic] it is a beautiful thing my self and comrads can sing it to a prfiction, I shal epxect to here you Pley it on the meldoien, when i get home if I ever do tell the rest of the folks that I should like to here from them as will as you and "Pa" what eals the folke around the track or the neighborhood I used to get a letter every other day regler but I hav not got a letter for too weeks be sides this but little do I care they need not rite if they dont want to it will suit me to a Perfiction. I hav got so that I dont Care for eny body or eny thing else thats my stile exately, well it is you now . . . give my respects to all

• • • • •

"Camp Mich" Dec. 28th 61

My one and much respected sister. Iit is with all the Plesure emaginable that I take the oppertuneity to answer a letter just received I just Came of from Picket guard we was out a bout '3' miles from "Camp," we was Put on there to guard Propperty I came very near shoot-ing one man he came after chickens I halted him at first he did not stop I thold him I would blow him through if he dident stop he then stoped and we took him Prisner he will weight now for a cortmartial

you spoke about "Practising Economy," that it is a good time now! I beg leaf to differ with you there is all the cance for spending money here. there is every things in the "Camp" that is emaginable epeshley fruit and eatabels that cost more than eny thing else for our daley rations is such that the men cannot keep from it. sence I hav been sick I hav spent a good eal for "Butter and Cheas" and for things that a person could eat you eat more butter at one meal than we can by here for 20 cts, if a man wants an apple he has to pay 5 cets a peace for them and every thing else in Proportion if it want for what little money we had we would starve to death. if I hv my helth after this Pay day I shal endevor to send $15 or 20 home every to months I hav spent a good eal more this term than I shal here after well it is time to gow to the hospitel I must gow and hav a tooth Puld I hav suffered more this fall with the tooth each than I ever hav before well now I will finish I hav just got back from the hospital I did not hav eny teeth Puled the Docters sed that it was the newralegy I also gave the Dockter the line that was in my letter he did not open it but he sed he would see what he could do. this Rigment is a gowing down hill like fun there is a bout 600 men in the rigment that is fit for duty be fore spring there will be nothing left. you spoke of the $15 draft I directed the letter my self the boys sed they would swair that I put the draft in the letter and Directed it my self "harve Dalleno" had one served the same way his had 20 in it there has been the time sence I sent it home that I could have got "20 for the 15 next Pay day" but there is no use to cry overy spilt milk it is gon if they can liv with it I can with out it

• • • • •

Camp Mich Jan 23d 1862

[By this time the Second Michigan Volunteers were part of the Army of the Potomac under General George B. McClellan, whose praises Gallup had begun to sing as early as December 13, 1861. The subsequent letters in the series are uninteresting.] As I hav a few moments this morning I thought I would Pen a few lines to you for the purpes of letyou know how I am get ing a long, well I am as well as can be expected and I hope that these few lines will find you injoying the Blesing it is very mudy to day with the exceptions of to day has rained for over a week the mudy is up to the op of our boots I tell you this Verginia soils is de light ful, it is very Plesant over head to day, there is a little prospect of a fight soon. I think in a bout 14 days there will be a battle on the Potomac River it will extend threu to Richmond if it does it will be one I tell you. I hope they will make a brake soon, I am getting tired of such times as we hav a Presant. we are geting new guns the miny Rifuls now look out for every time we draw a bead on the yeahoos somthing must come they are good for a man one mild they cary a half once Ball, they are slugs at that they are a savage looking gun the bayonets are a bout 18 inches long 4 square, I tell you what it is, if a man gets one of them thrue him is a going to feal it what do you think a bout it, there is a conciterable excitement to a bout going south it is repoited that we are a going to bee sat of from the division and sent to New orleans that would suit the Boys first trate I fear it is not so there is so meny reports a fliing that we cant tell much a bout it, my opinion is that we will never cross the river until we start for home that will be a bout the first of June not longer than that then I am done soldieren no more soldieren on my Plate

thats is waht the matter, we came in from Pickat, we was ad vanced a bout 6 miles from the old line with the expecttation of finding the enamy but our march was in vain we did not find eny thing of them there has not been eny of them within 20 miles of here sence the scirmish at accotink there was a bout 10,00 hundred of them there besides a Regt of Cavelry, three, co. of our Regt went out there and drove them from the village, there has been nun sene there sence, I dont think there is eny, of any account much short of Buls run or manases well I have told you all the nues so I will Close for this time give my respects to all inquiring friends

N.B. Fall in. Right Dressd. order Armes, Count off by toos from the Right, Right face, four Ranks from dubble file forwards march, Hault, and come to a sholder, order armes, stack armes. About face, Break Ranks, March. Now get your Pen and write to me, if you don't I will cortmartial you and sentane you to a co . . . knapsack drill for 60 cays and 4 dollars of your monthly pay stoped you nose Sis I bring you to it write soon as you get this.

Alias Franklin Thompson

By Betty Fladeland

Only men were allowed to enlist in the Union army. During the war, however, four hundred women—disguised as men—managed to sneak in. The most famous was Sarah Emma Edmonds of Flint. For years after the war it was thought that none of her fellow soldiers in the Second Michigan Infantry knew about her gender. But in 1963 a diary was discovered proving otherwise.

A few years ago the story of Sarah Emma Edmonds' service in the Second Michigan Infantry Regiment during the Civil War excited some attention and curiosity. There were at least three publications dealing with her life as Franklin Thompson, volunteer in the U.S. Army, but, incredible as it seemed, none of them could produce any evidence that Frank's true identity was known to any of her comrades. Recently, however, a new diary was acquired by the Michigan Historical Collections of the University of Michigan that does reveal without any doubt that at least two of her fellow soldiers did know, at the time, that Franklin Thompson was really a woman.

The diary, or journal, is that of Jerome John Robbins who enlisted in the Second Michigan Infantry at Leoni, at approximately the same time that Frank Thompson enlisted in Flint in May 1861. Robbins also worked in the army hospitals, and before the war was over he was promoted to assistant surgeon in the Second Michigan. At the end of the war, he entered the University of Michigan Medical School in Ann Arbor and was granted his medical degree in the commencement exercises of March 27, 1867. He practiced medicine for many years at Hubbardston in Ionia County and died in 1921.

The first mention of Franklin Thompson is in Robbins' diary entry for October 30, 1861, on which day he visited the army hospital and had a pleasant conversation with Thompson on the subject of religion Robbins' habit was to make a footnote on each person he mentioned in his journal, and of Frank he wrote:

> One of the few cherished friends made while at Camp Scott but not learning his value in conversation untill [sic] quite recently. He is an assistant in the Hosp. and one I think well calculated to win open the hearts of those about him.

A mystery seems to be connected with him hard to unravel.

Throughout October and November 1861, Jerome Robbins and Franklin Thompson were both on hospital duty. There are many references to their going for walks together, attending prayer meetings and conversing—mostly on the topic of religion. Robbins continued to be puzzled about his friend:

> I have which I receive as a blessing, the society of a friend so pleasant as Frank I hail with joy. Though foolish as it may seem a mystery appears to be connected with him which it is impossible for me to fathom. Yet these may be false surmises. Would that I might be free from them for not for worlds would I wrong a friend who so sincerely appreciates confiding friendship.

Before November ended, Jerome fathomed the mystery, but loyal to his friend, he sealed the pages of the diary on which the revelation was written. At the top of the page over the entry for November 16, 1861, is the note, "Please allow these leaves to be closed until the author's permission is given for their opening." It appears that some sort of gum or glue was used to fasten three pages together. The ink on the first of these pages has faded much more than that on the other pages of the journal, indicating that they were sealed for some time. The next two sealed pages were written in pencil, possibly to facilitate erasing should the author wish to obliterate this evidence without destroying or mutilating the whole journal. Several lines have been erased, much to the dismay of the researcher.

In the passage, Robbins gives some facts of Franklin Thompson's early life: that he was a native of New Brunswick, that his father's name was Thomas, that he left home at the age of seventeen to become a book peddler and that the reason for his leaving home was an unhappy love affair. In writing this, Jerome switches from the masculine pronoun "him" to the feminine "her" and then explains: "Though never frankly asserted by her, it will be understood that my friend Frank is a female, which accounts for the singularity of the use of pronouns." From the same entry it is readily apparent that Thompson and Robbins have had a disagreement. Robbins remarks about Thompson's willful and jealous nature. He writes:

God knows my heart that towards her I entertain the kindest feelings, but it really seems that a great change has taken place in her disposition or the real has been unmasked. . . . Perhaps a knowledge on her part that there is one in a Michigan home that I do regard with especial affection creates her disagreeable manner.

Piecing together this and other entries, it is quite obvious that Sarah Emma Edmonds had fallen in love with Jerome Robbins, but that Robbins had already committed his affections to a girl back home, an Anna Corey, to whom he intended to remain faithful. Throughout subsequent entries there are frequent references to Thompson's new reserve, his coldness or his being out of humor. Robbins wrote on Christmas Day:

The fault may be mine, but certain it is there is not so warm friendship existing between us as there formally [sic] has been, but though cold just now I cannot but pray for his welfare and that he may continue to be the Christian he has professed to be.

In the entries following his discovery of Thompson's sex, Robbins uses the masculine pronoun in speaking of Thompson but underlines it; for example: "I missed <u>his</u> presence much but this evening brought <u>his</u> pleasant face again."

In the summer of 1862 Robbins was taken prisoner by the Confederates. Although immediately paroled, he was kept in a parole camp until December. During that time he and Thompson corresponded, and immediately upon being returned to his regiment, he hunted up his old friend, who was by that time acting as an orderly for Brigadier General Orlando Poe. Their friendship was renewed in what seems to have been complete cordiality.

Robbins' diary entries through the end of 1862 and the early months of 1863 seem to substantiate several items in the story of Franklin Thompson that were hitherto not certain. For one thing, there are frequent references to the friendship between Thompson and Assis-

On May 17, 1861, Flint native Sarah Emma Edmonds—disguised as a man—enlisted in the Second Michigan Infantry as Franklin Thompson.

tant Adjutant General James Reid of the Seventy-ninth New York Volunteers. The December 20, 1862, entry includes the statement that "Asst. Adjt. Gen'l. Reed [sic] seems a fine fellow and is very fond of Frank." Again on December 25:

Quite recently I have become acquainted with a Mr. Jas. Reid. . . .With my limited acquaintance and my ever reliant Frank I can pronounce him one of Nature's noblemen and if I should choose to ever publish any of these scribblings he and his "pet" [Thompson] will figure somewhat as individuals who repose in the pleasantest arber [sic] of friendship.

The entry of April 4, 1863, indicates some jealousy on Jerome's part:

It is a sad reality to which we awaken when we learn that others are receiving the devotion of one from whom we only claim friendship— attention of which too we are deprived.

On April 17 and 18, 1863, Robbins recorded the news of Thompson's desertion from the army, and on April 20 of the departure of Lieutenant Reid, "Frank's particular friend." Robbins' first reaction to the report that Thompson was missing was that "he must have gone out of the picket line and found difficulty in getting back." But after what must have been an enlightening conversation with Reid, he wrote bitterly:

Frank has deserted for which I do not blame him. His was a strange history. He prepared me for his departure in part. Yet I did not think it would be so premature. Yet he did not prepare me for his ingratitude and utter disregard for the finer sensibilities of others. Of all others, whom I termed friends he was the last I deemed capable of the petty baseness which was betrayed by his friend R. at the last moment. . . . And while I own a slight disgust to such a character I am excited to pity that poor humanity can be so weak as to repay kindness, interest, and the warmest sympathy with deception [and] almost every attribute of a selfish heart.

What Robbins' diary reveals corroborates the item previously published from the diary of William Boston:

We are having quite a time at the expense of our brigade postmaster. He turns out to be a girl, and has deserted when his lover, Inspector Read [sic] and General Poe resigned.

It also substantiates the conclusion that Edmonds deserted from the army not because she was sick and afraid to go to the hospital, but because she was in love with Reid and did not want to be separated from him. A letter to Robbins which Edmonds wrote from Washington, DC, in May indicates that she did have some subsequent communication with Reid.

I dare not write you the particulars [sic] of anything now, until I hear from you and know where you are for fear it might fall into other hands. I wrote you from Sandusky 0. but have not heard from you yet. "Reid" wrote me that he had a long conversation with you about me—I want you to write me the import of it. Will you please do so? He says he wants me to come & visit his wife who is very anxious to see me.

But if Reid and Sarah Emma Edmonds had been lovers, it would be a bit unusual for him to be telling his wife about her and inviting her to their home. In the same letter to Robbins, Edmonds (who signs herself E. Edmonds) also speaks of seeing an "Ed" whose initials are E. H. H. and of visiting his family in Ohio.

Nor, apparently, has she completely recovered from her love for Robbins. She confesses as much in a letter to him.

Oh, Jerome, I do miss you so much. There is no person living whose presence would be so agreeable to me this afternoon as yours. How is "Anna"? I hope you have received a favorable answer to your letter sent just before I came away. I always remember you and sometimes her at the Throne of Grace.

Such an admission makes it seem plausible that Emma deserted because she could not bear to stay near Robbins and not have her love for him reciprocated. In a still later letter dated from Falmouth, Virginia, on January 16, 1865, she congratulates Robbins on "prospering so well in matters of the heart," but she cannot refrain from again referring to the old love:

Dear Jerome I am in earnest in my congratulations & daily realize that had I met you some years ago I might have been much happier now. But Providence has ordered it otherwise & I must be content. I would not change now if I could—if my life's happiness depended upon it. I do not love you less because you love another, but rather more, for your nobleness of character displayed in your love for her—may God make her worthy of so good a husband.

There is no further mention of Sarah Emma Edmonds in Robbins' diary entries after the spring of 1863, but her name appears in the lists of "Letters Written" and "Letters Received" he kept at the end of each volume. During the last year of the war he wrote to her twice and received from her two letters.

Although we are still confronted with how Emma "got by" in the army for so long, and why she did, we now know that the secret was not entirely her own. And although the several men who produced testimony for her after the war may have been completely truthful in their statements, it seems likely that others were protecting her in order not to jeopardize her chance to obtain a pension and to have the charge of desertion removed from her record. It is interesting to note that Jerome Robbins was not among those who furnished affidavits for her.

A China Doll for Abbie

By Larry Wakefield

*As Billy Voice left his Northport home to serve with the Twenty-sixth
Michigan Infantry, he promised his three-year-old baby sister
that he would bring her a china doll when he returned.
Voice died during the war, but he still kept his promise.*

As the Civil War entered its second year, President Abraham Lincoln called for more troops to man the Union army. Northport, a small village near the mouth of Grand Traverse Bay, was quick to answer. In August 1862 Billy Voice, along with twelve other men, joined a company being formed by Lieutenant Charles H. Holden for the Twenty-sixth Michigan Infantry. With pardonable pride and pugnacity, the men called themselves the Lakeshore Tigers.

Billy's family had moved to Northport from Traverse City in 1853. There his father had built a sawmill for Perry Hannah, who was later called the father of Traverse City. By 1855 Billy's father had established his own sawmill in Northport.

At twenty, Billy, the oldest of the Voices' three sons and two daughters, was the only family member old enough to enlist. The youngest was three-year-old Abagail, or Abbie, whom the family usually called Did because of her insistent "I did! I did!" when one of her brothers teasingly accused her of neglecting a chore.

Billy's family was proud he had enlisted, but little Abbie, his favorite, was heartsick. She idolized her big brother and couldn't bear to see him go. She wept bitterly on the eve of his departure. Trying to comfort her, Billy pleaded, "Don't cry, Did. If you'll stop crying I'll bring you a real china doll when I come back." But Abbie couldn't stop crying. She didn't want her brother Billy to go to war. She feared something dreadful would happen to him. "Billy, don't go," she begged. "Please don't go."

Although she couldn't possibly have known at the time, her fear was real. Something dreadful did happen to Billy. Just a few weeks after the Lakeshore Tigers left Northport to train in Jackson, Michigan, Billy died of typhoid fever, one of the many diseases that killed twice as many men during the Civil War than died in battle.

On September 26, 1862, the steamer *Buffalo* docked at Northport on a grim and solemn mission. It carried the body of Sergeant William H. Voice. A small, wooden box was strapped on top of Billy's metal casket. Inside was a beautiful china doll. Billy had kept his promise to Abbie.

Four soldiers accompanied Billy's body home. The family pressed them for details about the doll, but they knew nothing. Their orders were to see that the casket and box arrived safely at Northport. For the next sixty years the doll's story remained a mystery.

Billy's funeral on September 27, 1862, attracted the largest gathering of people ever held in Northport. The little log house that served as church and school could not possibly hold all those who shared the family's grief. All were intrigued by the doll.

Ceramic dolls during the Victorian period were usually purchased as just the head and shoulders—the body was made at home. After Billy's funeral, several Northport women formed a sewing bee to make a body for Abbie's doll. They also made it a lovely, white cotton dress and petticoat and placed the finished doll in Abbie's arms. Calling it the most beautiful thing she'd ever seen, Abbie vowed to keep the doll she named Jeanette for the rest of her life.

Abbie grew up and in 1878 she married her childhood sweetheart, Norman Morgan, one of Northport's most successful merchants. They were active in charitable work, particularly with the local Indians. Around the turn of the century, the Morgans sold their Northport interests, retired to Traverse City and continued their charity work.

Soon after World War I ended, Abbie learned about Herman Dunkalow, a resident living in a nearby rooming house who had been a medical corpsman in the Twenty-sixth Michigan Infantry. Now, at age ninety, he was ailing and had no family or friends. He needed someone to talk to.

Abbie's kind and generous heart couldn't resist an appeal like that. She found him in bed, too weak to get up but alert and talkative. Like many old soldiers,

Dunkalow liked to reminisce about the war and Abbie liked to listen.

Dunkalow mentioned how Civil War soldiers seemed closer to their families than those of World War I. He remembered one in particular—a young man in a Jackson hospital who was quite ill. He kept raving about a doll, Dunkalow said, begging everyone who passed his bed to get a doll for his baby sister. Doctors and nurses paid little heed to the young man's plea, believing him delirious. But Dunkalow was so touched he spent his last cent on a beautiful china doll with pink cheeks, brown eyes and black hair. Just the head and shoulders, he explained, that was all he could find in town. Dunkalow said the young man grew calm and peaceful once he saw the doll. He asked the medical corpsman to prop it up at the foot of the bed, where he could see it. It was still there when the soldier died that night. Dunkalow said it was he who sent the doll to Northport with the young man's body. He remembered the

Billy Voice had promised he would bring home a doll for his sister, Abbie. As he lay dying in a hospital bed, he begged a fellow soldier to buy this china doll. The doll—and Voice's body—were delivered home together.

man had seemed so determined about getting a doll for his sister. He thought it was the least he could do.

Abbie followed the old man's story with growing wonder and excitement. She could hardly wait for him to finish. Then she asked, "Do you remember the young man's name?"

"His name was William Voice," the old man replied.

Trembling with emotion, Abbie excused herself, saying she had an errand to run and would return in a few minutes. She rushed home, took Jeanette from her dresser drawer and hurried back to the old man's room. Holding the doll before him, she said, "This is the doll you bought. And I am Billy Voice's little sister."

The old man could hardly believe his eyes. But he recognized the doll and knew Abbie's story was true. His eyes filled with tears as he said, "I'll never forget the look on your brother's face when he saw that doll." He paused, as though reflecting upon that hospital scene so long ago, and then said, "I think your brother died a happy man."

A Michigan Soldier Views Slavery

Edited and with an introduction by George M. Blackburn

*As the Eighth Michigan Infantry marched through the South, Grand Rapids
gunsmith John C. Buchanan saw slavery and its effects firsthand.
During the course of the war, he wrote letters to his wife sharing his strong
feelings about slavery, emancipation and African American soldiers.*

As Union armies marched into the South during the Civil War, Northern soldiers reported their observations to friends and relatives back home. While Yankees were interested in much of what they saw in the South, perhaps the most exotic and fascinating feature of the Southern scene was the institution of human slavery. No one generalization can accurately describe the attitudes of the Northern soldiers toward African Americans and slavery, except possibly that personal contact with the colored folk led Yankees to think of blacks as human beings rather than abstractions, and, especially after the first months of the war, to consider how the African Americans could be employed to crush the Confederacy.

Obviously the conclusions a particular Northern soldier reached about the role of Negroes depended in part on the background of the soldier himself. Born in Ithaca, New York, in 1823, John C. Buchanan moved to Grand Rapids in 1842, where he pursued the trade of gunsmith until he enlisted in the Civil War. Commissioned as a first lieutenant in August 1861 in the Eighth Michigan Infantry Regiment, he was promoted to captain in 1862. He was wounded at Antietam and later, after several months of illness, he resigned his commission and was honorably discharged in May 1864. After service, he attended dental school and practiced dentistry in Grand Rapids. Buchanan was proud of his patriot family (his father had served in the War of 1812, his grandfather in the War of the Revolution) and was a strong Unionist. A devout Baptist, he saw the hand of a stern, just God in the Civil War. Though reared a Democrat, he became a Republican shortly after the election of 1856.

Buchanan's letters reveal him as an intelligent, articulate man who had very definite ideas about slavery.

He was convinced that God's wrath was directed against the "Peculiar Institution," because slavery was wicked and immoral. He was also certain that slavery would never survive the end of the war. These views he expressed emphatically on many occasions.

Though he never wavered in his opposition to slavery, he changed his mind on the question of enrolling blacks in the Union army. A strong antislavery man would obviously pity the "helpless Creatures" he observed during duty in South Carolina in 1861. So servile were the African Americans that he was sure they would never make good fighting material. Yet by 1863 he viewed the martial qualities of African Americans more favorably. They "do nobly in battle [and] vie even with Anglo Saxon[s]" as fine soldiers. What a "joke" upon Southerners to be forced to fight their former slaves.

No doubt there are various explanations for Captain Buchanan's change of attitude toward using black troops. Early in the war he was concerned about alienating conservative Northerners who were willing to fight for the Union but who drew the line at an antislavery crusade. As the war dragged on, however, it became more apparent that shooting rebels was dangerous business. Buchanan confessed in 1863 that "where the necessity exists, I would as soon that they [the negro troops] would shoot Mr. Reb as to do it myself." Finally, Buchanan could logically draw different conclusions about African Americans in such diverse states as South Carolina, Virginia and Kentucky. As he put it, "I have seen the two extremes" of slavery. Significantly, he first observed slavery in South Carolina and approved of enrolling African American soldiers only after he left that state. He noted that slaves in coastal South Carolina had not reached as high a cultural level as those in Virginia.

Thus it may well be that the varying attitudes of John Buchanan toward the African American in part reflected his own firsthand experiences with slavery. Few regiments in Northern service afforded such an extensive opportunity for varied experiences as did the Eighth Michigan Infantry Regiment, commonly dubbed the "Wandering Regiment." Rendezvousing at Grand Rapids in August 1861, the regiment was ordered to Fort Wayne, where it was mustered into federal service on September 16. After being stationed for a time at Washington, DC, the Eighth Michigan joined the expeditionary corps under General Thomas W. Sherman (who by the end of the war had the dubious distinction of being known as the "other" General Sherman), which accompanied the naval squadron that captured Port Royal and Hilton Head, South Carolina, in November 1861. The only western regiment in Sherman's command, the Eighth Michigan participated in several skirmishes and one important engagement at James Island, South Carolina, in June 1862. The latter was a disastrous attempt to strike at Charlestown and resulted in heavy losses for the regiment.

In July 1862 the Eighth Michigan was transferred to the Army of the Potomac, where it became a unit in the Ninth Corps under General Ambrose Burnside. During eastern campaigns in 1862, the regiment engaged the enemy in several battles, including Second Bull Run, Chantilly, South Mountain, Antietam and Fredericksburg.

After the battle of Fredericksburg, the Eighth Michigan, along with the Ninth Corps, was transferred to the west. After being stationed in Kentucky, the regiment moved to Vicksburg and, upon the fall of that city to General Ulysses S. Grant's forces on July 4, 1863, helped force Confederate evacuation of Jackson, Mississippi.

Removed to Tennessee, the Eighth Michigan fought in various engagements including the siege of Knoxville, where it won "imperishable honors." The unit reenlisted as a veteran organization at the end of 1863, returned to Michigan on furlough, recruited new members and then was ordered to the eastern theater of operations. As part of the Ninth Corps, the regiment participated in Grant's long campaign to take Richmond, from May 1864 until the fall of the Confederacy. The Michigan unit fought at the Wilderness, Chancellorsville, Spotsylvania Court House, Cold Harbor and various engagements connected with the siege of Petersburg, including the famous battle of the Crater. When the Confederate lines finally cracked in April 1865, the Eighth Michigan was one of the first regiments to enter Petersburg.

Truly it deserved the title the "Wandering Regiment" or as Mrs. Buchanan expressed it, "How strange it is that the 8th Michigan has such varied experiences."

The editing of the Buchanan letters is part of a larger undertaking in which the editor is engaged—research on a history of the Eighth Michigan Infantry Regiment. While official sources are essential for military history, personal narratives are necessary to fill in the human gaps. Many of the best accounts were printed in newspapers at the time. Typically, during the Civil War a company was formed by men from a certain locality, and often one of the men served as a correspondent and wrote letters to the hometown newspapers to keep friends and relatives abreast of the latest developments. Unfortunately, many of the newspapers of the towns from which the Eighth Michigan was recruited apparently are no longer extant. The companies were formed at Owosso, Alma, Grand Rapids, Flint, Jackson, Lansing, St. Johns, Hastings and Greenville; of these, only the newspapers of Lansing, Grand Rapids, Flint, Hastings and Jackson are known to have been preserved.

Only those portions of Captain John C. Buchanan's letters relating to his ideas about slavery are presented below. The letters have been altered only in punctuation and capitalization for purposes of clarity.

● ● ● ● ●

Annapolis, Maryland
October 10, 1861

Dear Wife

[The] streets [of Annapolis are] about the width of two Grand Rapids sidewalks, nasty, full of Contrabands, & red Clay. There is none of the Energy in the South so far as I have seen it, which characterizes the glorious soul expanding West. I was more disappointed in this City than in Washington.

● ● ● ● ●

Head Quarters 8th Michigan Reg
Naval School Annapolis
O[ctober] 17/61

My Own Dear Sophie

There was quite an excitement in Camp to day occasioned by a secesh coming in after a Runaway Contraband, & after the soldiers reamed the occasion of the visit they pounced [?] upon him until he used Intemperate Language & unless he had been protected, I think he would have lost his life in this Negro Hunt. As it was he got well frightened, & I presume will think twice before he goes into a Camp of northern Soldiers to reclaim Biped Property. It is quite an unfavorable Place to exercise any of [the] Traits of the Peculiar Institution. Contrabands are quite Plenty[ful] & if Maryland had only seceded they would many of them been loose, but of course they are protected at Present. This Disturbance or southern Rebellion, I am sure, will use up this very Peculiar Institution before it ends, but what can be done for that unfortunate Race I can not tell.

• • • • •

Beaufort, South Carolina
Dec. 22, 1861
My Own Dear Sophie

The squalid Poverty & wretchedness of these helpless Beings, who are turned loose by the flight [of] their Masters meets one at every Turn. . . . Because the Institution . . . has turned them to Ignorance & Bondage, in a Land of Intelligence & freedom with a double Damnation, it is a villiany [sic] which can not be excused, a Despotism which has no paralel [sic]. All the fine spun Theories of statesmen north & south, the exquisitely rounded Periods of labored arguments, the Philanthropic Developments of the Apologists of this accursed Peculiar Institution, characterising it as heaven Born, christianising, enlightening & elevating the Race, are worse than a Play on Words. A profanity almost unpardonable. There is more truth than Poetry in the Language of Another denouncing slavery as the "sum of all villianies" [sic]. There are, I understand from good authority, four thousand Communicants, mostly of the Baptist church. This is not an outgrowth of the system, but is a manifestation of an overruling hand, a Providence . . . bringing good out of Evil. A work which a God alone can do. These helpless Creatures look upon the Army as their Hope & are continually coming in, expressing their unbounded satisfaction at the Presence of the Yankees (This term with them includes the entire north & is the only class they are at all acquainted with) whom many of them expected & under whose protection they are free. The Question what can be done with & for them, is indeed one of grave Importance & needs a Wisdom, which can come from no other source than . . . the God of our fathers.

Before the Union army accepted African Americans into the ranks, it employed escaped slaves, termed contraband, to perform manual labor. After the Emancipation Proclamation, contraband were the first to join African American regiments.

• • • • •

Milne Plantation, Port Royal Island
South Carolina
Dec. 29, [1861]
My Own Dear Loving Wife

The measure proposed, or rather the suggestion of Simon Cameron [Lincoln's secretary of war until January 11, 1862] that it might be expedient to arm the Negroes, I am afraid will engender strife & divide the Councils of the nation & may embitter the minds of many who are really Union Men. I have seen none of these Colored Gemmen [sic] as yet who would be capable of fighting & will venture the assertion, such is their servility, that fifty of their Masters would put to flight a Reg. of them. Poor helpless Creatures, raised as a farmer Raises Stock, allowed a Peck of Corn a week for subsistence, a gill of salt, to season this . . . & with an abject servility which is painful, it would be equal folly to employ them on either side. All that can be consistently done to conciliate is right & proper. Do this. Then prosecute the War with the utmost vigor to its bitter end. The Peculiar Institution is inseparably connected with this Rebellion & I am persuaded in my own mind that its end is near. I think Providence will so direct that when this struggle closes, the sun will shine upon a nation of freemen. These Negroes have a truly wonderful Talent for music. I have never seen better time than in their singing & Dancing. All sing & all Dance from childhood to old age.

• • • • •

Dear Mother

This [the country around Beaufort] might [have] been made an Eden, but never while a portion of the human family are held in such a Bondage. Not alone the Physical System, but the soul is bound in the darkness of Ignorance, only here & there a ray of Light enters, or rather is permitted to enter the darkened understanding. . . . The darkness of ages is concentrated upon these helpless Beings, shut out from any means of Improvement, from Generation to Generation, father & son Mother & daughter born into, & doomed to perpetual servitude; every anxious glance after knowledge checked as a Crime, every aspiration of the soul looking toward a higher level of existence ground out as an Offence almost unpardonable. The thought suggests itself can they learn nothing by Observation. There is in this Institution an abject Servility a Cringing, which may be likened to that of a whipped Hound. Associated with one another, that is penned up like so many Hogs, often

Negroes are Born, raised, & die in old Age, on the same Plantation without intercourse with others from adjoining Plantations. Their World is narrowed down to quite a small Compass & perhaps their Desires to a corresponding limit. If this is the case they are salvable [Buchanan wrote above "salvable" the word "many".] Their food (& the Assertion always seemed fabulous to me) is a peck of corn a week & a gill of salt. . . . Under all these advantages, with Father & Mother (when they have them) who know nothing more of the world than the child when he comes into it, except indeed the hardening of the Muscles & a grotesque experience in Brothering, what advance would it be reasonable to expect in the rising Race. Every one has realized that knowledge in this state of existence is not intuitive. The slave Mother presses her child to her Bosom with all the seeming love & tenderness of the enlightened Christian mother but it is beyond her power to develop the Mind of her offspring & thus they live and thus they die. Oh what an accursed Institution this is, how full of wickedness & cruelty. If there had not existed another sin on this Continent, this is sufficient of itself, to call down the Judgements of a Just God & I think this unholy Rebellion may be traced to this Peculiar, very Peculiar Institution.

• • • • •

Camp 8 Mich, Hedgemans River
8 Miles South of Orleans
Nove 8 1862
My Own Dear Loved Wife

. . . The population I think in all charity are thoroughly secesh. That is the white portion; the Blacks all thoroughly union. Many a set of Ivory is displayed by these poor creatures. Although in point of intelligence they are far in advance of the South Carolina Negroes. I have seen I think the two extremes of this class: where the system of slavery has operated most heavily, debasing its victim to the level of the brute; & where more leniently, leaving traces of manhood, [though] still repugnant to every feeling of justice & right in all its phases. At a fearful cost the hitherto hidden wickedness of this thrice accursed institution is being developed, aiming in its dying throes to strike down the fairest governmental fabric the world ever saw. It seems passing strange that its steady advance has been so long endured by the north; more than endured, countenanced & sustained. God be praised its days of power are ended, ended forever. The hand writing on the wall. The finger of the most high has written it & its days are numbered & finished. I trust that all will be well in the final result. Well did Thomas Jefferson say in view of this evil, "I tremble for my country when I remember that God is just." The wisdom of the statesman could not fail to see the incongruity of freedem [*sic*] & slavery & did not fail to discern the coming evil hour when God should be seen in the vindication of right & punishment of wickedness.

• • • • •

Yazoo River, Miss
June 19 1863
My Only Loved One

I have seen Regs of Colored men & must confess that where the necessity exists, I would as soon they would shoot Mr. Reb as to do it myself. It is a joke upon their masters to lose their property & then have it turn round & fight them. Baalims [*sic*] Ass chiding the Prophet was not half as ludicrous as this. To be shot to death by a Negro is a very unchivalric exit from this mundane state. O tempous [*sic*] O mores.

• • • • •

Milldale, Miss
July 30 1863
My Own Dearly Loved Sophie

The raising of negro troops goes on & they do nobly in battle. [They] vie even with the Anglo Saxon. But it is the unkindest cut of all thus to expose their [Southern slave owner's] property to be shot or maimed while they are exposed to be killed by a human Machine which has always been subject to their nod. . . . Yours ever.

From Allegan to Andersonville

By Albert Castel

George W. Bailey of Allegan left his milling business to enlist in the Third Michigan Infantry. He saw action at Fredericksburg, Gettysburg and other major battles. But his real ordeal began when he was captured in 1864 and sent to the rebel prison at Andersonville.

Shortly before seven o'clock on the evening of June 4, 1861, George W. Bailey, a twenty-year-old miller, and two other young men set out on foot from Allegan, Michigan, to go to war. Their immediate destination was Grand Rapids, where, moved by "the patriotic spirit," they intended to enlist in the Third Michigan Infantry Regiment, then in the process of forming. At first all went well as they headed east toward Martin and the plank road that followed the route of present-day old US 131 to Grand Rapids. Then, abruptly, the lane they were traveling on appeared to end. For awhile they searched in vain for a continuation—there had to be one; after all, they reasoned, Lake Michigan is to the west and not east of Allegan! Finally they found it in the form of a "corduroy bridge"—logs laid in a row—across a "large swamp." While they passed over it, hundreds of frogs broke into a chorus that struck Bailey as being "as disloyal as any ranting" by Southern rebels. "Going-t' enlist, going-t'enlist, going-t'enlist," croaked the little frogs. "Dam-phool, dam-phool, dam-phool," bellowed the big bullfrogs. As long as he lived, Bailey never forgot this "prognostication of the frogs." He had good cause not to.

Once on the plank road the Alleganites made good time, especially after hitching a ride on a wagon, and arrived at 8:00 A.M. at the Grand Rapids fairground, where the Third Michigan was camped. Here they learned that Company F still needed men and accordingly sought out its captain. He welcomed them, they signed the enlistment papers and on June 10 they were, along with the rest of the Third Michigan, mustered into the Union army for a term of three years or the duration of the war, whichever proved shorter. Three days later the regiment marched to the Grand Rapids depot of the Detroit, Grand Haven and Milwaukee Railroad, boarded passenger cars (first class, no less) and, while the attending crowd cheered and a band played, went off to Washington, DC, and the war.

The regiment reached its destination on June 16 and, trudging down Pennsylvania Avenue through horrid heat, passed the White House, where on the east portico both President Lincoln and General Winfield Scott could be seen sitting "in plain view." It reached the war, or rather the war reached it, on July 21 at Bull Run—a much hotter and more horrid experience than marching along Pennsylvania Avenue. George Bailey, however, did not share the experience. He was in a hospital battling the measles—a common affliction of recruits from rural areas and one that often proved deadly. He survived, but in such a weakened condition that he was reassigned. Bailey returned to the hospital, this time as an orderly.

During 1862 and 1863 the Third Michigan participated in the Seven Days Battles, Second Bull Run, Fredericksburg, Chancellorsville, Gettysburg and other lesser but no less serious engagements such as at Grovetown, Virginia, on August 29, 1862. There it went into action with 246 men and, according to Bailey's diary, it "was under hot fire more than eight minutes and came out with 115 men." By the end of 1863 the regiment's strength, which had totaled 1,039 when it left Grand Rapids, had dwindled to scarcely a third of that number. Even as a noncombatant, Bailey had also become well acquainted with the hardships and miseries of war as his 1863 diary entries testify:

> Friday, June 19: Rained most of the day and night. Third corps [in which the Third Michigan served] left Centreville at two P.M. and marched to Gum Spring . . . where we arrived at midnight, tired, wet, and hungry.

> Saturday, June 20: Cold and rainy. All quiet. We laid in camp today. Water is scarce, every spring is guarded for some General's use and we have to go from one and a half to two miles, and then take it out of a dirty creek.

Friday, July 3 [Gettysburg]: Clear and warm. The fighting today has been very heavy. The Third Michigan lost about 30 men killed, wounded and missing yesterday. I am at the Third Corps hospital, assisting dress of the wounds of my unlucky companions.

Saturday, July 4: Clear in forenoon and hard rain this afternoon. There's scarcely any firing today. This is the third Fourth of July that I have served for Uncle Sam and hope that he will not have any claim on me a year from this day.

Monday, July 6: Rain most all day. Orders to march, but did not go. There is a very bad odor begins to arise from the battlefield. The dead are most all buried, but not as they should be.

As the July 4 entry demonstrates, Bailey, after two years, had enough of the war. It is not surprising to read in his diary for September 21, 1863, that he had refused to reenlist as a "veteran volunteer" despite the inducement of a thirty-day furlough for doing so: "It may be a big thing, but I for one can't see it. Three years of soldiering will suit me."

Bailey spent the winter of 1863-64 performing routine hospital duties and counting the days until his enlistment expired. With spring's arrival, the Federal forces in Virginia, now commanded by Ulysses S. Grant, proposed to confront Robert E. Lee's Confederates in what all hoped would be a final, victorious campaign. Part of the preparations included sending all sick and unfit men to Washington and returning all soldiers hitherto detailed to hospital duty to the ranks. As a result, when Grant's army crossed the Rapidan River into the Wilderness on May 3 and 4, Bailey was again marching with his company, a rifle on his shoulder.

In his diary Bailey described what happened next:

Thursday, May 5: Clear and warm. Marched at 5 o'clock A.M. and advanced about ten miles where we met the enemy. The 3rd Michigan ordered to the left, and deployed as skirmishers when they immediately engaged the enemy losing 18 killed and about 50 wounded.

Friday, May 6: As soon as it was light, the 3rd Michigan went in and fought and lost heavy. At 10:30 A.M. we were in a rifle pit and the enemy advanced. Our support all left us and the enemy flanked us on the left at 11:00 and Geo. W. Bailey, Dan Wilson of Co. F, and several others of Co. K

George Bailey had this photograph taken in spring 1864 while his regiment was camped near Brandy Station, Virginia. By summer he was a prisoner of war trying to survive the horrid conditions at Andersonville, the war's most notorious prison.

were taken prisoners.

Saturday, May 7: After we were taken yesterday, we went about three miles to the rear. Today at 12:30 P.M. we fell in and marched to Orange Court House where we arrived at 10 P.M.

From Orange Court House Bailey traveled by foot and rail with hundreds of other Union prisoners through Virginia and the Carolinas to Georgia. There, on May 23—just seventeen days before he was to be discharged from the army—he

Arrived at Andersonville...where we [were] put in an enclosure of 16 acres with a stockade 20 feet [high] all around. There was [sic] 15,000 prisoners when we came, and there are about 1,000 of us. We are crowded very much.

Officially named Camp Sumter, Andersonville was the most notorious and dreaded of all Confederate prisons. It contained no shelters for the inmates except what they improvised with blankets or by burrowing into the ground. A fetid swamp covered one-third of the enclosed area. Through it ran a shallow, filthy stream, the sole source of drinking water—and also the only drain for human waste from the "sinks" (latrines) that by July were serving about thirty thousand prisoners, many of them suffering from diarrhea and dysentery. No medicines were available; rations by Northern standards were meager and poor. Nearly thirteen thousand Union soldiers died in this "hell hole" during its fourteen months of operation. Although not intended to be, it was, in effect, a death camp.

While at Andersonville a prisoner had two choices: try to escape or try to survive. Bailey chose the latter, being sustained, as his diary tells us, by hopes of parole, rescue or the war's end:

Monday, May 30: Clear and hot. More prisoners came in. . . . Rumors that all the prisoners are to be exchanged on or before the 10th of June, hope it will be true. Drew rations: 7 loaves for 18 men, 3 oz. meat and about 3 oz. mush. One of the boys bought some beans and we had soup for supper.

Saturday, June 4: Rained all day. I left home three years ago today at 7 o'clock P.M. and walked to Grand Rapids in the night to enlist. Wish I was home today. Rumors that Richmond was taken with 30,000 prisoners by General Grant.

Monday, June 6: Cloudy, some rain. It has been rumored all last week that they would begin parolling [sic] today, but it was false. Rations: raw meal 1/2 pint, cooked meat 3 oz., salt 1/4 oz. I have been a prisoner one month today.

Thursday, June 9: Rained most of the day. When it did not rain the sun was out very hot. . . . I have been in the U.S. Army three years this day and if I were inside our lines I would be discharged.

Monday, July 4: Rain most of the day. 9 A.M. K. Parrish and Moe G. Powers and myself have just had our 4th of July breakfast. It consisted of corn flakes and corn meal coffee.

Wednesday, July 20: Clear and hot. The Rebels are afraid our calvary [sic] will make a raid here and release us. They began to fortify around the prison this morning.

Thursday, July 21: The rebels still building rifle pits and we hope they will soon have a chance to use them.

Wednesday, July 27: Cloudy but warm. Dame rumor is very busy again. She says we are all to be exchanged and paroled next month.

Thursday, July 28: In order to terrify the prisoners, the Rebels thronged [sic] a solid shot over camp this afternoon. About 300 prisoners came in from Sherman.

Sunday, July 31: The Rebels have been hard at work all day falling [sic] trees around the stockade and fort. It is reported that our calvary [sic] is coming here to relieve us.

There was a foundation in fact for this report. On July 26 Major General George Stoneman set out with two thousand cavalry from Sherman's army to besiege Atlanta and liberate captive Union officers at Macon, Georgia, and on to Andersonville to free the prisoners, all of whom were enlisted men. Perhaps fortunately for those prisoners, given Confederate measures to prevent their rescue, Stoneman failed to take Macon. On July 31 he was captured along with many of his men, as Bailey soon learned:

Tuesday, August 2: 442 prisoners came in. They were captured near Macon. It is reported that Major General Stoneman was captured also.

Despite, or rather because of, disappointment over the failed rescue attempt, rumors of an exchange and parole continued to run rampant at Andersonville.

Early in September it seemed that the rumors were finally coming true. Starting on September 6, trains began hauling away thousands of the prisoners, among them Bailey, who departed in a boxcar loaded with fifty-nine other men on the night of the tenth.

Were they on their way to freedom? No. The Confederates merely were removing most of the prisoners from Andersonville so that General John Bell Hood's army in Georgia, which had just been forced to evacuate Atlanta, would not have to worry about another attempt to free them and thus be able to swing north of Atlanta in a campaign designed to compel Sherman to retreat by cutting his railroad supply line to Chattanooga, Tennessee. The only exchange taking place for Bailey and his fellow captives was one hellhole for another.

The new prison camp was at Florence, South Carolina, and also consisted of a stockade without any shelters

When George Bailey arrived at Andersonville on May 23, 1864, conditions in the new stockade already were poor and overcrowded. Bailey endured more than six months at the South's most notorious prison until he "told the surgeon a good story" during a routine medical exam and was paroled.

other than those the prisoners created. Bailey and five comrades spent the night of October 9—"the coldest night I have seen in three years and over"—huddled beneath "1 and 1/2 blankets stuck up and one rubber blanket under, and we came very near to freezing." These conditions and above all loss of hope that they would ever be paroled caused hundreds of the prisoners to join the Confederate army—they were called "galvanized Yankees"—to escape what seemed certain death. The mortality rate at Florence was higher than at Andersonville because so many of its inmates had already been weakened by their stay at Camp Sumter. "I for one cannot blame them," Bailey wrote in his diary, yet he resolved to "try to stand it until after the [presidential] election." Should Lincoln win reelection—and thanks to Sherman's capture of Atlanta and Sheridan's victories in Virginia's Shenandoah Valley that appeared fairly certain—then Bailey expected the rebels would realize that they were doomed to defeat and cease their futile struggle, ending the war.

Lincoln did win, and although the war continued, his victory had an impact. Beginning in late November the

Confederates paroled many Florence prisoners. Most, Bailey noted, were either sick or convalescent. When his prison detachment received medical exams on December 7, "I told the surgeon a good story," with the gratifying result that he was able to write in his diary that evening that he was "now outside, and have just signed the papers" for parole. Undoubtedly, Bailey felt greater joy signing those papers than he did when he wrote his name on the enlistment roll at the Grand Rapids fairground in June 1861.

On December 12 Bailey and 804 other ex-prisoners steamed out of the Charleston, South Carolina, harbor aboard the truce boat USS *Crescent City*. Three days later they disembarked at Annapolis, Maryland, while "a brass band played Hail Columbia, the Star Spangled Banner and several other pieces," and then marched to "the barracks and got our supper and turned in for the night." The war finally was over for Bailey, and with this entry he concluded his diary.

Still, Bailey remained in the army. Given a furlough, with instructions to report to Detroit for mustering out on being notified, he returned to Allegan in time for

Christmas. But no instructions came and, owing to a mix-up that will not surprise anyone familiar with military bureaucracy, he was officially listed as a deserter. Not until April 14, 1865, the date of Lincoln's assassination, did he receive—ten months and five days overdue—an honorable discharge.

As was the case with most Civil War veterans, Bailey's postwar career contained no experiences comparable to those he had known in the army, something for which, like most other former soldiers, he probably felt thankful. In 1867 he married an Allegan woman, and fathered eleven children, two of whom died in infancy. Starting in 1872 he worked as a United States railroad mail clerk, a position he held (except for a brief interval in the early 1890s, when a Democratic appointee superseded him) until failing health compelled him to retire in 1903. The partial disability pension he had obtained in 1890 as a consequence of scurvy contracted while in Andersonville and Florence was increased from eight to twelve dollars a month when he retired. On February 20, 1905, he died at his home—which still stands at 601 Trowbridge Street in Allegan—and was buried in Oakwood Cemetery, the customary iron marker of the Grand Army of the Republic beside his grave.

Were the bullfrogs in the Martin swamp correct? Was George Bailey a "dam-phool" when he walked to Grand Rapids on that June night in 1861 to join the army? One might say he was: Bailey's military service was devoid of glory, filled with misery and poorly rewarded. But then so was that of the vast majority of his fellow soldiers. Although in later years he sometimes complained about the paltry veterans' pensions and the government's failure to acknowledge, either with money or at least a "cheap medal," the sufferings of former POWs such as himself, he took great pride in having been one of the "boys in blue." He had every right to do so. While no hero, he did his duty as best he could, risked his life and health and conrtibuted to the preservation of his nation. No more can be asked of any soldier.

Guns, Grain and Iron Ore

By Albert A. Blum

*At the beginning of the Civil War, Michigan had a firm agricultural
and industrial base. Ships left Michigan's many Great Lakes
ports loaded with a variety of goods ranging from
grain and livestock to copper and iron ore.*

Michigan entered the Civil War as an agrarian state and emerged with a firm industrial foundation. In 1858, for example, the state produced only 22,876 tons of iron ore. By 1866, that figure had grown to 296,713 tons. Though the war fostered such growth, it was not a prerequisite for Michigan's industrial development.

When the Civil War began, the United States economy had just survived the depression of 1857. As wartime products were substituted for peacetime goods, consumer and government demand far exceeded supply. At the same time, the army vied with wartime industry for the existing labor supply. Prices increased and inflation resulted. The war also damaged the nation's financial structure. The loss of nearly $300 million of uncollected Southern debts shook Northern banks. Unsecured paper depreciated, and thousands of Northern banks failed or were suspended. The Midwest suffered greatly since the mining, manufacturing and agricultural components of its economy were especially dependent upon seasonal credit to start up spring production.

Wartime demands, however, also spurred the nation's economic development by causing new services, workers and production techniques to substitute for those siphoned off into the war economy. Michigan's economy expanded overall during the Civil War. But the war was not the only stimulus. The extension of Michigan's transportation system, parts of which had been developed prior to the war, also facilitated the state's growth.

Before the 1850s the Mississippi River had been the shipping outlet for midwestern grain and other produce. The Civil War, however, forced the Midwest to turn to the numerous railroad trunk lines that connected its farmland via Great Lakes steamers to eastern markets.

In 1860 Michigan had less railway mileage than any other northwestern state, except Minnesota. Michigan's

779 miles of operating track were composed almost entirely of three roads: the Central and the Southern, which connected Chicago and Detroit, and the Detroit and Milwaukee Railway, which ran between Detroit and Grand Haven. By 1870 Michigan had more than doubled its railroad mileage to 1,638 miles. This increase included a short line from Marquette to Champion and another from Negaunee to Escanaba, which provided an outlet to Lake Michigan for iron ore. During this same period, the total railroad mileage in the United States increased from 30,626 to 52,922 miles.

More important to Michigan was the 1855 completion of the Sault Ste. Marie locks, which linked Lakes Superior and Huron. The Sault locks, then the largest in the world, provided an important shipping outlet for the Upper Peninsula's mining regions. During their first year of operation, the locks carried 15,000 tons of copper and iron ore; in 1864, the last full year of the Civil War, approximately 284,000 tons passed through them.

Improved transportation also helped the steady growth of Northern agriculture, though a scarcity of farm labor caused by army enlistments and the migration of the farming population to work in the mines initially caused problems. The reasons for agricultural prosperity during the war included (1) the need to feed the army, which at the close of the war numbered one million men, (2) the increasing population of the country, (3) the improved mechanization of the farm and (4) the large foreign markets available for exports.

The initial farm labor shortage was soon offset by the use of women in the fields, by the influx of European immigrants and by the use of labor-saving farm machinery, such as the McCormick reaper, the gang plow, the thresher and the improved mower. As a result, the North was able to feed both its armies and its growing population.

Michigan's population growth of 58 percent in the 1860s was partially due to the response of eastern farmers and foreign immigrants to the Homestead Act of 1862, which offered citizens 160 acres free after five years of continuous residence.

From January 1, 1863, to June 1866, some 762,075 acres of Michigan land were distributed to 5,997 homesteaders, while the state land office sold an additional 530,000 acres.

Despite the increased national production of grains during the 1860s, prices remained at approximately the same level because the growing demand for these products carried off the surplus. Harvests in the years 1860 to 1862 in England were below normal. United States exports to England between 1860 and 1865 reached 100,578,665 bushels of wheat and 9,253,732 bushels of wheat flour. How much of these exports came from Michigan is impossible to determine; however, Michigan was producing a growing share of the nation's grain.

When Southern secession deprived the North of its prime source of cotton for clothing, the North turned to wools, and Michigan quickly became an important wool producer. Michigan's agricultural growth was also evident in the expansion of its farm products and farm-related manufacturing products.

During the 1860s Michigan's mining and lumbering industries expanded along with agriculture. The output of iron ore, copper, salt and lumber in Michigan during the 1860s surpassed previous records and contributed significantly to the industrial growth of the North.

In the Upper Peninsula, limited capital, poor transportation, unusually high costs of materials and the failure to adopt smelting had hampered early iron-ore operations. The transportation difficulty was lessened by the completion of the Sault locks and the railroad between Marquette and Ishpeming. Indeed, as historian George Fuller observed, "The canal made the ore trade and the ore trade made the canal." Between 1856 (the first full year the canal was in operation) and 1860 the amount of iron ore shipped increased by a factor of almost twenty. The Civil War and the industrial expansion of the 1860s caused Michigan iron-ore production to expand dramatically in the Marquette range, though the greatest growth in tons produced occurred after the end of the Civil War.

The Sault locks also permitted exploitation of many copper deposits in the western Upper Peninsula. By 1870 the three main copper districts—Keweenaw, Ontonagon and Portage Lake—were being worked by twenty-four mines. During the war Michigan produced over six thousand tons of copper annually—70 percent of the nation's supply.

Both iron and copper mines faced acute labor shortages caused by the increasing number of men serving in the army and the difficulty of attracting laborers to work in the isolated mining districts. Congress made several attempts to alleviate this manpower shortage. Under the Contract Labor Act of 1864, authorized persons could make contracts in other countries to import workers. Offers to foreign workers often included draft exemption and liberal wages. Several Michigan mining companies raised ninety thousand dollars to send agents to Sweden to recruit workers, many of whom, upon reaching the United States, refused to work in the mines and emigrated elsewhere or enlisted in the army.

Michigan also became a major producer of salt during the 1860s. Salt had been found in 1840 south of Grand Rapids and in Midland County. The discovery of richer veins along the Saginaw River, coupled with the wartime destruction of the salt works in Virginia and southern Ohio and the inability of New York mines to meet national demands, allowed Michigan to fill a void. Moreover, Michigan's mines were in an excellent location for market distribution, especially for the nearby Chicago meat-packing industry.

Timber was another important Michigan resource. Unlike iron and copper, which remained untapped until adequate transportation made them profitable, noncommercial lumbering began in Michigan as soon as the first settlers arrived. Commercial milling of lumber, however, had to wait until the 1840s. By the 1850s lumbering in Michigan had become an established industry with an annual cutting of 400 million board feet.

Many of the Illinois banks that had provided much of the early financial backing for Michigan's lumbering industry did not have a firm financial basis. When the war broke out, the securities of many of these banks, based primarily on Southern state bonds, became worthless. Illinois bank-issued money quickly lost its value, and the collapse of the banks forced many lumber camps and mills to shut down. What little lumber was produced remained unsold or brought low prices when desperate mill owners flooded the Detroit market with lumber normally routed westward to Illinois.

As the financial crisis slowly passed, lumbering rebounded. A prime construction material, lumber was needed for the war effort, as well as for railroad expansion. As a result, capitalization in Michigan lumbering more than doubled between 1860 and 1870 and lumbering establishments and employment increased. In 1864 Michigan cut 620 million board feet. By 1870 Michigan led the United States in lumber production.

The 1860s were years of expansion for manufacturing industries in the United States, particularly in the North. Wartime manufacturing had to satisfy the needs of the military, the civilian population and international trade. Though the added demand of the army can be estimated, how much of this was new demand and how much a redistribution of goods from civilian to military consumption is difficult to assess. The slow rate of growth in manufacturing during the first years of the war has been attributed to the disorganization or complete breakdown of financial and product markets. Southern secession cut off the supply of certain manufacturing goods and raw materials, particularly cotton, and reduced Southern demand for Northern products. The near collapse of Northern banking also caused plant shutdowns. As a result, many manufacturing goods had to be imported. Northern manufacturing, however, expanded markedly as the Civil War progressed, though it is impossible to determine how much of this expansion would have taken place without the war.

During the Civil War army arsenals cast bronze cannon and copper was used to make brass army buttons and belt plates. To meet the high demand, these Houghton County miners were kept busy hand-drilling copper for the Northern war effort.

The war's demand for improved armor and more powerful artillery stimulated interest in a new steel-making process. The Bessemer process, which was first introduced in the United States in 1862 in Wyandotte, south of Detroit, was not fully developed until 1864. Lake Superior iron ores were highly suitable for the Bessemer process because of their high purity and low phosphorus content. The process, which was not adopted by other steel producers until after the war, put Michigan at the forefront of modern steel production. It is difficult to ascertain the war's impact on the growth of metals manufacturing, but one expert, Victor S. Clark, concludes that the war "affected the technical progress and the organization of the metal working and engineering industries more than it did the volume of their production, because the direct demands for ordnance and other military uses did not counterbalance the checked market for structural iron and railway equipment."

Growth in manufacturing increased the number of workers in Michigan

Michigan, like the rest of the North, suffered a manufacturing slowdown during the early war years, but then took part in the expansion that followed. Michigan manufacturing, however, probably responded more to conditions prevailing in the North at the outbreak of the Civil War than to the war itself. For the first time, the expanded railroad system and Sault locks provided the means to cheaply get Michigan products, particularly raw materials, to markets. Manufacturing quickly reacted. Processing plants for raw materials appeared, and durable goods industries developed. Michigan built industries that used its iron, steel, copper and lumber for the manufacturing of heavy articles. Iron manufacturing increased markedly during the decade, most notably providing small firearms, steam engines, boilers, iron bridges and railroad equipment.

industry by 70.5 percent (from 236,987 to 404,164) between 1860 and 1870. The nation's labor force increased by only 50.9 percent (from 8,287,043 to 12,505,923) during the same period. The limited data on how much workers were paid and what prices they paid for goods during the Civil War decade necessitates a dependence upon regional and national estimates. Two distinct trends emerged nationally during the 1860s. First, wages remained relatively stable for the first two years of the Civil War but then rose sharply over the next three years. During these same five years, the cost of living nearly doubled. Second, during the postwar five-year period, some wage rates advanced at a more moderate rate than during the war, while others dropped. Consequently, daily average wages in 1870 were slightly lower than those in 1865 and 1.5 times as great as wages in 1860. Prices during 1860-70, however, rose moderately and did not return to prewar levels. Thus, while annual earnings of nonfarm employees rose, their real earnings fell. Wages in Michigan also rose drastically from 1860 to 1865 but grew little or decreased in the postwar years. The mean annual wage in Michigan manufacturing went from an 1860 level of $290 to $333 in 1870. During the same period the national average rose from $289 to $378. In general, higher prices kept real wages down in Michigan, as they did in the United States. Also, wages did not rise as much as they might have because many of the workers who entered the army were replaced by lower-paid women, boys, unskilled laborers and immigrants.

The Civil War was not the only stimulus for Michigan's industrial growth during the 1860s. First, Michigan increased in population by almost 60 percent during the 1860s. Demand for food, clothing, housing, transportation, iron and steel soared as the population grew, and industry expanded to meet the demand. Second, the completion of the Sault locks, as well as railway expansion, made it easier to transport Michigan's natural resources.

The Civil War differed from later wars in that there were few "war-contrived" goods—goods that existed only for the conflict. The Civil War demanded few capital-intensive, highly complicated articles. The military, however, needed items that normally would have entered civilian consumer markets. The economic effect of such military demands is difficult to determine for "if government demands merely replace civilian demands for the same commodities, it is possible that no increase in demand over and above the probable nonwar situation occurred." For example, according to *The Reinterpretation of American Economic History* (1971):

It has been shown that the consumption of iron attributable to small arms production during

the war was only one percent of total U.S. iron output between 1861 and 1865. The amount could have been used to lay 650 miles of railroad track. The shortfall in mileage built during the war below the 1865-1870 level was seven times that amount. Thus, any expansion in iron output based upon arms production was more than offset by the effects of the war upon railroad construction.

The war may have had, indirectly or directly, negative effects on economic growth. The breakdown of financial markets slowed production and economic development; not until several years after the Civil War did the economy of the Midwest recover from that collapse.

The war also jeopardized the labor force. By war's end, Michigan's total contribution of manpower to the federal army was 92,220. (This does not include the Michigan men who enlisted in regiments of other states.) The loss of these workers slowed Michigan's rate of industrialization and brought about a shift in the sex and age composition of the manufacturing labor force. With a labor shortage, mechanization was encouraged; yet it is difficult to separate the introduction of labor-saving machinery induced by this shortage from that caused by the continuing evolution of industrial science. Moreover, the workers' real wages declined during the Civil War as prices rose faster than wages.

Thomas C. Cochran has argued that "aside from commercial banking, the Civil War appears not to have started or created any significant new patterns of economic institutional change." This was true in Michigan. The state was at the stage where all the factors of industrialization were present: rising population, presence of valuable natural resources, improved transportation facilities and the beginning of new industrial processes. These factors, not the Civil War, catapulted Michigan into economic prominence.

Rendering Invaluable Service

By Steven Dunker

Michigan was one of the few states that sent an engineer regiment to the Western Theater of the war. The First Michigan Engineers and Mechanics built bridges, forts and roads in Tennessee and Georgia while earning an impressive record on the battlefield.

They built bridges, storehouses and pontoon boats, repaired Union-held steamboat docks and railroads and destroyed miles of Confederate railroads. They even fashioned a gunboat out of a converted ferry. They did not seek the honor and glory achieved in battle, but they frequently worked while under enemy fire. They were the men of the First Regiment Michigan Engineers and Mechanics, some of the finest engineers to see action during the Civil War.

The First Regiment Michigan Engineers and Mechanics was the brainchild of Grand Rapids residents Wright L. Coffinberry, a civil engineer; James Sligh, a merchant; Baker Borden, an architect and builder; and Perrin V. Fox, a contractor and bridge builder, who decided to form a Michigan engineer regiment. They all became captains in the regiment. Thirty-five-year-old William Powell Innes, also of Grand Rapids, who had supervised the construction of the Detroit and Milwaukee Railroad from Detroit to Grand Haven, was chosen commander on the premise that his prestige would garner the new regiment the same respect of regular U.S. Army engineers. This would include the monthly pay of seventeen dollars received by engineers, instead of the thirteen dollars received by infantrymen. Recruiting began in mid-August 1861.

In early October 1861 the First Regiment Michigan Engineers and Mechanics, then known as the Michigan Fusiliers, rendezvoused at the Calhoun County Agricultural Society grounds, named Camp Owen for the occasion, in Marshall. The regiment mustered into federal service on October 29. Training was delayed since the quartermaster in Detroit did not have the required engineering tools. Finally, on December 17 the 1,032-man regiment left Michigan to join General Don Carlos Buell's Army of the Ohio in Louisville, Kentucky.

Many of the men who enlisted in the First Michigan Engineers and Mechanics had no desire to see combat.

In fact, those who enlisted did not seek the honor and glory achieved in battle. They enlisted with the assurance that they would not be on the front lines. John Weissert of Hastings noted that "from Grand Rapids many have enlisted in our regiment. They are very good citizens and well-off. They thought like myself—if there is drafting they would have you put in front—no chance for survival."

Once in Kentucky, the engineers were soon building roads, bridges and storehouses and performing a variety of diverse tasks, such as floating grounded barges. The regiment was split into four battalions of two and three companies. To diffuse their skills throughout the region, each battalion was attached to one of the Northern army's four largest divisions in Kentucky.

One problem needing resolving before the engineers could prove an efficient tool for the Union army was their salary. Prior to leaving Michigan, the paymaster paid the engineers the thirteen dollars a month infantrymen received instead of the promised seventeen dollars. The regiment's officers convinced the men that the matter had been corrected and the paymaster would meet them in Kentucky with due pay.

This did not happen and the men became angry. William Calkins of Grand Rapids complained, "We have been having a flare-up in our regiment and I don't know how it will come out. Our colonel has used fraud and disseption [*sic*] ever since our first enlistment and he has got caught at it." As the payless months passed, the men became more irate. On February 24 Calkins wrote, "The first of March the boys are going to bolt on the account of our pay and we expect them to be mustered out then."

The problem was that Congress had not authorized the extra pay. The bill to do so was opposed on the grounds that thousands of engineers would be paid to build railroads that would be used by private enterprise after the war. The legislation was passed in July 1862; however, only existing engineer units received the bonus.

In early April 1862 most of the Michigan engineers, except Companies A and K, began moving to Pittsburg Landing, Tennessee, with Buell. But the Michiganians, who guarded the slow-moving supply trains, did not arrive until a week after the Battle of Shiloh, Tennessee. At Pittsburg Landing, they constructed a steamboat landing, repaired roads and built fortifications. Next, they moved to Corinth, Mississippi, to build roads and position guns for a siege of the enemy forces located there. After the Confederates evacuated the city, the engineers opened one hundred miles of the Mississippi and Charleston Railroad from Corinth to Decatur, Alabama, building ten bridges on the way. In July the engineers moved to Huntsville, Alabama, where they were joined by Companies A and K. At Huntsville the regiment also completed a 160-foot-long bridge built of cotton bales and fashioned a gunboat from a converted ferry and a sawmill engine.

On January 1, 1863, the second day of the Battle of Stones River, Tennessee, the First Michigan Engineers was ordered to Lavergne, Tennessee, a position in the rear of the army, to guard the supply train. Commanding a small force of only 391 men, Colonel Innes put the wagons in a semicircle and built light breastworks of logs and brush. Confederate cavalry units raided the huge wagon trains of General William S. Rosecrans' Northern army. Outnumbering the Michiganians ten to one, Confederate cavalrymen attacked the engineers' position seven times during the afternoon. On one occasion the rebel commander sent a flag of truce to Colonel Innes and demanded his surrender. Innes reportedly replied, "We don't surrender much." The Michigan officer refused the offer and his men repulsed the rebels on every occasion.

General Rosecrans described the engineers conduct as gallant, but a newspaper correspondent recorded:

Forty-four-year-old John Hiesrodt of Tuscola County wears the First Michigan Engineers and Mechanics state-issued uniform—complete with the engineers' castle-hat insignia—given to the men before they left for Kentucky in December 1861.

The scene was at times thrilling beyond description. The rebel horde, exasperated at the successful resistance of the little force, dashed their horses against the circular brush fence, which was only breast high, with infuriated shouts and curses. But the Michigan troops were cool and determined; they loaded fast and aimed well, and, as the troopers rushed on upon all sides they were met with staggering volleys almost at the muzzle of the muskets. Horses and riders recoiled again and again until they despaired, and soon swept away through the dense forests, leaving over fifty of their dead upon the field, which were buried by our forces. The ground around that small circle of brush was strewn with dead horses of the rebel troopers, and with their clothing, guns, etc. Truly this was one of the most gallant affairs of the campaign.

The engagement lasted five hours; the engineers suffered two dead, nine wounded and five missing.

In late June 1863, the Michigan engineers began working on the Nashville and Chattanooga Railroad. By September they had built five bridges, including the most-impressive Elk River Bridge. When the Pioneer Brigade (soldiers assigned to a special three-thousand-man unit from their regular units to clear roads, construct bridges and dig trenches) at Elk River informed General Rosecrans that it would take them six to seven weeks to complete the bridge, the impatient commander sent for the Michigan engineers. Innes seemed pleased with the assignment. The *Detroit Free Press* reported that "Colonel Innes told General Rosecrans that the Michigan engineers would build the bridge in eight days, provided the Pioneer Brigade were kept away."

Finished in the promised eight days, the bridge was 450 feet long and 58 feet high. Shortly thereafter, the regiment built another bridge—350 feet in length—over the Duck River. According to regimental historian Charles Sligh, "The building of these bridges in the short space of time in which they were accomplished was among the remarkable engineering achievements of the war and brought the highest commendations from the commanding generals. Their building resulted in restoring railroad communications that were of vital importance to the Union armies."

One of the engineers' most important accomplishments during the war occurred following the Union defeat at the Battle of Chickamauga, Georgia, in late September 1863. When the battle ended, the Northern army retreated to Chattanooga, Tennessee, where it became entrapped by Confederate forces.

The Michigan regiment's first project while trapped was to finish a pontoon bridge across the Tennessee River, north of Chattanooga. The Pioneer Brigade had unsuccessfully attempted this on October 5, 1863, damaging some of the boats in the process. The engineers did the necessary repair work and completed the bridge in two days.

Breaking the Confederate siege required a more dangerous undertaking. Brown's Ferry was chosen as a second bridge site; however, it was under enemy observation. Materials for the bridge would have to be floated down the river at night.

Before a bridge could be attempted, additional pontoon boats had to be built. Although some lumber was found in Chattanooga, it was unsuitable for pontoon construction. Captain Perrin V. Fox, commanding Companies C, D and K, creatively fashioned a pontoon that could be constructed out of this lumber. The army's chief engineer said it would not work, but Fox appealed to General Rosecrans, who ordered him to proceed. When Fox's prototype passed all the requisite tests, fifty-one additional pontoons were ordered constructed.

The lumber for these specially designed pontoons required further cutting, but the Confederates had dismantled the Chattanooga sawmills. Area slaves located the hidden sawmill parts and the engineers reassembled the mills. Caulking material was unavailable, so baled cotton was substituted. Nails were carried over the mountains by dispatch riders. With all the pieces in place, the engineers assembled the pontoons with help from three infantry regiments. The fifty-two pontoons were assembled in less than twelve hours.

The bridge material was loaded on the pontoons during the night of October 26, 1863. The next night the engineers and the Eighteenth Ohio Infantry floated the loaded boats down the river. At 4:30 A.M. on October 28, General William B. Hazen's brigade was ferried across the river to drive away any Confederates in the area of the bridgehead. Then, assisted by approximately one hundred men from the Twenty-first Michigan Infantry, the engineers erected the bridge. The construction team worked under fire from an enemy artillery battery until it was silenced by Union cannon. A Chattanooga correspondent recorded that "during the hottest and thickest of the fight, [as] the shells were falling thick and fast all around him," Fox's men accomplished the task in just three hours without suffering any casualties.

With the completion of the bridge, water-borne supplies were landed at Brown's Ferry and shuttled overland, out of enemy artillery range, to Chattanooga's hungry garrison. The starving Northern soldiers, happy for hardtack, dubbed the route the "Cracker Line." General George Thomas, commanding the Army of the Cumberland, offered the Michigan engineers "the highest praise" for their work on the bridge.

On September 21, 1864, the Michigan engineers, excluding Companies L and M, were ordered to join General William Sherman's armies in Atlanta, Georgia.

In Atlanta the engineers, now commanded by Major John B. Yates, found themselves destroying as much rebel property as they did constructing or repairing bridges and earthworks. According to Sligh, "for three or four days" in mid-November the Michiganians tore up railroads leading into the city, burned the ties and twisted the iron rails. The engineers also "destroyed the depot buildings, besides many others that might be of use to the enemy in our absence." Sligh noted that during the night of November 15, the "sky was bright with fires from burning buildings throughout the city." On November 16 the Michigan engineers left Atlanta to participate in Sherman's March to the Sea. On the way to Savannah, Georgia, the regiment built bridges and corduroy roads to aid the army's movement and destroyed much enemy property. During the nearly four weeks it took to reach Savannah, the Michigan engineers burned anything—especially railroads—that might be of assistance to the enemy. After the capture of Savannah, the Michigan engineers spent a month in the coastal city. Flint engineer James Greenlach described it as "a very nice place, the most so I think of any southern city" that he had seen in two years of fighting in the South.

In late January 1865 the engineers sailed from Savannah to Beaufort, South Carolina. By early February they were marching north with Sherman's army through the Carolinas. The march proved even more arduous than the trek through Georgia. Winter rains had caused a great deal of roadwork. During one six-day period the engineers marched about sixty-nine miles, repairing roads and bridges. On another occasion, Greenlach wrote that they had marched all day; then, because a dam broke, they built a footbridge before eating supper. He lamented, "We worked all night in the rain and in the morning the water had falen [*sic*] so that what we had built was ordered to be taken away so our nights work in the rain did not amount to anything in reality."

On March 19 the Michigan engineers, after spending the morning repairing a road, moved forward to defend the Union line, which was coming under attack. As the engineers advanced to their assigned position, "small crowds of pack animals, coming out of the woods, and from the front, seemed to indicate to an observer the likelihood of our repulse." Colonel Yates advanced the Michiganians towards the woods in line of battle. According to Sligh:

> While doing this the movements of infantry in front and on the right with the accompanying noise of battle seemed to show that the enemy would soon be upon them. The Colonel, following the movements of infantry on his right, took a better position. Then facing the enemy he ordered the men, who had been provided with shovels from our tool wagons, to throw up hastily a temporary earthwork in their front. They worked lively. At the same time it was reported that the enemy were massing on our left. Colonel Yates exhorted his men to stand firm, by saying, "We will whip the rebels." The men stood firm and kept in line. After the enemy had been checked and the troops deployed in front, we moved to our position on the left, where a very strong line of works were soon thrown up. The action from this time (5:30 P.M.) until dark was very heavy indeed. The rebels, massed in front, made several charges to take our battery, holding on desper-

ately for half an hour, during which time the guns poured in grape, canister, shot and shell. The noise occasioned by the incessant rattle of musketry, mingled with the loud, sharp cracking of artillery and the dense smoke, made it for a time one of the sharpest battles of the war.

In late March 1865 all twelve companies of the First Michigan Engineers were reunited at Goldsboro, North Carolina. One veteran engineer recorded on March 22. "We will have a few days rest, and be prepared to take part in the grand final overthrow of the great rebellion." However, the war was quickly ending.

After General Joseph Johnston surrendered his Confederate army at Bentonville, North Carolina, in late April 1865, the Michigan engineers journeyed to Washington to march in the Grand Review. Most of the men hoped to be mustered out. Instead, they were ordered to Louisville, Kentucky, where they arrived on June 14. They then went to Nashville, Tennessee, where they worked on the city's defenses. During the next three months, Colonel Yates wrote regularly to the adjutant general, requesting that the Michiganians be mustered out. This request was granted on September 22. The First Michigan Engineers arrived in Jackson, Michigan, where they were paid and disbanded on October 1, 1865.

The value of the First Michigan Engineers is best evidenced by the accolades they received from numerous Union commanders. On Sherman's march, commanders were often anxious to have the Michigan engineers move with their units. In February 1865 General Henry W. Slocum wrote, "If it is not absolutely necessary to retain all the engineer troops with the Right Wing, I earnestly hope that at least one company of the First Michigan may be sent to this wing." But one of the finest tributes the Michiganians received came from the unit's first commanding general, Don Carlos Buell, who wrote in late 1862, "I cannot omit to make mention of the Michigan regiment of Mechanics and Engineers. It has not only rendered invaluable service in its appropnate duties during the past year, but at Chaplin Hills . . . [and] other occasions it has, in whole or in part, gallantly engaged the enemy. I . . . commend Colonel Innes . . . for the efficient services of this fine regiment."

"Fighting is Not Very Funny Business"

By Roger L. Rosentreter

*Sam Hodgman of Climax was a typical Civil War soldier.
He entered the army in 1861 with great expectations. Instead, he found that
the common soldier experienced little glory and much suffering.*

The guns at Charleston, South Carolina, had barely cooled in April 1861 when thousands of men, from both the North and South, rushed to answer the call to arms. Samuel C. Hodgman—thirty years old and working in his father's shoe shop in Climax—organized a company of volunteers. He studied the manual of arms and drilled his company regularly in the small village between Kalamazoo and Battle Creek. But the state had no need for his services. Michigan already had four regiments in service, and Governor Austin Blair had temporarily suspended accepting new enlistments. Since many leaders predicted a short war, it was frustrating for those yearning to serve to be rejected.

Finally, when it appeared that he would never get to war, Sam was ordered to Detroit's Fort Wayne. On June 22, 1861, he enlisted as first sergeant of Company I, Seventh Michigan Infantry. He soon began writing home, creating a record of what war was like, not for a hero or great leader, but for a common soldier.

Camp life appealed to Sam, and he fell into the daily routine with ease. A typical day involved rising at 4:30 A.M., breakfast, drill all morning, lunch, lounging until 3:00 P.M., more drill, supper, parade at 7:00 P.M. and tattoo at 9:00 P.M. One of Sam's comrades recalled that "the whole affair seemed so like a picnic, so romantic for us all who had been accustomed to hard work on the farm."

In August the Seventh Michigan moved to Monroe, where it was uniformed, mustered into federal service and ordered to Washington, DC. Writing home, Sam told his parents that at numerous stops they were greeted "with the greatest enthusiasm." The Seventh remained in Washington one week and then moved thirty miles up the Potomac River and encamped in a wheat field with easy access to a clear stream. Here the men spent the autumn perfecting their soldiering.

In October the Seventh received orders to drive the Confederates out of the Virginia countryside bordering the river. But they saw no rebels. "The only thing we won was the right to return to camp," complained a fellow sergeant. With the exception of a "mud march" in December, the Seventh saw no further action during the winter of 1861-62. The men built winter quarters, drilled, paraded, went on picket and fatigue details, played cards, had snowball fights and complained. In February they cheered Northern victories in Tennessee and North Carolina and burned an effigy of Confederate president Jefferson Davis.

As the newly formed Army of the Potomac waited, Sam criticized the high command for keeping the Seventh "out of harm's way for fear that some of them might get hurt" and glumly predicted, "We seem destined to earn our laurels not by what we do, but by what we don't do." The regiment's colonel posted a sign that read "Headquarters Grin and Bearit."

Finally, in March 1862 the Seventh was ordered to help capture Harpers Ferry, Virginia. They arrived to find it had already fallen. The regiment then journeyed to Virginia's Yorktown Peninsula to participate in the war's first great campaign.

Sam began the Peninsular Campaign optimistic that the army, which consisted of over one hundred thousand well-trained and well-equipped men, would "sweep everything before it." But the only thing they initially encountered was bad weather. The smartly polished soldiers who had set off to end the war became caked with mud and soaked from the continuous cold rain. Roads were impassable; supplies were delayed. The infantry pulled wagons and artillery through the mud, and the rebels retreated before the slow-moving Northern army.

In the campaign's first battle, the army besieged the Confederate works at Yorktown. Sam's spirits rose in early May as the date neared for a massive artillery bombardment that might end the siege. But the rebels withdrew and foiled the Northern plan. "I don't know where we shall fight them," Sam wrote dejectedly. "We have been chasing them sometime but they beat us in running. Possibly they may keep us following them till 'yellow jack' comes to their aid." "Yellow jack" (yellow fever) soon came to the rebels' aid. By late May Sam's company was reduced to 50 percent. By July 1, 20 percent of the army was in field hospitals suffering from various diseases.

The Seventh finally received its baptism of fire at the Battle of Fair Oaks on May 31, 1862. Sam spent the day in a field hospital with a severe case of "bilious diarrhea." The disease so weakened him that he did not participate in any of the campaign's remaining battles.

The fighting ended in early July, but the Army of the Potomac remained on the peninsula until August. The sick rolls grew longer, the mud deeper and the pessimism stronger. Scurvy appeared. Sam wrote, "Our living is generally hard bread, pork and bacon, beans and rice and occasionally beef. When we want a change we reverse the order." The Seventh was down to a quarter of its original enrollment. Sam was losing confidence. "The boys in this regiment and many others are very much disheartened by the prospects of the war. Many are willing to bet that the South will be recognized [by Great Britain and France] in less than 30 days."

In mid-August the Army of the Potomac returned to Washington. Though Sam claimed that "we are pretty well worn out," the army was soon on the move. They headed toward western Maryland where Robert E. Lee's Confederates were moving north. On September 16, near Sharpsburg, Maryland, Sam wrote that he did not expect to see the enemy for quite awhile.

He was wrong.

On the morning of September 17, Sam's division marched to assist the army's right flank. They encountered little resistance as they moved into a wooded area. Then, suddenly, rebel fire came from the front and left. Standing near the regimental flag, Sam attempted to rally some of his comrades. "They [musket balls] were flying all around . . . and like plums in a pudding were bursting in every direction. . . . It seemed almost a miracle that any escaped." Sam went down, wounded in both legs. Eventually, he hobbled to a field hospital two miles behind the lines. A week later he was transferred to an army hospital in Philadelphia.

Sam had lived through the bloodiest single day of the war—Antietam. His regiment was part of Major General John Sedgwick's division. Through a foul-up, the division went through a gap in the Union lines and exposed its left flank. The Seventh was on the division's extreme left when the Confederates attacked. Sam and his regimental comrades numbered 360 as they entered the West Woods; only 138 left unscathed. Casualties from both sides at Antietam totaled 25,000.

Sam remained in the Philadelphia hospital for three months. With "over 4,000 beds," the hospital was huge and Sam hated every minute there. "It [the hospital] is about the same as a state prison. The fare is much the same and we have not much more liberty." A firm believer that a furlough would recuperate him more quickly, Sam repeatedly sought a chance to go home. When prospects looked dim, he lashed out against the government. "Our government seems to be afraid that sick & wounded might have a little enjoyment if they gave them a chance to get home."

As the weeks turned into months, Sam warned his brother to stay out of the army. "Instead of the end being nearer it seems to grow farther off all the time. Every victory of our troops seems more of a victory for the rebels than it does for us. They seem to gather strength while our army is, half of it or more, in the hospital." He also no longer had any delusions about a soldier's life. In November he wrote, "Fighting nowadays is not very funny business, especially when the balls fly as thick as they did at Antietam."

In January 1863 Sam returned to the Seventh just in time to break camp and participate in one of the war's most futile campaigns. It soon began to rain; snow followed. Sam wrote, "Our army is at present stuck in the mud and can do nothing in the way of forward movements." The army did not engage the enemy, and soon it returned to its original encampment near Fredericksburg, Virginia.

Spring brought better health and optimism. "We are having the best time so far that we have ever had since we came to the fields," Sam wrote. "Our troops are all in good spirits and ready to fight." Though the army undertook a major campaign in May, the Seventh had only a minor role and did not leave Fredericksburg.

Mid-June brought action. Lee's army was headed north, and the Army of the Potomac sometimes covered thirty miles a day in its effort to thwart the invasion. On June 22 Sam was promoted to captain. On July 1 the Union army's lead elements clashed with the Confederates at Gettysburg, Pennsylvania.

Located near the army's rear, the Seventh was still outside Gettysburg on the evening of the battle's first day. The next day the regiment, along with other elements of the Second Corps, positioned itself behind a rail fence and a stone wall, just to the left of a small clump of trees. Sam was on Cemetery Ridge—the center of the Union line.

Friday morning, July 3, the battle's third and final day, dawned hot and humid. The rebels renewed their assaults on the Northern right flank, but around 10:00 A.M. the fighting stopped and silence pervaded the battlefield. The men of the Seventh crowded behind their barricades wondering if the battle had ended. Around noon they heard two single cannon shots, which began a massive rebel bombardment of Cemetery Ridge. During the two-hour barrage the men of the Seventh hugged the ground behind whatever cover they could find. Suddenly the firing stopped. After the smoke cleared away, thirteen thousand Confederates moved out of the trees less than a mile away. As they

Samuel C. Hodgman of Climax eagerly sought an opportunity to go to war. On June 22, 1861, he joined the Seventh Michigan Infantry. During his nearly three years in the army, he discovered that the common soldier experienced little glory and much suffering.

marched across the open fields, Union cannon and muskets took a dreadful toll. The rebels pushed on, but only several hundred reached their destination—the clump of trees to the Seventh's right. The fighting was hand to hand. Sam recalled, "We stuck to our barricade and fought till they—what were left of them—were glad to come into our lines or skedaddle double quick."

The two armies stayed in their positions the next day, burying their dead and resting. The battle had cost the Seventh a third of its strength. Sam was unscathed. On July 5 he and the Seventh joined in the pursuit of the Confederates, who had begun the long return trip to

Virginia. The rebels got away and the Seventh spent most of July marching around the Virginia countryside having little contact with the enemy.

Sam and the Seventh spent late August in New York City quelling draft riots. By mid-September they were back in Virginia. On October 5, 80 percent of the Seventh's 1861 enlistees reenlisted for another three years or the duration of the war. Sam did not. He had already fixed his sights on the end of his three-year hitch. Following his return from New York, he reminded his parents that he had only eleven months to serve. (As an officer Sam could have resigned anytime, but he apparently felt compelled to stay in for his original three-year enlistment.)

In early November Sam's regiment was on the move again. Major General George Meade was planning to flank Lee's army. Command foul-ups and bad weather plagued the Northern army, and in late November they discovered the rebels positioned directly in front of their advance. Meade issued orders calling for a frontal assault on the entire rebel line. To get to the enemy's works five hundred yards away, the men would have to cross an open valley, ford the flooded Mine Run Creek and re-form to continue the attack. Even for the best veterans, the chances of success were slim if not nonexistent. Sam predicted that only one in twenty would ever reach the enemy's lines. "None would have flinched but the bravest knew that they were going to meet almost certain death." Sam's predictions were never tested. The attack was called off and the army returned to its winter quarters.

But as he lay there looking at the near-impregnable Confederate works, Sam decided that he had had enough soldiering. He had witnessed murderous assaults by both armies at numerous battlefields. The assaults when successful were disastrous; those that failed were calamitous. War had changed. The well-entrenched position was becoming predominant, and the improved distance and accuracy of weapons made frontal assaults on entrenched positions suicidal.

Sam also had personal reasons for wanting to leave the army. In September he realized that of the six men who left Climax with the Seventh in 1861, he was the only one still in service. He had not fully recovered from the typhoid fever he had contracted on the Peninsula, and his leg wounds often hurt, especially in cold weather. He was tired of the rigors of campaigning. At Mine Run, he wrote, "the weather was so cold that much sleep was out of the question as it took a good share of the time to keep the fires going." In December 1863 Sam concluded, "I am pretty well worn in the service. All tell me I look ten years older than I did when I joined the regiment."

He had also begun to look toward the future. During the fall of 1863 he began corresponding with a woman in Ohio. Soon there was talk of marriage. Prior to Mine Run he wrote, "If I get out alive I shall be thankful. At Gettysburg I would have given a leg to have my life warranted without a moments [sic] hesitation. I don't feel so now."

In December the Seventh received a thirty-day furlough. It arrived in Monroe on New Year's Day 1864.

Though the residents were "tickled to death" to see them, Sam saw little to admire. The Seventh had only 160 of its original complement of 900 and "brought back a flag staff with a few rags of silk and fringe hanging to it—nothing to admire either."

On March 1, 1864, Captain Samuel C. Hodgman was honorably discharged with a surgeon's certificate of disability. His resignation came only two months before the Army of the Potomac undertook the campaign that ended at Appomattox on April 9, 1865.

Returning home Sam married his correspondent, Ella M. Weeks of Sandusky, Ohio, and started a family that eventually included four children. His postwar years were checkered with poverty and sickness. He suffered from a worsening case of rheumatism, probably aggravated by his military career, and held a variety of different jobs. He moved to Florida during the 1880s and became a minister in 1894. Sam died six years later in Haines City, Florida.

Sam Hodgman was an average Civil War soldier. His military career started with great expectations and ended in the realization that the common soldier experiences little glory and much suffering. He did not serve the duration, nor did he commit any singularly courageous act during his years of service. But Sam Hodgman, like so many others, learned that war, so often perceived as exciting, is in reality only tragic.

Their Greatest Battle Was Getting into the Fight

By Hondon Hargrove

In 1863 Michigan was authorized to raise one regiment of African American volunteers. Thousands of black men rushed to the recruiting booths and enlisted in the First Michigan Colored Infantry. Proving their loudest critics wrong, the First showed themselves to be gallant fighters.

Thousands of volumes have been written about the Civil War, but the complete contributions by blacks are not generally known by most Americans. During, and even long after, the war only a handful of publications noted their involvement; school textbooks pointedly and consistently omitted references to them. Meanwhile, white officers and enlisted men wrote books and stories for magazines and newspapers about their heroic experiences and their units, most of which were widely read. Relatively few such tomes were written about black soldiers.

When the Civil War began, President Abraham Lincoln issued the first of many calls for voluntary enlistments. All the troops raised were white. This was not because black men refused to apply—hundreds of free men appeared at recruiting stations but found the doors closed to them.

As the war progressed, abolitionist organizations offered to aid in raising black regiments. Frederick Douglass claimed he could raise an army of ten thousand slaves and freedmen within thirty days. Similar offers were made in Washington, New York, Cleveland, Detroit and Pittsburgh but to no avail. Reasons given for rejecting blacks included that this was a white man's war, whites would not fight alongside black soldiers and blacks would not or could not fight. Another reason—not readily admitted—was that accepting a black man as a soldier meant that he would be free and must then be considered an equal.

By late 1862 attitudes began to change. The North was becoming disheartened about the long casualty lists and escalating costs of the war. Objections to using black soldiers decreased. Discontent also surfaced among many high-ranking Union commanders. In 1862, without federal sanction, three U.S. Army department commanders organized and committed to battle several black regiments in South Carolina, Kansas and Louisiana. Finally, the January 1, 1863, issuance of the Emancipation Proclamation opened the doors for black Americans to become soldiers in the Northern armies.

Recruiting for black regiments began immediately. Most Northern states adjusted their laws to accommodate the use of black soldiers, and some, like Massachusetts, began raising black regiments. Several other states—Pennsylvania, Rhode Island and Connecticut—quickly followed suit.

This was not the case in Michigan. In 1862 the state legislature passed laws prohibiting the enlistment of black men in its militia, further delaying the recruiting of a black regiment. During the interim the state was swamped by aggressive recruiting teams from other Northern states, and Michigan black men enlisted in large numbers elsewhere.

It did not take long for black citizens and their white friends in Michigan to begin mobilizing support for raising a black regiment. Many black men, well known for their views and leadership roles, became extremely active. Among them were George de Baptiste, John D. Richards, William Lambert, William Webb and Dr. Joseph Ferguson. Clergymen of both races were also active. Mass meetings throughout the state were held in black churches, where nationally known figures exhorted the people. Such gatherings occurred at Detroit's Second Baptist Church and the Lafayette Street African Methodist Episcopal Church. Many prominent citizens, organizations and one of Michigan's most powerful newspapers exerted political pressure to raise a black regiment.

However, the Democrats and Republicans held broad differences of opinion on the use of black soldiers.

The *Detroit Free Press*, the political organ for the Democratic party, generally vilified the black race. It extolled the black stereotype as lazy and shiftless, editorially warning that Southern blacks were going to move in wholesale numbers into Northern cities, take over all the jobs, raise the crime rate and demand social equality. In May 1863 the *Free Press* declared, "The city is being over run by Negroes." This was a ridiculous claim since Wayne County's entire population of 75,284 included only 1,570 black residents.

The Republican party and the *Detroit Advertiser and Tribune* usually took positions favorable to blacks. The *Tribune* strongly supported efforts to raise a black regiment. Editor Henry Barns held forceful abolitionist sentiments and was reputed to be a leading supporter of the Underground Railroad. Barns proved to be a tireless advocate in the fight to gain a black regiment for Michigan, and according to Michigan historian Norman McRae, "without his efforts, there would not have been a [Michigan] Negro regiment."

Barns also undertook persistent editorial and political efforts that soon proved successful. After Barns lamented in an editorial on April 16, 1863, that two hundred men were enlisted in Detroit for the Fifty-fourth Massachusetts Colored Infantry, he directed his energies toward the power structure in Washington. On July 24, 1863, Michigan governor Austin Blair confirmed in a letter to Secretary of War Edwin M. Stanton that Barns had applied for authority to raise a regiment of colored troops in Michigan. On August 12 Michigan adjutant general John Robertson informed Barns that he was "fully authorized and empowered to raise and organize such a regiment."

Enlistments were for three years or the war's duration. Pay was ten dollars per month; three dollars was deducted from the monthly pay for clothing. (White soldiers were paid thirteen dollars per month, with no such deduction.) Unlike the enlisted men, officers in black units were authorized the same pay as officers of white regiments.

Barns accepted a commission as colonel of the new regiment, designated the First Michigan Colored Infantry. Recruiting began immediately at Camp Ward, located near an army barracks on Clinton Street in Detroit. The selection and certification of commissioned officers (all white) by the secretary of war followed regulations. Appointments were made as each company was mustered into service, and all officers were required to appear before examining boards in Cincinnati or Washington, DC.

When the regiment was mustered into federal service on February 17, 1864, its officers compared well with those in other regiments. Most, except for Colonel Barns, had seen active service and many were from Michigan. Lieutenant Colonel William T. Bennett hailed from South Carolina; chief surgeon Wesley Vincent and chaplain William Waring were from Oberlin, Ohio (the location of the first college in the North that admitted black students equally with whites). Staff officers included Major Newcome Clark of Clarkston, Adjutant James A. McKnight of Ann Arbor and Quartermaster Patrick McLaughlin of Detroit. Two of the company commanders later became well-known judges following the war: Captains Edward Cahill of St. Johns and Jonathan B. Tuttle of Alpena. Other regimental officers hailed from Bath, Ypsilanti, Lowell, Grand Rapids and Kalamazoo.

Initially, recruiting did not proceed as rapidly or smoothly as anticipated. Impediments included continued enticement by recruiting agents from other states, unequal pay, the generally hostile environment in Detroit and Michigan for black soldiers, discrimination, no rights to citizenship or voting, segregation and the deplorable living conditions at Camp Ward. One report indicated that "the barracks were unfit for human habitation and there is not a barn or pig-sty in the whole city of Detroit that is not better fitted for human habitation than Camp Ward."

Despite the many difficulties, recruiting improved and the exacting and serious training program left the new soldiers little time to complain. Early in October 1863 the first of many interactions with the public occurred. Church groups from Detroit conducted Sunday services at Camp Ward and were invited to witness dress parades in the afternoon. During one such parade the recruits showed "good proficiency in drill, stepping to the music of the drum like veterans." The *Tribune* further noted, "They make very cheerful, obedient soldiers and will be an honor to the State of Michigan."

Famous dignitaries visiting the camp included Sojourner Truth, the fiery orator and abolitionist leader, who spent two days intermingling with the soldiers, preaching at church services and speaking with the men individually and in groups. Local citizens also made contributions to the regiment. After learning that fifteen members of the First Michigan had formed a band, J. Henry Whittemore donated $528 for "instruments manufactured expressly for this band." In January 1864 the Colored Ladies Society presented a set of colors to the regiment in a ceremony at Camp Ward.

Near the end of 1863 the First Michigan made a successful railroad tour of communities in the southern Lower Peninsula. Stops were made at Ypsilanti, Ann Arbor, Jackson, Kalamazoo, Marshall, Cassopolis and Niles. At all the locations, the men were well received and their newly formed band won many accolades. After a review in Jackson, Governor Blair declared, "This is the first time I ever saw Negro troops and I am very proud of your general bearing. Take courage and do your duty nobly."

The tour created a favorable impression among other Michiganians who had never seen black soldiers. The men who had been on the tour were pleased with their success, but jubilation turned to anger and discouragement at the deplorable conditions of their barracks at Camp Ward. Despite initial frantic efforts by the staff to improve the living quarters, the situation changed little. On other occasions the men of the First suffered other indignities.

In March 1864 the Tenth Michigan Infantry refused to march behind the black band at a parade welcoming the return of another Michigan regiment home. The *Free Press* noted, "The declaration that the colored band is superior to the band will only be received by those who consider that an African is a little better than a white man." The *Tribune* reported that the white band's price was exorbitant and since the black band "could furnish as good, if not better music, they were requested and patriotically offered their service for a nominal sum."

Frequent altercations also occurred between the black soldiers and Detroit civilians in saloons, stores and on the city's streets. Newspaper accounts were highly critical of their behavior and inflammatory and derisive headlines were common: "Raid of the First Ethiopians," "Unruly Soldiers of the 1st Colored Infantry Attack Patrons in Detroit Saloons" and, of a dance given at a public hall, "Grand Artillery Shake Down—The Colored Citizens and Soldiers Indulged in a Hep." Generally, most incidents were not as horrendous as reported and probably not any different from those involving other regiments in the area.

Despite these developments, Colonel Barns intensified the vigorous training program. Officers and noncommissioned officers worked well together in molding a closer relationship between themselves and the men in instilling an *esprit de corps*.

Typical of the regiment's noncommissioned officers was Parker Bon, who had served as a cook in the officers' mess at Fort Wayne. He also had listened to the

At Camp Ward in Detroit, members of the First Michigan Colored Infantry learned skirmish drill, as these volunteers from an unidentified African American unit demonstrate.

officers' discussions about tactics and strategy and observed their conduct of drill and field exercises. He joined the First Michigan on September 16, 1863, and was soon promoted to sergeant major, serving in that capacity until the war's end.

On February 11, 1864, a full review was held on Woodward Avenue. A week later the First Michigan was mustered into federal service with an enrollment of 895 officers and men. On March 28 the First Michigan entrained for Annapolis, Maryland. Predictably, the *Free Press* proclaimed, "The First Regiment of the Corps d' Afrique took their departure from the city. Its departure secures the peace and tranquility of our city."

It was raining heavily when the First Michigan arrived in Annapolis. They were then denied permission to use some empty barracks because of potential trouble with white troops stationed there. Their disappointment vanished the next day when, after passing in review, they were highly praised by Generals U.S. Grant and Ambrose Burnside.

On April 12, 1864, Colonel Barns resigned and command passed to Henry L. Chipman, who was promoted to colonel. A former regular army officer who had seen action, Chipman led the regiment throughout the rest of the war.

On April 19, after a long ride on transports, the First Michigan arrived at Hilton Head, South Carolina. On May 23 its designation was changed to the 102nd United States Colored Troops (USCT) and control was

As soon as African American regiments were formed and sent south, abolition groups turned their efforts to educating black soldiers. In South Carolina, white teachers proudly stand behind their black pupils who pose with their reading primers in their laps.

transferred from the state of Michigan to the army's newly created Bureau for Colored Troops.

The true test of any regiment is its performance on the battlefield. That is where the questions "Can they fight?" and "Will they fight?" are answered, and the men of the 102nd USCT responded with a proud "yes!"

Most of the regiment's combat operations did not involve the entire regiment, a common practice for newly formed black (and some white) units. The 102nd spent approximately thirteen months on picket or outpost duty, which usually meant minimal contact with the enemy and six months in direct combat, usually in small units. About six months were spent in marching or traveling on trains and transports. The entire field duty was in Florida, South Carolina and Georgia; most of the time they were surrounded, and often outnumbered, by Confederate troops so that even fatigue duty and working on fortifications required constant combat preparedness.

After the 102nd arrived at Hilton Head, detachments were sent to picket duty on St. Helena and Jenkins Islands and at Seabrook and Spanish Wells on Hilton Head Island. After a few weeks the regiment occupied Port Royal and was assigned to fatigue duty and construction of fortifications. On August 1 it was sent to Jacksonville, Florida. The next day, following a twenty-one-mile march to Baldwin, the regiment did more picket duty and destroyed railroad tracks. When suddenly attacked by a strong rebel cavalry force, the

Michiganians stood their ground, repulsing and driving the enemy from the field.

On August 15 the 102nd began a long march through eastern Florida, ending at Magnolia on the St. John River, where it spent ten days building fortifications and on fatigue duty. It embarked on transports arriving at Beaufort, South Carolina, on August 31. In September it was sent to different points on Coosa and Port Royal. In October the enemy attempted to surprise the rebel garrison at Lady's Island but were repulsed and driven from the field.

In November and December, detachments of the 102nd were involved in heavy fighting as parts of larger Union forces. Union general William T. Sherman ordered the destruction of the Charleston and Savannah Railroad around Pocotaligo and a division of five thousand men, commanded by General John P. Hatch, was formed. Three of the First brigade's regiments were black—the 32nd, 34th and 35th USCT. The 2nd Brigade was composed of four black regiments—the 54th and 55th Massachusetts and the 26th and 102nd USCT.

The 102nd detachment consisted of 12 officers and 300 men and on November 30 a correspondent noted, "Here our forces sustained a charge and charged in return. In this affair the 102nd covered itself with glory[;] our regiment maintained the steadiest line of battle and fought with the greatest determination of any troops. The wounded refused to go to the rear, but kept on fighting."

With greater strength and firepower, the Confederates overcame the Union defenses and a general retreat was ordered. In front of the 102nd sector three cannon were abandoned. Men from Company D of the 102nd rushed forward to recover them but were beaten back with heavy losses, including the death of Captain Arad E. Lindsay.

Lieutenant Orson W. Bennett then gathered thirty men around him and again attacked the enemy. After several unsuccessful efforts to recover the artillery pieces, Bennett "gallantly led a small force fully 100 yards in advance of the Union lines and brought in the guns, preventing their capture." Bennett was one of two officers of the 102nd awarded the congressional Medal of Honor.

In December 1864 the 102nd—fighting alongside white regiments and the 54th Massachusetts—experienced heavy fighting at the Tillifinny River. On December 7 the 102nd was attacked by a strong force but repulsed the enemy with heavy casualties. The following day the 102nd was one of several regiments that attempted to destroy the railroad.

In January 1865 the companies on duty at outposts returned to Beaufort. In late January the entire regiment moved to Pocotaligo. On February 7 the 54th Massachusetts and the 102nd crossed the Salkehatchie River, marching at night in a heavy rainstorm, and drove the enemy out of their barricades and fortifications. On January 8 companies B, E and I, commanded by Major Clark, made a reconnaissance near Cuckold's Creek. A rebel cavalry picket was attacked and forced to withdraw behind their works. Having destroyed the railroad and breastworks, the 102nd remained there until February 14. After a series of marches and skirmishes, it arrived at the defenses at Charleston; then on March 9 it took transports to Savannah, Georgia, where the two wings of the regiment rejoined.

Two detachments were again formed, one commanded by Colonel Chipman, the other by Major Clark. Between April 11 and 18 Chipman's wing participated on a hazardous expedition from Charleston to join a union force on the Santee River at Nelson's Ferry, seventy miles away. They marched through enemy territory where they met and drove off a large cavalry force after a brisk and vigorous fight. Another lively engagement near Camden also ended in victory. Major Clark's detachment moved out on April 5; following a hard march and minor skirmishes, the Michiganians met the enemy in great force at Boykins. Working with the 54th Massachusetts, it flanked the rebels, spiritedly attacked them and drove them in great disorder toward Statesburg. The next day the two detachments of the 102nd were reunited and executed a successful flank movement in a skirmish at Singleton's Plantation. These actions resulted in forcing the panicked enemy to abandon their strongly fortified position. On the morning of April 21, Companies A, B and C, under the command of Major Clark, were attacked by two hundred rebels. After a lively skirmish the rebels retreated with heavy losses.

This action ended the regiment's combat record. In late May 1865 the 102nd was on occupation duty in Summerville, Branchville, Orangeburg and Winnsboro, South Carolina. In September the Michiganians returned to Charleston where they were mustered out of federal service on September 30. The men of the 102nd were disbanded in Detroit on October 17, 1865.

The regiment's total enrollment included 1,673 men. Losses totaled five killed in action, seven dead of wounds and 118 dead of disease.

Eleven black soldiers who served in the 102nd are buried in Detroit's Elmwood Cemetery. In death they are not segregated as they were in life.

Those Damned Black Hats

By Roger L. Rosentreter

*The Twenty-fourth Michigan Infantry was raised after Detroiters felt
embarrassed that a mid-1862 call to arms had resulted in a riot in their city.
Less than a year after mustering into federal service, the Wayne County
regiment—now part of the Iron Brigade—had the dubious distinction
of suffering 80 percent casualties in the war's greatest battle.*

On July 15, 1862, Detroit residents gathered to discuss ways to fill the six new Michigan regiments recently requested by the federal government. The meeting erupted into a riot as opponents of the war tore down the rostrum and manhandled the speakers. Outraged local citizens sought to relieve the city's embarrassment by agreeing that Wayne County would raise an extra regiment to be added to the six being formed across the state. Judge Henry Morrow of Detroit Recorder's Court, who had seen action in the Mexican War, was appointed colonel of the new regiment, and Wayne County Sheriff Mark Flanagan, who led the deputies that subdued the rowdies at the July rally, became the lieutenant colonel of the newly designated Twenty-fourth Michigan.

Mustered into federal service on August 15, 1862, the Twenty-fourth trained in Detroit for two weeks before leaving for Washington, DC. The regiment was assigned to the capital's defense until October, when it joined Brigadier General John Gibbons's Iron Brigade, which had formed in the fall of 1861 when the Second, Sixth and Seventh Wisconsin and the Nineteenth Indiana Infantries were brigaded together. The brigade was the only all-western brigade in the Army of the Potomac.

Gibbons replaced the traditional kepi cap worn by most Union soldiers in the East with black, broad-rimmed felt hats. The hats soon became the brigade's mark of distinction. At the Battle of South Mountain, on September 14, 1862, Gibbons's men fought so courageously that Major General Joseph Hooker referred to them as the "iron" brigade. Several days later at the Battle of Antietam, the Iron Brigade suffered 42 percent casualties. These losses prompted the Northern command to add a fifth regiment to Gibbons's brigade. Gibbons requested and received a western regiment: the Twenty-fourth Michigan.

On October 9, 1862, the Iron Brigade was assembled to welcome the Twenty-fourth Michigan. On one side of the parade ground stood the veterans—lean, suntanned, their uniforms worn from a year of campaigning. They stared across the field to the Michigan men, whose newness was evident not only by their crisp uniforms, but by their numbers. The nine hundred men in the Twenty-fourth equaled all the other men in the brigade combined.

The arrival of the Twenty-fourth was not without incident. One member of the Twenty-fourth recorded that the Michiganians received a "pretty cool reception, we had come to reinforce them, and supposed that they would be glad to see us." The veterans were neither delighted nor relieved; they refused to accept the Michiganians, who they believed were bonus men.

The newcomers would have to prove themselves under fire; two months later the Twenty-fourth received that opportunity. At the Battle of Fredricksburg, the Iron Brigade was stationed on the far left of the Northern line. Ordered to silence rebel horse artillery, the brigade advanced with the Twenty-fourth in the lead. For the Michiganians, nothing the rebels could do was half as bad as the cold contempt they had received from the brigade's veterans. When rebel cannon fire unnerved the green troops, Colonel Morrow halted his men and—while under fire by unseen enemy snipers—they coolly went through the manual of arms.

The Twenty-fourth Michigan suffered thirty-six casualties. However, they had "seen the elephant" and were worthy of inclusion into the Iron Brigade. The regiment's historian noted after Fredricksburg that "the greatest cordiality ever prevailed" between the Michiganians and the brigade.

In late May 1863 the Twenty-fourth bivouacked on the Rappahannock River near Fredricksburg. For the Army of the Potomac, there was evidence that rebel forces across the river were preparing to move. On several occasions the Twenty-fourth struck its tents and stood ready to march, only to have the orders reversed and the tents repitched. One veteran complained of "excessive readiness." The men would lie "hour after hour on the ground in the hot sun with everything packed for marching," only to be ordered to fall out.

During this period of uncertainty, thirty-four-year-old Michael O'Brien, a private in the Twenty-fourth, noted that "I don't think there will be any more fighting" on the Rappahannock that summer. O'Brien predicted the next battle would be near Manassas in northern Virginia, where he hoped that "it must be our turn to make them run this time."

During the first week of June, Robert E. Lee's Army of Northern Virginia left Fredericksburg and headed north. On June 12 the Iron Brigade broke camp and followed. It had not rained for six weeks and the sun blazed down. Spurred on by inaccurate reports that they were racing with the rebels for the heights around Manassas, the men marched twenty miles a day through the choking dust.

On the third day of the march, the Twenty-fourth halted. The three days had been cruel—especially with water often unavailable, except for an occasional mud-hole or slimy marsh—and at least three members of the Twenty-fourth died of sunstroke on the march. The men made supper and prepared to camp for the night. However, the preparations had not proceeded far when the march was resumed.

Clouds of dust—hanging heavily in the damp night air—enveloped the men. Covered with a mantle of white, they looked like a ghostly procession as they plodded on. After marching all night, the Twenty-fourth arrived at Manassas. Following a four-hour stop, the Iron Brigade moved on to Centerville, where the westerners, "tired, sore, sleepy, hungry, dusty and dirty as pigs," rested for one day. They had covered seventy-five miles since leaving their camp on the Rappahannock River. At Centerville the Iron Brigade discovered that Lee's army was in western Maryland and headed for Pennsylvania. After an evening's rest, the brigade moved on. The sun remained hot and the weather humid, but the marches covered fewer miles.

The shorter marches allowed the men to enrich their diet with livestock from nearby farms. On one occasion a Michiganian confiscated a couple of geese and convinced the regiment's drummer boy to place them inside his drum. A little while later Colonel Morrow noticed that the young drummer was shirking his usual

On July 1, 1863, Wayne County lawyer Henry A. Morrow, commander of the Twenty-fourth Michigan Infantry, was wounded during the Battle of Gettysburg and taken prisoner. Convincing his captors that he was a surgeon, Morrow managed to escape and return to his command three days later.

efforts. Morrow rode up to the boy and said "Why don't you beat that drum?" The startled musician motioned for the colonel to come closer. Morrow leaned down and the boy whispered "I've got a couple of geese in here." The colonel straightened up and gravely said, "Well, if you're sick and can't play, you need not." That evening the colonel also enjoyed roast goose.

Between June 19 and 25 the Iron Brigade camped several miles south of the Potomac River, near Edwards Ferry. During the one-week bivouac, the Twenty-fourth frequently heard heavy firing to the west, where Union cavalry skirmished with the Confederates advancing northward. According to Lieutenant Lucius Shattuck, the Twenty-fourth Michigan "habitually turned out at two or three o'clock in the morning." The men would "hold [their] blankets and sit down on them to hold [their] tempers and await orders." On June 25 the Iron Brigade crossed the Potomac into Maryland.

Moving back into the North was a delight for the westerners. One veteran described it as moving "out of the barren desert of Virginia into the land of thrift and plenty."

As the soldiers passed through the Maryland towns, citizens cheered them. Near Poolsville, Corporal Orson Curtis recalled that the homesick soldiers saw "a most beautiful sight . . . a large school of children . . . who gazed upon the soldiers as they marched by." Curtis added that "one cannot imagine . . . the cheerful feeling such a sight induces." But the Wayne County native also noted that "this reminder of home brought tears to many an eye."

Thirty-five-year-old Frederick Neff of Detroit wrote his wife, "We are glad to put our feet on Maryland's shore, we are at last out of the enemies country and where we can see smiling faces when we march along the roads. When we were in Virginia, we saw nothing but sour looking people." But "as soon as we got into Maryland, we were cheered by all the people and we saw the glorious stars and stripes waving from every window and doorstep."

Maryland residents—often young women—offered the marching soldiers drinks of cold water, which were gratefully accepted. According to historian Bruce Catton, the wolf-call whistle was unknown to soldiers of that era. But they had an equivalent—an abrupt significant clearing of the throat or cough that burst out spontaneously whenever a line of march went by a nice-looking young woman. One veteran recalled that at such times "the men seemed terribly and suddenly afflicted with some bronchial affection."

On June 30 the Iron Brigade crossed into Pennsylvania—the first infantry units of the Army of the Potomac to enter Pennsylvania. About noon the brigade bivouacked near Marsh Creek. They were 160 miles from the Rappahannock River and about six miles from Gettysburg.

To the men of the Iron Brigade it was appropriate that they led the Army of the Potomac into Pennsylvania. A recent organization of the army had left them the First Brigade, First Division, First Corps. As one veteran noted, "If all the armies of the United States were in one line, the Iron Brigade would be on the extreme right." The numbering system appeared as no mere coincidence. The colonel of the Sixth Wisconsin noted, "We deserve the title."

On the evening of June 30 a certainty of the impending battle began to have "a perceptible effect" upon the Iron Brigade. According to one veteran, the men "were a little more serious than usual, and there was less chaff and bandiage among them." Private John Ryder predicted, in what would be his last letter home, "I expect we will have a great battle shortly." Ryder

noted in resignation that if battle "has got to be done, let it come, and we will look for the best."

The men of the First Division were up at dawn on the morning of July 1 preparing a frugal breakfast of hardtack, pork and coffee. The chaplain of the Twenty-fourth, the Reverend William Way, called the regiment together for prayer. But the day's events were forecast—as the men prayed—ammunition was distributed.

Shortly after 8:00 A.M. the First Division was on the Emmitsburg Road, headed for Gettysburg. The First Division's other brigade, commanded by Lysander Cutler, led the procession; the Iron Brigade followed behind. The Second Wisconsin was followed by the Seventh Wisconsin, the Nineteenth Indiana, the Twenty-fourth Michigan and the Sixth Wisconsin. The file closers, twenty men from each regiment, completed the division's line of march. Wedged between the infantry was Battery B, Fourth U.S. Artillery. Major General John Reynolds, who commanded the army's left wing, the First, Third and Eleventh Corps, rode with the First Division.

The sun shone brightly and only a few scattered white clouds dotted the sky. The men seemed relaxed. One member of Battery B, who watched the Iron Brigade cross Marsh Creek, noted that "because they had served together a long time . . . there was a great affinity between the artillerymen and the westerners." This relationship expressed itself in cheers and good-natured chaffing as the foot soldiers passed the artillerymen. "Find a good place to camp," "Tell the johnnies we'll be right along" were the salutations that passed from the cannoners. The infantrymen responded with, "Better stay here, the climate up there may be unhealthy just now for such delicate creatures as you."

Lieutenant Colonel Dawes of the Sixth Wisconsin ordered his musicians to the front. With drums beating and fifes shrilling, the Iron Brigade marched north to the battle cry of "The Campbells are Coming." But above the music the men soon heard the dull boom of artillery and the crackling of musketry.

At the first sound of fighting, General Reynolds rode forward. Near the Lutheran Theological Seminary west of Gettysburg he found Brigadier General John Buford and two brigades of Union cavalry resisting the advancing Confederates. The seminary was located on Seminary Ridge. Five hundred yards to the west lay McPherson's Ridge. Further west lay Herr Ridge, which was occupied by the rebels.

Reynolds sent a courier to Major General George Meade, who had assumed command of the Army of the Potomac several days earlier, announcing that he would fight the rebels "inch by inch, and if driven into the town," he would "barricade the streets and hold him back as long as possible." Reynolds also ordered Wadsworth to bring up his division to aid Buford's beleaguered cavalrymen.

The pace quickened. Noncombatants and pack mules were ordered to the rear, and the file closers joined the Sixth Wisconsin. When the Iron Brigade reached the Codori House, one mile south of Gettysburg, it left the Emmitsburg Pike and hastened toward the sound of battle. The Sixth Wisconsin was left in reserve at the seminary; the remainder of the brigade advanced toward the crest of McPherson's Ridge. Colonel Morrow halted the Twenty-fourth to have his men load their rifles, but there was no time and they had to load while on the run. It was about 10:00 A.M. General Reynolds was instantly killed by a bullet as he watched the Iron Brigade move into position, and the westerners raced over the crest of McPherson's Ridge and crashed into the advancing Confederates. The stunned Tennesseans and Alabamans in Brigadier James Archer's brigade reeled as volleys were exchanged at a range of forty yards.

As Archer's men struggled with the Second and Seventh Wisconsin, the Nineteenth Indiana and the Twenty-fourth Michigan moved to the left through a wooden ravine and on to the rebels' exposed right flank. Yells of surprise and consternation rose from the startled Southerners. They had expected militia or cavalry. According to legend, at least one Confederate shouted, "There are those damn black-hatted fellows again. T'aint no militia, it's the Army of the Potomac."

The sound of firing intensified as the Wolverines and Hoosiers seized the initiative. The Twenty-fourth swarmed across the Willoughby Run and overlapped Archer's rear and flank. Within minutes the rebels were overpowered. Many threw down their weapons; others fled to the safety of the woods on Herr Ridge. Hundreds of prisoners were taken, including Archer—the first general of the Army of Northern Virginia to be captured in the war. During the fighting, Lieutenant Colonel Flanigan of the Twenty-fourth went down with a shattered leg that was later amputated. Abel Peck, who had sworn to defend the colors with his life when the regiment had left Detroit, was killed.

While the Twenty-fourth routed Archer's brigade, Brigadier General Joseph Davis's brigade of North Carolinians and Mississippians pressed Cutler's men north of the Chambersburg Pike until the Sixth Wisconsin went forward and flanked the rebel position.

It was now about 11:00 A.M. Archer and Davis had suffered 50 percent casualties. In a terse communique, Confederate major general Henry Heth—whose division included Archer's and Davis's brigades—reported: "The enemy had been felt and found to be in heavy force in and around Gettysburg."

Both sides re-formed their positions and the battle line stretched farther north from the Chambersburg Pike as more troops poured into Gettysburg. Still holding the Union left, the Iron Brigade withdrew to McPherson's Woods. The brigade's position was also strengthened by the addition of Colonel Chapman Biddle's brigade, which was stationed to the left of the

Detroiter George C. Gordon was wounded and captured at Gettysburg while in command of Company I. On February 14, 1865, Gordon successfully escaped from a rebel prison in Virginia and rejoined the Twenty-fourth.

Iron Brigade, and Colonel Roy Stone's brigade, which was placed on the brigade's right.

The Iron Brigade's new alignment, however, put the Twenty-fourth in an awkward salient in the center of the line. The Nineteenth Indiana was to its left and the Second Wisconsin was to its right. The right flank of the Twenty-fourth curved back to connect with the Second Wisconsin, while its left extended down a hillside to a deep hollow. The regiment's two wings formed the sides of an obtuse angle, and in the foliage, the left flank was scarcely visible to the right. The position was also completely dominated by rebel gunners on Herr Ridge. Colonel Morrow recognized that the position could not be maintained for long and only at great cost. Three times Morrow requested that the line be formed on the elevated ground in the rear. Each time, he was told "The position must be held."

The Iron Brigade also received one additional reinforcement—John Burns, a Gettysburg resident and veteran of the War of 1812. Despite taunts from the soldiers, Burns was determined to fight and brought his own rifle. The seventy-four-year-old volunteer positioned himself with the Second Wisconsin and according to one veteran, he "did much to create good feeling and stimulate the courage" of soldiers waiting for the battle to resume. Before the day ended, Burns suffered three wounds—at least one of which was treated by the assistant surgeon of the Twenty-fourth Michigan.

About 3:00 P.M., as the battle raged along the Union right flank, General Heth ordered his brigades forward. According to Colonel Morrow, the rebels came "yelling like demons." Brockenborough's Virginians, Pettigrew's North Carolinians and the remnants of Archer's brigade led the first wave. Behind them was a second line that included two brigades of North Carolinians and a brigade of South Carolinians.

Pettigrew's brigade had the formidable task of clearing the Iron Brigade out of McPherson's Woods. Heth went down wounded and Pettigrew resumed the attack, which came under heavy artillery and musket fire as it neared McPherson's Ridge. As the North Carolinians started across Willoughby Run, Colonel Morrow gave the command to fire and a solid sheet of flame tore through the Confederate ranks. However, the rebels quickly re-formed and the Twenty-fourth began suffering heavy casualties.

The disadvantage of the terrain prevented the Twenty-fourth from bringing its full firepower to bear. But a more serious problem developed when the rebels pressured the Nineteenth Indiana to withdraw. The Twenty-fourth was caught in a deadly crossfire, with bullets coming in from the front and the left. Thirty-one-year-old Captain William Speed, who had served as Detroit's city attorney before the war, attempted to swing two companies of the Twenty-fourth at right angles to protect the left flank when a bullet pierced his heart. Lieutenant Gilbert Dickey, one of the first graduates of what is now Michigan State University, rushed to help Speed, but he too was killed.

Unable to resist the Confederate onslaught, the westerners withdrew to the eastern edge of the woods. According to one Wisconsin soldier, "Every tree [became] a breastwork, every log, a barricade, every bush, a cover." And Confederate major J. T. Jones noted, "The fighting was terrible. The two lines were putting volleys into each other at a distance of not greater than twenty yards."

Pressured on three sides by the overwhelming rebel advance, the Iron Brigade withdrew to a third line of defense in the ground between McPherson and Seminary Ridge. Among the Twenty-fourth, Major Edwin Wight was wounded in the face. Colonel Morrow directed the regiment's fourth color guard—the previous three color-bearers were dead—to plant the flag to rally the Michiganians. The soldier was instantly shot down. Morrow seized the standard, but twenty-two-year-old William Kelly, insisting that while he was alive the colonel would not carry the flag, took the staff. He was immediately shot dead. Another private grabbed the flag, but he, too, was killed. Morrow once again took the flag. But as the brigade retreated to the crest of Seminary Ridge, a bullet creased Morrow's skull and he went down wounded. The command of the Twenty-fourth passed to Captain Albert M. Edwards.

During the retreat up Seminary Ridge, twenty-four-year-old Captain Malachi O'Donnell tried to rally his men. O'Donnell, who had worked for the *Detroit Free Press* before joining the Twenty-fourth, had been given a sword by his newspaper colleagues. At that time O'Donnell promised that "in the hands of an O'Donnell [it] will never cause a blush to mount the cheeks of these kind friends." O'Donnell waved that sword until he was killed. Elsewhere, twenty-three-year-old John Welsh, who was carrying a wounded comrade, was struck by a bullet that killed him and the man he was trying to save.

At the crest of Seminary Ridge, the Iron Brigade positioned itself behind a barricade of rails that had been prepared earlier in the day. The rebels paused, realigned themselves and sent a strong column toward the rails. Marshaling both their depleting energy and ammunition, the westerners let loose a smashing volley.

Colonel Robinson of the Seventh Wisconsin noted that the rebels "went down like grass before the scythe." An advancing North Carolina lieutenant, who had a similar impression, wrote that "the earth just seemed to open and take in that line which five minutes ago was so perfect." But the rebels re-formed and kept coming.

During the melee, the flag of the Twenty-fourth became lost. When Captain Edwards found it, it was inside the barricade in the arms of a dead soldier. The soldier, whose identity remains unknown, had managed, even in death, to keep the standard upright. Edwards, who had entered the service in 1861, reportedly grabbed the flag—now reduced to a few shreds—and defiantly waved it as the battle raged. Nearby Sergeant Augustus Pomeroy, who was too disabled to hold a rifle, used his good hand and his teeth to tear cartridges for his comrades on the line.

The positioning of twelve cannon beside the rail barricade slowed the Confederate advance, but the day's end was now in sight. The Union right had collapsed. Outflanked, heavily pressed on the front and the ammunition nearly exhausted, the First Division withdrew—under order—to the newly prepared defenses on Cemetery Hill.

Despite the stress and strain of the day, the Iron Brigade made an orderly retreat down the Chambersburg Pike. The Union soldiers on Cemetery Hill looked down on a wild panorama of retreat. Thick smoke lay on the ridge, and in the late afternoon sun, retreating Yankees could be seen turning now and then to fire a defiant volley. The retreat was not a rout. Colonel Charles Wainwright, an artillery officer in the First Division, noted no panic. Wainwright even claimed that the men were "talking and joking" as they hurried along. If they were joking, it stopped as they passed through Gettysburg. All lines of the Union retreat converged in the town and the streets were clogged with cannon, wagons and ambulances. Retreating regiments collided with each other and got hopelessly intermingled. Rebel gunners hit the town from distant positions and soldiers were wounded by bricks and other flying debris. Yankees and rebels unexpectedly ran into each other as smoke settled over the town and nobody could see which way he was going. Finally, the rolling country beyond the town was reached. Captain Edwards—still carrying the flag of the Twenty-fourth—led twenty-six survivors up Cemetery Hill. He later reported that all the men were in "good order." Edwards placed the flag beside a battery to guide other Michiganians to the position and then he sat down on a tombstone.

Twenty-six-year-old Augustus Pomeroy of Salem was wounded at Gettysburg. Pomeroy's wound healed and by November 1863 he was back with the Twenty-fourth.

Many of the Twenty-fourth's wounded men who had been housed in makeshift hospitals in Gettysburg, fell into Confederate hands. One of these was Colonel Morrow, who made the most of his capture. After being wounded, Morrow was taken to Gettysburg, where his wounds were treated by local residents.

Colonel Morrow removed his shoulder straps and masqueraded as a doctor. He is credited with persuading the Confederates to send out ambulances to retrieve Northern wounded from the extreme parts of the battlefield. Morrow even claimed that he ran into Confederate Lieutenant General Richard S. Ewell, who told him that the Twenty-fourth was foolish for not having surrendered after being so badly shot up. Morrow allegedly responded, "The Twenty-fourth Michigan came here to fight, not to surrender." On July 4 Morrow eluded his captors and rejoined his regiment.

On the morning of July 2, Captain Edwards took the roll and found three officers and ninety-six enlisted men remained ready for duty. Edwards consolidated his command into four companies. The former University of Michigan English major must have noted in a manual that the survivors of a battle should be lauded for their bravery, so he prepared a declaration.

I congratulate you, brave soldiers, upon your splendid achievements of July 1. . . . The enemies [*sic*] dead in front of your line attest your valor and skill, again you have merited a nation's gratitude; again you have shown yourself worthy of the noble state you represent and the glorious cause for which you are fighting. Our joy in the glory of our arms is mingled with sadness for the heroic dead on the field of honor, but the memory of our lamented comrades inspire your hearts with new life and zeal to emulate the heroic virtues and avenge their untimely fall.

The Twenty-fourth had gone into battle with 496 men. Its losses totaled 80 percent of the regiment's strength, including 22 of the regiment's 25 officers (eight had been killed in action). No other Northern regiment at Gettysburg had lost so many officers. Nine men died carrying the regimental standard. Company B went into battle with 51 men; by day's end only 11 men were unscathed. Sergeant Charles McConnell survived and he wondered why. A bullet had gone through his pants and another through his shirtsleeve. During the retreat he was knocked down by a musket ball that struck his knapsack and went through ten thicknesses of his blanket.

Brigade and corps losses were equally frightening. The Iron Brigade suffered 65 percent casualties. The First Corps had gone into battle with 9,500 men; its losses exceeded 6,000 men. Rebel casualties were equally appalling. The Twenty-sixth North Carolina, which had opposed the Michiganians, suffered a casualty rate of 75 percent. Six hundred of the regiment's 800 men became casualties that day, and at least 14 different men earned the colors.

Through their dogged, desperate fighting, the Twenty-fourth Michigan and the rest of the Iron Brigade had allowed the Army of the Potomac to concentrate along Cemetery Ridge. The possession of that key ground helped the North win the Battle of Gettysburg—a victory that forever robbed Lee's army of its offensive power.

During the remaining two days of the Battle of Gettysburg, the Twenty-fourth saw limited action. On the second day the Twenty-fourth saw no action. Early on the third day, it fired upon the enemy from the safety of solid breastworks along Culp's Hill. On the third day of the battle, the Twenty-fourth rushed to Cemetery Ridge with other units to reinforce Union troops resisting the massive rebel assault on the Union center. But the Twenty-fourth was not engaged. On July 6 the Iron Brigade moved south to follow Lee's retreating army. In late August 1863 the Twenty-fourth was back on the Rappahannock River.

The Twenty-fourth actively participated in the 1864-65 Virginia campaign. However, the Michiganians, as well as the Iron Brigade, would finish out the war only shadows of their former selves. In early February 1865 the Twenty-fourth was withdrawn from the Union siege lines around Petersburg, Virginia, and sent to Springfield, Illinois, to do guard duty at the draft rendezvous. On May 4 the Twenty-fourth Michigan served as the military escort for President Abraham Lincoln's funeral procession. Two months later, Michigan's black hats were mustered out of service.

"I Am an American"

By Jessie Moore Loveridge

*In early July 1863, as the nation's attention was focused on
Northern victories at Gettysburg and Vicksburg, Colonel Orlando Moore
and the Twenty-fifth Michigan Infantry stood off a significantly larger
rebel force at Tebbs Bend on the Green River in Kentucky.*

In the *National Tribune* of November 22, 1928, a beautiful tribute is paid to Colonel Orlando H. Moore, who with only two hundred men of his regiment, the Twenty-fifth Michigan Infantry, defeated General John H. Morgan with his entire division of three thousand men at the Battle of Tebbs Bend, Kentucky.

When General Morgan, under flag of truce, demanded immediate and unconditional surrender of the entire force under his command, Colonel Moore quietly replied, "I am an American and the Fourth of July is no day for me to entertain such a proposition. I must therefore decline."

The ensuing conflict was desperate for three and a half hours, almost a hand-to-hand fight, but General Morgan's loss was so great that he withdrew from the field.

The skillful selection of Colonel Moore's battlefield in the narrow bend of Green River, where the high bluffs afforded some protection for his very few men, and the wonderfully well-drilled troops excited the admiration of General Morgan, who sent a message to Colonel Moore that "he promoted him to the rank of Brigadier General."

General Morgan and General Basil Duke became excellent friends of Colonel Moore, after the war, on account of their great admiration for him as a man of the highest honor.

While still on the battlefield, Colonel Moore issued this order to his men, giving them all the praise for their bravery, never claiming any credit for his own good generalship:

Special Order No. 42
My brave, my noble men, it is with pride and pleasure that I congratulate you upon the great victory won today. While you numbered but two hundred men, the enemy numbered thousands.

Our brave companions who fell, fell gallantly fighting for their Country and in defense of the starry flag. Their names deeply inscribed on the pages of memory, will be wreathed ever in bright laurels of fame, and though 'tis hard to part with over noble dead, we know 'tis sweet in the cause of our Country to die. Although no marble slab have we placed o'er their heads to mark their last resting place, although no monumental pile have we erected over their graves, yet in the hearts of the people of our Peninsular State will be erected a monument that will perpetuate their names to all eternity.

The importance of this victory is beyond measure, for General Morgan was pushing on to Louisville, where all of the western military and naval supplies were stored, including ordnance, commissary, clothing, and medical supplies, amounting to millions of dollars, which would have been captured by General Morgan and sent to the South. This is the first time General Morgan had ever met with defeat and he changed his course and never besieged Louisville.

The military career of Orlando Hurley Moore began in 1856 when he entered the service of the United States as second lieutenant in the Sixth U.S. Infantry. His first tour of duty was in Kansas during the political difficulties in organizing that territory into a state.

In 1857 he made a march with the command of General E. V. Sumner on the expedition against the Cheyenne Indians, of eighteen hundred miles, enduring many hardships; one time the command was without any subsistence stores, except the beef cattle, for seventeen days.

Lieutenant Moore, then only thirty-one years of age, was selected by the administration as the leader of a secret mission to investigate trouble brewing on the Pacific Coast. He had proven himself a man of exceptional executive ability and fine discernment, eminently fitted to conduct such an expedition with undaunted courage, yet with extreme caution and consideration for others.

Three states—California, Oregon and Nevada—wanted to secede from the Union and establish a "Pacific Republic." These states were far removed from the seat of government in Washington at that time. There were no transcontinental railroads and no postal or telegraphic communications and there was a vast intervening territory inhabited mostly by hostile Indians.

San Francisco was garrisoned by brave and loyal men but commanded by officers whose sympathies were entirely with the Confederacy.

A plan was formed by those sympathizers to take the Pacific states out of the Union.

Lieutenant Moore, with his regiment, was ordered at once to Benicia, California. Benicia was the stronghold on the Pacific Coast and was commanded by General Albert Sidney Johnston, who afterward became a Confederate general. He was even then plotting to deliver the government stores within his department over to the Confederacy.

In 1858 Lieutenant Moore marched with his regiment from Fort Leavenworth, Kansas, to Benicia, making a march of twenty-one hundred miles, probably the longest continuous march on record.

The officers were mounted, but the troops, being infantry, were obliged to march the entire distance, through almost impassable mountain roads and vast deserts. The women rode in ambulances, and the camp supplies were carried by mule-driven wagons.

Arriving in Benicia, they found every official was a sympathizer with secession and Lieutenant Moore was obliged to study law and was admitted to practice before the Superior Court of California, in order to execute legal papers secretly.

General Johnston tendered his resignation from the army and the cabal awaited notice of its acceptance in order to put their plans into execution. They were to seize Benicia Barracks and then Mare Navy Yard, Alcatraz and Fort Point, but the Administration had been advised by Lieutenant Moore of Johnston's purposes and General Sumner was put on board a California-bound mail steamer outside Sandy Hook so that no one of the traitorous spies swarming Washington should know of the grand old hero's departure.

General Sumner went by the Isthmus of Panama and arrived at Benicia quite unexpectedly on the same mail steamer that brought to General Johnston an acceptance of his resignation from the United States Army.

The Twenty-fifth Michigan Infantry is best remembered for its victory at Tebbs Bend, Kentucky, on July 4, 1863. It was there that Colonel Orlando Moore of Schoolcraft rejected rebel demands to surrender by declaring, that as an American, he could not entertain the thought of surrendering on Independence Day.

Within an hour General Sumner relieved General Johnston and assumed command of the Department of the Pacific.

It was magnificent work that Lieutenant Moore did for his country for at the breaking out of the Civil War, those three states—California, Oregon and Nevada—united with the Union and sent troops to the front that were as loyal as any sent out by any of our Northern states.

This is a bit of unwritten history of our country for it was a "secret mission."

At the beginning of the Civil War, Lieutenant Moore asked for active service at the front and was given command of the Twenty-fifth Michigan Infantry, which was rendezvoused at Kalamazoo. The regiment was made up of young boys from the first families of that locality.

Colonel Moore drilled them like "regulars" and loved them with the devotion of a real father. Their headquarters was in Louisville, Kentucky, and Colonel Moore was provost marshal of that city.

After a long bitter siege Colonel Orlando Moore entered the city of Atlanta with the rest of William T. Sherman's army on September 2, 1864. The day before, rebel troops intentionally set off explosions that demolished a Confederate ordnance train and factory and then evacuated Atlanta (above).

In compliance with orders, he organized a provisional division of troops consisting of nine regiments, for immediate field service, and within ten days it joined General Sherman's Army in Rome, Georgia.

Colonel Moore was then assigned to the command of the Second Brigade, Second Division, Twenty-third Army Corps and participated in the Tennessee Campaign, in the battles of Franklin and Nashville.

For two years Colonel Moore was serving as brigade and division commander with only the pay of a colonel, desiring to do that much more for his country.

The same brilliancy of action characterized all of Colonel Moore's military service, especially the capture of Fort Anderson, North Carolina, the stronghold of the Confederacy.

Colonel Moore was a man of the most modest and retiring nature. But he was idolized by his command and was furnished with a petition signed by every field and staff officer of his division recommending him for promotion, which petition he laid aside as a keepsake, in grateful remembrance of his friends. To be colonel of the Twenty-fifth Michigan Infantry was the greatest honor he desired.

About the first of July 1865, Colonel Moore's volunteer command was mustered out, and he returned to duty again in the regular army, and, with his family, was stationed in the South during Reconstruction and then in various garrisons on the frontier, participating in almost continual Indian warfare, and was with General Alfred A. Terry's command during the Custer massacre.

At this time he was lieutenant colonel of the Seventeenth U.S. Infantry.

Colonel Moore was always a friend of the Indians, who trusted him implicitly and were influenced by his wise counsel to avert hostilities many a time while railroads were built through their territory.

Moore retired from the army in April 1884 because of the effects of sunstroke he had received in the Rocky Mountains during a campaign against the Indians. He died on October 31, 1890, in Dearborn. He was buried in Tulare, California.

Dearest Ben

By Albert Castel

*On August 27, 1861, Benjamin Wells and Melissa Hoisington were married
in Fabius Township. Three days later Wells left to join the
Eleventh Michigan Infantry. During the three years that Ben was away,
Melissa wrote a steady stream of letters to him at the front.
They are a stark reminder of hardships women faced on the homefront.*

There is no end of extant letters by Civil War soldiers, but only a comparative few of the many letters by their wives, mothers, sisters and sweethearts survive. This is understandable. The soldiers were participating in dramatic and historic events; hence their letters were considered worth keeping. In contrast the women for the most part had no such exciting tales to tell, and the majority of their letters simply disappeared.

But if understandable, this imbalance between warfront and homefront letters is unfortunate. Civil War women, with a handful of rather aberrant exceptions, did not fight in battles, and few of them outside the South experienced personally the terror and devastation of war. Yet emotionally and psychologically it was as much their war as it was their menfolk's. They, too, were part of the great cataclysm of 1861-65.

Hence, when the historian comes across letters—many letters, long letters, expressive and poignant letters—penned by a soldier's wife, the historian has found something most valuable. Such are the letters written by Melissa Wells to her husband, Benjamin Franklin Wells of the Eleventh Michigan Infantry.

In Melissa's letter to Ben of June 12, 1864, we learn how her letters came to be preserved: Ben sent them back to her precisely for that purpose. "I will soon," she wrote, "have all the letters I have written to you. ... I am sure you take more pains than I would to keep such trash. ... Just read them and burn them. ... But then it is all right if you want them kept—I will keep them for you until you get home and then if we cannot find anything else to amuse ourselves with, we will make a bonfire of them some night."

Let us be glad that bonfire never occurred and that Ben, who lived until 1925, continued to keep the letters. In them Melissa still lives, as do thousands of other women of her time.

Susan Melissa was born May 1, 1840, the eldest of four daughters of Abishai Hoisington, a moderately well-to-do farmer and brickmaker in Fabius Township, near Three Rivers, Michigan. In the spring of 1861 she became engaged to Benjamin Wells, a twenty-six-year-old native of Ohio who came to Three Rivers in his mid-teens and worked as a mason, occasional schoolteacher and laborer in her father's brickyard. When the Civil War began, there was no question that Ben would enlist. In August 1861 he, Melissa's forty-five-year-old father, her brother Wallace and thirteen other Fabius Township men joined the Eleventh Michigan, a regiment recruited principally in St. Joseph and adjoining counties. Probably because they believed, as did the vast majority of Northerners and Southerners in 1861, that the fighting would not last long, Ben and Melissa got married on August 27, three days after most of the Eleventh Michigan was mustered into service at nearby Centreville. Four months later, the regiment left for Kentucky. Melissa was pregnant with their first son, Frank.

During the next two years the Eleventh Michigan vainly chased John Morgan's raiders in Kentucky, fought on the bloody battlefields of Stones River and Chickamauga and helped storm the Confederate lines at Missionary Ridge. Ben, who also suffered two severe bouts of illness, received an ample taste of the hardships and horrors of war.

December 20, 1863
Dearest Ben:
    I have spent many gloomy and unhappy hours since you have been in the South. I hope I may never experience such feelings again for it is suffering indeed. Many times have I received a letter from you and would think that perhaps it was the last I would receive. . . . Many such times have I seen during the past

Although there are no known photographs of Ben or Melissa Wells or their farm, this 1864 Saginaw homestead is typical of the farms that women managed while their husbands were in the army.

two years, for instance when you were sick last winter and all communications cut off from Nashville . . . and then again last spring when you took relapse and was sick with the fever at Murfreesboro and when Brother Wallace sickened and died. . . . I often think I never knew what trouble was until since the commencement of this horrid rebellion, but how many others there are who have learned the same by bitter experience. . . . How I wish you could come home soon—by Christmas anyhow. . . . Don't you think it would be a merry Christmas? I think it would. I have paid but little attention to the holidays for the last two years for I felt that I could not enjoy them very well as long as my companion was in the army, but if he will only come home now I think I can enjoy myself as well as the rest. The sleighing is nice and we would have a fine sleigh ride. . . . I wish you were here tonight to see me and Mary [one of Melissa's

sisters, also a soldier's wife and the mother of two small children, who lived with her] perform with our babies. . . . You think we have a fine time with so many little folks, do you? And you think you can imagine how we look on the occasion? Well if you imagine right you can see a good many frowns and scowls when they all cry and scream at once, and sometimes the young hopefuls get a good slapping to assist them in tuning their harps. . . . Such things are any thing but pleasant, that is true, but you need not make sport of us, for it is bad enough to have to stand it without being laughed at. But never mind, you may have all the fun at my expense that you like and I will comfort myself with the thought that when you get home you will have to take a part in some of those interesting scenes.

Ben did come home on leave—his first and last of the war. It was a bittersweet time:

January 20, 1864

These ten short days [that you were home] were soon past and they did not seem more than half as long as any other ten days. Time always passes swiftly away when we enjoy ourselves the best. It is one week ago tomorrow since we parted; that was a sad parting indeed, very unlike the meeting. . . . You say perhaps I did not think you was very sociable after we started from home [for the railroad station]. You need not excuse [blame] yourself on account of that for even at that time I thought you did not feel much like talking, that is, if your feelings were in accordance with mine, for I could not have been very sociable had I tried ever so hard. . . . I am well aware that things did not go on as orderly and regular as they should [in the house] . . . but I hope you will excuse me and I will try and make things more pleasant for you when you come home again. I would have been glad if you had enjoyed it much better than you did but it is but little you know what a trouble it is to take care of so many small children and the hindrance they are in regard to the work about the house. . . . The children will be older some time and when you get home to stay I hope you will realize all. . . . I know that it is the duty of every wife to make home as pleasant and attractive as possible for her Husband, but I fear in many instances I have fell far short of my duty. But be that as it may I cannot help it now.

On February 8 Melissa again "was seated with pen and paper preparing to communicate my thoughts through this silent language to the absent one who is perhaps thinking or writing even now to me."

You know when we parted we promised to write to each other often and now if we will only do so all will make better feeling all round, don't you think so Benny? I do at least, but I guess I will not say anything more about it for you will think I am finding fault. But I do not mean it as such for I know you have done as well as I have and if anything better. However I will have to stop writing for a while and get Frank to sleep for he is clinging to my dress and crying as loud as he can scream for me to take him. Sweet blessings of matrimony. Don't you wish you were in my place? If I had half a dozen such I

would make a regular business of taking care of them and no one would expect me to do anything else.

Melissa's criticism offended Ben and not without cause. As one of her subsequent letters revealed, he had sent her nearly two hundred letters since going off to the army, an average of almost two a week! His reproach to her came quickly, and she responded on February 14:

I feel you mistake my meaning many times *Dear Ben* and my letters fail to accomplish the aim they are written for. In the first place I never meant to complain of you for not writing more often. I do not think I have any reason to complain of you for as a general thing you have done much better than I have [when it comes to writing]. . . . I am sure I do not remember you making any promise that you have not fulfilled and when I spoke of our promise to write often to each other I did not intend to infer that you had broken your promise. I am very sorry that you understood me so. . . . I am well aware that we all have our peculiarities and imperfections and I have never looked for perfection in any one. I know that I have many failings, many more than I wish I had, but I would not hurt your feelings even more than I would [the feelings of] any one else and I certainly do, and hope you will ever find in me all that could be expected of a true and devoted wife, for without you life would not be very bright or cheerful, and I long for the time to come when we will enjoy the society of each other and then we will know each other's peculiarities better and I hope have a better understanding between us.

Later Ben traveled to Detroit on behalf of the Eleventh Michigan to collect and take back a consignment prepared for his regiment by the women of the Soldier's Aid Society. It was a welcome vacation from the army that for a while seemed like it might be extended indefinitely, for the Detroit women tried to obtain his services in escorting shipments to the troops on a permanent basis. Melissa regretted their lack of success:

February 27

I am very much disappointed that the Ladies of Detroit did not succeed in gaining permission for you to remain there. . . . I think the Ladies of Detroit were doing a noble work. . . . The Ladies of 3 Rivers are doing considerable for the

Soldiers Aid Society and I am sure they cannot employ their time to any better advantage or in any better cause. I think it is the duty of the woman as well as the men to do all they can to assist in suppressing the rebellion and what they are now doing must be of some help toward it, for it is promoting the comfort of the Soldier and perhaps prolonging their lives.

The Eleventh Michigan comprised part of the mighty host Sherman was gathering to invade Georgia, his goal: Atlanta. Early in May 1864 the invasion got under way. The consequent fighting was almost continuous and often ferocious. Along with thousands of other wives, Melissa anxiously followed the course of events:

May 22
Another long week of anxiety and suspense has passed and still I am waiting . . . to know the results of the great battle in which my absent one has been participating. . . . News of great battles, great victories, great defeats reach us every day and yet I am ignorant of the fate of my Husband. . . . It seems as though there had been lives enough lost to crush two rebellions but we cannot always see things in their true state. There is much to do and it takes time to perform so much. . . . Perhaps you will think I am very much discouraged by writing as I do . . . but you must excuse me, I cannot always feel contented and happy and know that you are daily exposed to such danger. . . . But such is the horrors of war and we must bear the consequences even though our hearts are breaking. . . . How many times have I thought of the many hopes and anticipations we used to have before we were married. . . . We did not know then that our Country was in such a perilous situation or that we were tottering on the brink of war. It seems as though we must have been very blind. . . . Dear Ben, how I wish you were home today. A more beautiful day never graced the earth. I agree with you that Spring is the most pleasant season of the year. Our tastes are very much alike in that respect if no other. It seems hard that we cannot enjoy the pleasures of Spring together. . . . If we ever have a home where we mean to settle for life, let us have it surrounded with fruit trees. . . . Do you ever think of those two large apple trees in Father's door yard where we have passed so many happy hours in

the days of our courtship? . . . Oh for a renewal of those dear old times.

Around this time, according to a memoir written by Melissa and Ben's second son, Clayton, one of Ben's officers accused him of disobeying an order that in fact he never received. Ben was placed under arrest and "confined to camp." Possibly this affair, which eventually ended in his release without a court-martial and with his sergeant's rank intact, explains why by June he was engaged in nursing duties. Melissa had mixed feelings about his new assignment—evidently he did not mention the arrest:

June 12
I think . . . you will make an excellent nurse to attend the wounded Soldiers, but I hope you will not make yourself sick with the care and attention of so many. If there were more women to attend the sick and wounded it would be much better. There are thousands who are daily idling away their time who could volunteer their services to relieve the wants of the many poor suffering Soldiers in the Hospitals. How I wish it were in my power to administer to the sick and wounded Soldiers. . . . I can assure you it would be done with willing heart and ready hand.

As Sherman's rendezvous in Atlanta drew ever nearer, so too did the August 24 expiration date of the Eleventh Michigan's three-year term of service. In every letter, Melissa referred to this much-desired event. When Ben teasingly wrote her that he might reenlist, she was indignant:

July 8
You wanted to know what I would say if you should reenlist again for three years. I really hope if any such thoughts are passing through your mind you will banish them at once. I really do not know what I would say, but I fear my wrath would rise a little and might tell you to enlist for life while you were at it. I am afraid I would be tempted to hunt me up another man if you were . . . to stay three years longer. Do you suppose I could find another that I would like as well as I do Ben? I rather imagine it would puzzle me some. But of course you were only joking.

While awaiting Ben's return, Melissa kept busy being a "farmer and housekeeper":

I have just finished hoeing the potatoes today and came out feeling pretty well with the exception of some lameness in my arms and a pair of hands pretty badly blistered. You see it is a new business for me and comes rather hard at first—but I think I will get used to it. . . . It takes me a good while for I cannot work very fast. . . . I like farming first rate with the exception of hoeing potatoes. . . . It is most too much like work and not enough like play.

With the arrival of August and Ben's "release" a few weeks away, Melissa became increasingly joyful:

August 1
You are right in thinking that I am expecting a merry time when you get home. . . . I guess you are the same Ben you always was, that is if I can judge any thing by the tone of your letters. I cannot discover any change, but one thing I cannot agree with you. I do not think we will settle down or rather sober down and be old folks right away, for that would not agree with my natural disposition. . . . I think we will have smiles and kind words and acts and what more do we want to make us happy?

She humorously imagined how they might live once Ben was home:

August 7
I suppose you forgot I will not promise to saw the wood but I will agree to make the fires in the morning. I can well afford to do that. I made fires all last winter and so am pretty well used to it. I will bring the wood in if you will see that it is sawed . . . and as for your lying in bed in the morning until breakfast is ready, I have no objections to make if you lay until noon but I will not promise you how much you may sleep. . . . If you can sleep and put up with being teased and tormented at the same time you are at liberty to do so and if necessary you shall have your breakfast on a server.

But Melissa also experienced fear that Ben might be killed during his last days of service. She could not, she wrote on 7 August, "help a feeling of dread stealing over me every time I knew of any one going to the Post Office for fear the worst would come, and I have actually felt relieved when there would be no letter for me rather than . . . one directed [addressed] in a strange hand bearing sad tidings for me":

August 14
I have heard several times that the Regt was not going to be discharged until sometime [later than August 24] on account of one of the companies not being installed into service until that time. James King [another Fabius Township soldier serving in the Eleventh Michigan] wrote home to that effect, I was told. I wonder if it is true.

It was true.

When August 24 arrived, the men of the Eleventh Michigan, now in the trenches outside of Atlanta, were told that they had to remain until an order came relieving them from duty. Outraged by what they considered to be a breach of contract, a large number of them "bolted" and refused to do "extra duty for 'Uncle Sam,'" to quote the diary of Private Daniel Rose of Company A. This was mutiny in the face of the enemy and could have led to serious consequences. But the necessary authorization came through, and on August 27 the regiment took a train to Chattanooga, where it remained until September 18. While there, it participated in operations against Confederate cavalry raiders. Finally, it traveled back to Michigan and on September 30 was mustered out at Sturgis. Although the war would go on for another seven months, for Melissa and Ben it was at last over.

During the years that followed, Melissa gave birth to two more children, Clayton and a daughter named Eunice. Ben tried his hand first at brickmaking and then at farming, but he achieved little success at either and supplemented his income with teaching. On January 22, 1883, after a prolonged and painful illness, Melissa died at the age of forty-two. Ben had her buried in a little cemetery on their farm overlooking Corey Lake. The grave, marked by a tombstone that has been broken off at the base, still is there.

The Capture and Escape of Edwin Bigelow

Edited by Frank L. Klement

On August 30, 1862, Edwin Bigelow of Davisburg mustered into Company B, Fifth Michigan Cavalry. On January 1, 1863, he began recording his daily activities in a small diary. He continued to write entries through his subsequent capture by rebels during a skirmish at Buckland Mills, Virginia, his escape and eventual rescue. This diary excerpt begins on May 15, 1863.

Friday, May 15. The company were relieved from duty on the Ox road. Nothing new. Recd a letter from Mate.

Saturday, May 16. Our whole company went on picket on the Lawyers road with Co. H & I of the 7 Mich. This night one of Co. I's men stole my breast strap.

Sunday, May 17. Still on picket on the Lawyers road. No news of any consequence. I think more of our company by being brot in contact with others so much rougher. Wrote a letter to Mate.

Monday, May 18. Were relieved from picket at 2 P.M. All quiet.

Tuesday, May 19. The Co. went on camp guard. Two patrols went out at night to Centerville. I wrote a letter to Geo. and Recd one from Hamp [Hamilton].

Wednesday, May 20. The Co. were relieved at 9 o'clock from camp duty. I wrote a letter to Dr. Crooks.

Thursday, May 21. Went on picket at Hawkers mills. I wrote a letter home.

Friday, May 22. Still on picket at Hawkers mills. Recd a letter from Mate, by Rob. Traded bits with him.

Saturday, May 23. Were relieved from Picket at 2 o'clock and returned to camp Gray.

Sunday, May 24. At Cavalry Out-Post all day. I received three letters, one from Mother Stinson, one from Olive & one from George. I wrote a long letter to Mate, one to Mr. Phillipps, & one to Ellen. To day we were made glad by the news of a victory of Grant at Vicksburg. May he be as successful in all his undertakings if worthy ones.

Monday, May 25. We were sent out to Hawkers Mills with Capt. Purdy Com. Co. H. at 1 o'clock P.M. Nothing of consequence transpired.

Tuesday, May 26. On picket all day. No news, only heard that Lieut. Col. [Russell Alger] was to be our Col.

Wednesday, May 27. Were relieved at 2. P.M. and got our pay soon after arriving at camp.

Thursday, May 28. Were on camp gard [sic] all day. I acted as Officer of the [day] during the A.M. I wrote a letter to George [and] one to Olive. I sent Twenty dollars home in George's letter.

Friday, May 29. Were relieved from camp guard this morning at 9 o'clock. I received a letter and six papers from Mate and wrote a letter to her.

Saturday, May 30. Went on picket on the Lawyers road and had charge of a relief. No news from the war.

Sunday, May 31. Still on picket & still nothing new.

JUNE

Monday, June 1. Were relieved from picket and returned to camp.

Tuesday, June 2. Detailed 24 men, 2 Sgts [and] 3 corpls. to go on picket at Hawkers Mills with Lieut. Haire—all under command of Capt. Purdy. Wrote a letter to Hamp.

Wednesday, June 3. The rest of the company went on picket on the Ox road at 3 o'clock P.M. Received a letter from George.

Thursday, June 4. This morning our picket had a visit from Mosby [and his Raiders]. One Corpl. & Horse were wounded belonging to Co. M. Col. Gray went out and lost six or eight men taken prisoners but did not accomplish anything. Wrote a letter home & one to Uncle Ed[mund].

Friday, June 5. To day our company with several others went out on a scout but found no enemy and returned about 4 o'clock. Recd a letter from Mate.

Saturday, June 6. The Company did camp duty from 4 o'clock P.M. I wrote a letter to Mate.

Sunday, June 7. Went out to Chantilly to see if the force who were coming in were our men or rebs. They were the 2nd Penn. We were relieved from camp guard at 10 o'clock A.M.

Monday, June 8. A part of the company did picket duty on the Ox road to-day. The rest did picket duty on the Fox road during the night.

Tuesday, June 9. The rest of the Co. did picket duty on the Ox road. No news of consequence.

Wednesday, June 10. The company were relieved from picket on the Ox road by Co. C. I spoke to Maj. Trowbridge about a recommend & he said he would give me anything.

Thursday, June 11. Expected to go on picket on the Lawyers road but hearing of Mosby's approach we were kept back for him. I wrote a letter to George and sent five dollars. I also received a letter from Mate.

Friday, June 12. Went on picket on the Lawyers road at 1 o'clock P.M. I had tea at Mr. Bennett's with the Capt. [Purdy] and Lieut. [George R.] Barse [of Detroit].

Saturday, June 13. Still on picket. I reed a letter from Amos Stinson.

Sunday, June 14. Were relieved from picket and moved our camp to beyond Vienna and are now under the command of Col. Alger.

Monday, June 15. To day we fixed a good place for our tents and horses.

Tuesday, June 16. Went on picket, and our company picketed from Leesburg Pike to the Potomac. The Capt. [Purdy] and myself went in swimming. It was a shady place on the bank of the river with high rocks around us but nice large trees on the flat.

Wednesday, June 17. To day we were relieved from picket and resumed to camp. No news of importance—only Hooker's Army were near Fairfax.

Thursday, June 18. In camp all day. I reed a letter from Home & wrote one to George. Also received a letter from Marietta.

Friday, June 19. To day I busied myself by writing to Olive & Mary till afternoon when we had orders to pack everything and go to Fairfax C[ourt] H[ouse], which we did. I received a letter from Mate and wrote a short one in answer.

Saturday, June 20. Were in camp all day waiting orders to march but received none. Heard that the main body of Lee's Army were marching on Washington.

Sunday, June 21. To day we received orders and marched at 10 o'clock for Warrenton and camped near New Baltimore. Heavy firing heard toward Ashby's Gap.

Monday, June 22. This morning we went to Warrenton and staid till 4 o'clock P.M. We then marched to Kelly's Ford and back to within about 7 miles of Warrenton, having marched till about 3 o'clock A.M.

Tuesday, June 23. To day we came from our camp near Kelly's Ford, back to Ga[i]nesville & staid all night.

Wednesday, June 24. To day we went to our old camp near Fairfax and received orders to march at 3 o'clock the next morning for Harpers Ferry. Reed a letter from Lyman & answered it sending $1.00. Also wrote a letter to George. Reed three papers from E. A. H.

Thursday, June 25. We marched at 3 o'clock [in the morning] for M.D. [Maryland] and camped at night about five miles from Edward's Ferry. We crossed the Potomac . . . [editor writing illegible], the water came up to our horses [sic] shoulders.

Friday, June 26. This day we came as far as Fredrick City where were met with a fine reception, the ladies waving flags & scarfes. . . . [illegible writing] The city is the finest I ever saw and contains the best farms. The city is also a little beauty. We camped near the city in a large meadow and had plenty of food for the horses.

Saturday, June 27. Left camp near Fredrick and went to within a mile of Emmetsburg. This is quite a rebel town and not much of a place being nearly destroyed by fire. I wrote a letter to Mate and had it mailed here.

Sunday, June 28. This morning we went to Gettysburg and staid all day. This is a fine place and we were reed with much joy by the inhabitants. The rebels had just left the day before. There are a goodly number of pretty girls to welcome us.

Monday, June 29. To day we resumed to near Emmetsburg and there waited for the infantry and artillery. Then went to within a few miles of Littlestown.

Tuesday, June 30. This morning we went to Littlestown and there found a good many of our cavalry. We fed our horses and then one company went out on a scout. I was left with ten men to guard a road and wait the return of a company of the sixth, but they did not come so I remained all night. Our forces had a sharp fight at Hanover and whipped the rebels. I wrote a letter to George.

JULY

Wednesday, July 1. To day I joined the Co. again at Hanover, and the regiment went to Abbieville [Abbotsville] and from there to [East] Berlin where we camped for the night. Our regiment received a compliment from the Maj. Genl. [Pleasanton] for good conduct in the fight at Hanover.

Thursday, July 2. Marched to near Gettysburg and joined the main army. Had a little skirmish at dark. We were in the saddle all night and just in the morning had a little rest.

Friday, July 3. This day we left our camp and attacked the rebel army on the left, and after a hard fight enemy checked. Our regiment did noble executions. Lieut. Hickey was wounded and has not returned yet, but is reported to be in the hospital. We lost Maj. Ferry who was shot dead. Maj. Trowbridge had his horse shot under him. John Norton was taken prisoner. Chas. Yates is missing, supposed to be wounded.

Saturday, July 4. We marched to near Emmet[s]burg and then into the mountains. We met the enemy at dark. Our Company deployed as skirmishers and were in the woods fighting all night. Sgt. Brenner was shot and I guess will die. We captured quite a number of prisoners and a large train. There were about 1600 prisoners.

Sunday, July 5. This day we marched to Smithsburg and remained till dark. We had a skirmish with the enemy who were guarding the pass

Taken prisoner at Buckland Mills, Virginia, on October 19, 1863, Edwin B. Bigelow of Davisburg endured almost five months of captivity at Virginia's Belle Isle prison. He escaped on March 13, 1864, while being transferred to Andersonville, Georgia.

and trying to cut us off, but we gave them the slip, and went to near Boonsborough and camped till daylight. We rested only three or four hours.

Monday, July 6. To day we went to Hagerstown and there met the enemy, and after a little skirmish went down to the Potomac where they were crossing the river. We attacked them and after a hard fight we [were] obliged to withdraw, but not till we destroyed some

forty or forty five wagons. We rode all night and had only a few hours to rest.

Tuesday, July 7. We rested to day and much needed it too. There was nothing very stir[r]ing only at 4 o'clock we were called out to repel an attack but it was not made. Wrote a letter Home. Wrote one to Mate.

Wednesday, July 8. This day we again went out and had a sharp fight, and drove Stewart [Stuart] back with considerable loss. Our loss was comparitively small. We came to our old camp near Boonsboro at night.

Thursday, July 9. We rested and got our horses shod. Drew three days [sic] rations and a large supply of ammunition.

Friday, July 10. Remained in camp near Boonsboro all day.

Saturday, July 11. Left camp near Boonsboro and went to near Hagerstown and remained all night.

Sunday, July 12. This [morning charged the rebels on Hagerstown] capturing 40 or 50 prisoners and two pieces of artilery. Among the prisoners were two Maj[ors]. Our Company were on the right and staid till about 11 o'clock P.M. Col. Gould was wounded.

Monday, July 13. Remained in camp all day. Got pretty well rested.

Nothing new.

Tuesday, July 14. Today we went to Falling Waters and charged through town but the rebs were all gone except some stragglers. In the P.M. we went below the town and got there just as the 6th & 7th Mich. charged some rebel infantry and routed them, but our loss was considerable. This day we captured nearly 2000 prisoners and one piece of Artillery.

Wednesday, July 15. We went to near Boonsboro and remained all night. Nothing new.

Thursday, July 16. To day we went to near Berlin and camped for the night. Recd our mail there. I received two letters from George, two from Mate, one from Hamp., one from Lyman, one from Mr. Tindall.

Friday, July 17. To day we crossed the Potomac at Berlin and went to Sni[c]kers Gap. Had a little skirmish and took three or four prisoners. Had two men wounded. Our regiment took and held the gap. This night I think I suffered more than any one night before.

Saturday, July 18. We remained in the Gap all day and were relieved at night by the 1st V.A. We went about 8 miles to camp and got there about 2 o'clock.

Sunday, July 19. We left camp near Snikers Gap and went to near Ashbys Gap where we encamped.

Monday, July 20. To day we took possession of Ashbys Gap without any fighting; the enemy retreating upon our approach. Recd a letter from George.

Tuesday, July 21. Remained all day at camp near Upperville. Had a letter from Olive.

Wednesday, July 22. To day we left our camp near Upperville and went to about 7 or 8 miles from Manassas Gap, where we camped for the night. Had Inspection in the A.M. also wrote a letter to Olive.

Thursday, July 23. This day we marched from our old camp to within 15 miles of Culpepper—a place called Amesville—and a long march it was.

Friday, July 24. To day we went out for a fight and our company went to the left to guard a road. Heard pretty heavy firing in front at about 1 o'clock. We were ordered back to camp and then went out on picket.

Saturday, July 25. On picket all day, no news. Genl. Hill's corps went by toward Culpepper. They held Thornton's Gap. We were relieved from Picket and went back to Amesville for the night.

Sunday, July 26. To day eight companies and a part of the 6th went out to Jefferson[ton] to forage. We got very little. I called it a thieving expedition.

Monday, July 27. To day we went out to do picket duty at Hart's Ford on the Rappahannock. We have comfortable quarters and easy times. Wrote a letter to George.

Tuesday, July 28. Still on picket. We are having a good rest. To-day I received a letter from George & two from Mate.

Wednesday, July 29. On picket. Still nothing new.

Thursday, July 30. On picket yet. Are having a first rate time.

Friday, July 31. Were relieved from picket and went to Warrenton Junction.

AUGUST

Saturday, August 1. Are at Warrenton Junction. We have a very poor camp. I wrote a long letter to Mate in the evening. To-day the men resumed from Washington who went after new horses. They all had a grand spree at Washington, Officers & men.

Sunday, August 2. A very warm day. Did a little except run about camp attending the common duties. I wrote a letter to Carrie Wilson for C. Blunden and some in it for myself. Also a little more in the one to Mate of the night before.

Monday, August 3. To day all passed off quietly, as usual.

Tuesday, August 4. This morning about 2 o'clock we were all called up by the bugle and fifteen went out of our company, with a good many others on a reconoisance [sic] to Falmouth and up to Stafford C[ourt] H[ouse] where we remained all night.

Wednesday, August 5. To day we resumed to camp all tired and hungry. Our horses had nothing till we arrived back to Warrenton Junction.

Thursday, August 6. In camp all day no news.

Friday, August 7. To day I have been quite unwell. In the P.M. we moved our camp into a better part of the woods.

Saturday, August 8. Remained all day in camp. Recd a letter from. Alice & one from Mate & one from Olive.

Sunday, August 9. To day we had inspection but I did go out I wrote a letter to Alice & one to Mate. Recd a letter from Henry.

Monday, August 10. To day we moved our camp again. No news.

Tuesday, August 11. We went to do picket duty and camped about five miles from the reserve. I received three papers from Mate. Our detachment is under command of Capt. [Wellington W.] Gray.

Wednesday, August 12. This day we went to Stafford's Church and back to Falls Church.

Thursday, August 13. To day we went to Aquia Station and back.

Friday, August 14. We remained in camp all day. I was detailed to act as the Q[uarter] M[aster] of the detachment.

Saturday, August 15. This day we started for Aquia by the way of Stafford's Store having orders to take all male citizens able of bearing arms. We took 12. We camped about five miles from Stafford's store.

Sunday, August 16. We went to Stafford C[ourt] H[ouse] and back to camp, taking about thirty citizens with us.

Monday, August 17. This day we left our old camp and went to Falmouth to do picket duty. The rebs fired on us from across the river. We did not return the fire. They showed a flag of Truce & when our men showed themselves they fired again but did no dammage [sic].

Tuesday, August 18. To day they fired on our pickets again in the morning but not after noon. To day I recd a letter and three papers to Mate.

Wednesday, August 19. No firing today. All quiet. At night I went to a house near by and remained all night.

Thursday, August 20. I was quite unwell to day so staid at Mrs. Little's all day and night.

Friday, August 21. Went back and did duty as Q.M.

Saturday, August 22. Got relieved from the Q.M. department and reported to my company. We all went to the Lacy House on picket duty. Received a letter from home. I wrote a letter to Alice & a note to Maj. Trowbridge.

Sunday, August 23. At the Lacy House all day. At night about 9 3/4 o'clock we were attacked by the rebs and lost seven horses & three men—Corpl. [William H.] Pepper, S. [Stephen W.] Thompson, & A. [Alva] Roe. Cpl. Cook was wounded in the arm. Four horses were shot. I wrote a part of a letter to Mate.

Monday, August 24. This day we were relieved from the Lacy House and went to Capt. Gray's head quarters. I finished the letter to Mate & sent it off.

Tuesday, August 25. At camp all day. No news of any consequence. We had a very hard storm at evening.

Wednesday, August 26. I went down to the Lacy house and superintended the burying of the horses killed during the attack Sunday night. I got my dinner & supper at Mr. Heffron's.

Thursday, August 27. On picket all day no news of the army doing anything.

Friday, August 28. This day we were relieved from picket by the 1st Mich. and returned to near Hartwood Church.

Saturday, August 29. We were to have an inspection to day but did not. I received a letter from Mate.

Sunday, August 30. To-day we had a Regimental Inspection. I wrote a letter to George and one to Mate.

Monday, August 31. This morning we were aroused at 2 1/2 o'clock and saddled ready to march. We mustered for pay.

SEPTEMBER

Tuesday, September 1. To day we went to Port Royal and expected a fight but the rebs went across the river and we were cheated out of it.

Wednesday, September 2. We scouted around the country and the battery shelled a couple of boats the Rebs had captured from us. In the P.M. we started back for camp and went about 15 miles and encamped.

Thursday, September 3. We came back to Hartwood Church in our old camp. Recd a letter from George.

Friday, September 4. Remained all day at camp. Received a letter from Maj. Trowbridge now Lieut Col. of the 10th. Recd 2 papers from George. Sergt. Merwin and 8 men went to Washington, on the cars from the Junction, after horses.

Saturday, September 5. All day in camp. Nothing new. Recd a letter from Mate & 3 papers.

Sunday, September 6. All day in camp. Had company inspection at 9 o'clock. I wrote a letter to Mate & one to George.

Monday, September 7. In camp all day. I drilled the Co. in saber drill. I wrote a letter to Uncle Spencer & one to J. Worden.

Tuesday, September 8. The same old story. Drill with the saber.

Wednesday, September 9. In camp all day. Drilled the men with the sabres on horseback.

Thursday, September 10. In camp as usual. Received a letter from George. Drilled on horseback.

Friday, September 11. In camp all day. Drilled as usual.

Saturday, September 12. Left our camp near Har[t]wood Church and went to near Kelley's Ford with the whole division.

Sunday, September 13. To day we crossed the Rappahannock at Kelly's Ford and met the enemy about six miles from Culpepper. We were here joined by [Brigadier General John] Buford's & [David McN.] Gregg's cavalry. We then fought the rebs to the villiage [sic] capturing 3 pieces of artillery and about fifty men. We camped near the town. Again we gave Stewart [Stuart] a good thrashing.

Monday, September 14. This morning we again started for our friends and found they were across the Rapidan supported by Infantry. We had a little fight across it. Chas. Blunden was wounded in the leg. About 11 o'clock we went down on the bank of the river on picket. I had command of our company.

Tuesday, September 15. We have been all day on picket without a mouthful to eat.

Wednesday, September 16. To day our Regiment was called out to stop the advance of the Rebs (who drove the 6th & 7th back) at double quick but when we got down there they were all on their own side of the river. I had command of the Co. and staid till night, when being quite unwell I returned to camp.

Thursday, September 17. To day we left the Ford, being relieved by the Infantry & went into camp about five miles from Culpepper.

Friday, September 18. We remained all day in camp.

Saturday, September 19. This day we changed our camp ground about 1/2 mile off. I received a letter from Mate, one from Geo., one from Uncle Ed[mund], & one from Sarah Thompson. Also three papers from Mate & one from Uncle Spencer.

Sunday, September 20. This day we had Regimental Inspection and Dress Parade. Capt. [John E.] Clark was appointed Maj.[;] Lieut. [William O.] North, Capt.[;] [and] Sergt. [George W.] Longberry [Lonsbury] made Lieut. I wrote a letter to Mate. I received one from Geo. Merwin.

Monday, September 21. This morning we left camp and went to Madison C[ourt] H[ouse]. Our Co. charged through the place, but the Rebs had gone double quick. We camped here all night.

Tuesday, September 22. To day we went across the Rapidan and moved down the river. Met the enemy about 4 o'clock but they were too strong and we retreated across the river and went into camp about 10 o'clock.

Wednesday, September 23. This morning we left early and went toward Culpepper. The Rebs. close after us & attacked as we were crossing Robison [Robertson] River but did not do much damage. We went into camp near Culpepper. I received a letter from Olive & one from Serg't Howe. Wrote a letter to George.

Thursday, September 24. To day we fixed our tents to stay a couple of days but were ordered out on picket at James City.

Friday, September 25. On picket all day. I did not have to do much. Received a letter from George.

Saturday, September 26. We were on picket all day.

General George A. Custer of Monroe took command of the Michigan Cavalry Brigade on the eve of the Battle of Gettysburg. On the afternoon of July 3, the Fifth Michigan Cavalry participated in a series of mounted charges that checked the Confederates.

Nothing new. Were relieved about 3 o'clock and went to the reserve. I wrote a letter to Mate & received one.

Sunday, September 27. This day we were in camp all day and I wrote a letter to George & one to Olive. We got our pay also. I received a letter from Ellen.

Monday, September 28. We moved our camp across the road in a more pleasant place. Had inspection by Maj. [George A.] Drue [Drew].

Tuesday, September 29. To day we moved our camp again to James City. Ed. B. [Sergeant Edwin Bulson] went out and got some potatoes.

Wednesday, September 30. In camp all day. In the P.M. Ed & I went out and got about 1/2 bushel of sweet potatoes for which he gave $2.00 secesh money.

OCTOBER

Thursday, October 1. A part of our Co. was on duty but I did not have to go out. We all went out to see the race between Kilpatricks horse & a Lieut's in Battery M. The battery horse beat. I received a letter from Hamilton.

Friday, October 2. This day it rained all day. I wrote a letter to Hamilton and one to Mr. Curtis. I received one from George.

Saturday, October 3. To day we went out and saw another race by John Allen's and the Colonel's *bay*. The Col's horse beat. I wrote a letter to George.

Sunday, October 4. To day we had Company Inspection and Dress Parade which took up all the time we had to write & c [etc.]. I wrote a long letter to Mate in the evening. I received a letter from Wm Pepper, who, with S. Thompson, A. Roe, G. Lord, & C. W. [Charles W.] Yates, had just been paroled by the *Rebels*. They are at Colledge Green Barracks, Annapolis Md.

Monday, October 5. To day we had a Division Review by Maj. General Pleasanton. After which we went to a horse race again. I received a letter from H. [Henry] McWethy & wrote one to Pepper.

Tuesday, October 6. We had drill in the A.M. by the Officers & Serg'ts & in the P.M. Squadron drill. I wrote a letter to H. McWethy.

Wednesday, October 7. We went at daybreak with Co. G. on a scout and did not stop to feed or rest till we resumed to camp. We marched about 30 miles, took one prisoner. He belonged to a N[orth] C[arolina] Reg[iment] & was going to his Uncle's to get some new clothes, being very ragged & barefooted.

Thursday, October 8. In camp all day. Nothing new.

Friday, October 9. To day we went to see Capt. North's horse race with Frank Neal [Nash?]. At night our Battallion packed up to go on picket. I recd a letter from George, one from Mate, & one from D. C. Howe.

Saturday, October 10. This morning we went out to the front but the Rebs were driving our Pickets in and we all fell back to General Killpatrick's head quarters just back of James City where we gave the Rebs all they wanted. We camped here all night.

Sunday, October 11. This morning we left near James City & fell back to Culpepper without a fight but there we had quite a brush. We fell back till near Brandy Station where the Rebs got clear in our front so we were completely surrounded. We formed for a charge by brigades, and with three times three cheers charged on the traitors and they got out of the way double quick. We then took position with the battery and gave battle. The Capt. was wounded in a charge & S. Smith missing.

Monday, October 12. We crossed the Rappahannock the night before and marched all night, going to Har[t]-wood Church and this day we went to Kelleys Ford & U.S. Ford Md. Our Co. did picket duty all night at U.S. Ford.

Tuesday, October 13. This morning we went up to Bealton's Station and drew rations—all but Hard tack which we ought to had had the day before. We went to near Gain[e]sville and camped all night.

Wednesday, October 14. This morning we went to near Bull Run and camped again for the rest of the day.

Thursday, October 15. We moved across the river and got rations this morning.

Friday, October 16. In camp all day near Bull Run. I wrote a short letter to Mate & one to George.

Saturday, October 17. In camp all day near Bull Run.

Sunday, October 18. To day we went out to welcome Col. Kellog [Michigan congressman F. W. Kellogg] after which we made a move to the front. We drove the pickets in and camped for the night, our company being on picket.

Monday, October 19. At Buckland Mills had a pretty hard fight and Beckwith, Thayer, Astrander, Markham, Schultz, Wilson and my *very humble* self got taken prisoners. Brink was mortally wounded. We were marched about ten miles to Warrenton and put into the old jail. Maj. Clark, Lieut. Barse, Capt. Lee, & another Lieut. was [*sic*] captured this day in the fight.

Tuesday, October 20. This morning we were started off at day break withhout any rations. We had to march over thirty miles to Culpepper. We got there about 10. o'clock P.M. In about an hour we got a few hard tack a piece.

Wednesday, October 21. We remained all day in Culpepper but got no more rations this day, just at dark we got on the cars and went as far as Rapidan Station & from there we had to walk to Orange C[ourt] H[ouse] where we were put into the basement of the C[ourt] H[ouse] with nothing but the bare ground to lie upon till morning.

Thursday, October 22. We went today to Gordonsville and in the P.M. drew some H[ard] T[ack] & Bacon. We were put in a warehouse and kept till morning.

Friday, October 23. We were put on the cars at daylight and started for Richmond where we arrived about 4 o'clock in the P.M. We drew 4 H[ard] T[ack] & a piece of bacon. We were put into an old Tobacco warehouse with about 1000 others.

Saturday, October 24. This morning we were taken to Bell Isle [Belle Island in the James River] and divided into squads. I got a tent and 20 of us had to stay in it. We get 1/2 loaf of bread with a little beef & a pint of soup per day. Some of the prisoners here have been on the Island over 4 months. It rained all day & a good many of the men had no tent to stay in. Those that had could not sleep it was so cold.

Sunday, October 25. This is the 1st Sabbath of my imprisonment & the 2nd day on Bell Isle. It is a beautiful day overhead but one of misery here. This morning one of the guards shot one of our Serg'ts for being on the top of the embankment. He died in a few minutes.

Monday, October 26. To day was spent on the Island as usual. Had rumors that we would be taken off to-morrow. There [are] three or four hundred that have no tents, and those who have nearly freeze at night. We are allowed two sticks of wood to every 20 men.

Tuesday, October 27. The sun shines brightly this morning but it almost seems like a mockery upon our misery, yet we ought to feel very thankful for the warmth it brings us. We have rumors again of an early parole.

Wednesday, October 28. We are all here on this miserable little Island yet, but to-day's paper states we will be paroled by the 5th of Nov. We are very willing to be paroled or exchanged. I saw a good example of a Union Soldier in the person of an East Tenn'ean whose Aunt and Wife were both shot by the traitors. He was tried before four Justises for murder but they could not prove him guilty. He has four children but they are with his father.

Thursday, October 29. Thank God one more day has passed and we have one less to *stay*, not live, on Belle Isle, Richmond. Our boys are all pretty well as yet. [General] Geo[rge] Kenzel lost $10.00 by a set of Thieves.

Friday, October 30. All day wishing we were off for home but no home yet for us.

Saturday, October 31. One week ago today we came on to this miserable Island. All are anxious, yet continue to hope for the best.

NOVEMBER

Sunday, November 1. This is the 2nd Sunday of our captivity which ought to be devoted to our Lord but you see nothing done but picking lice and lie around playing cards. We had an addition of some 400 more poor fellow prisoners, mostly from Burnside's Army.

Monday, November 2. Two weeks to-day I with 14 others were taken prisoners and during that time have suffered more and seen more suffering than I ever saw before in all my life or in any six times the same length of time.

Tuesday, November 3. We are still on the Island growing weak & fainter every day for the want of sufficient food. Gen. Neal Dow came and looked at us and promised to do all he could for us as soon as he got back. He has been a prisoner since the siege of Port Hudson and is exchanged for General [John] Morgan. I wrote a short letter to Lieut. Hickey.

Wednesday, November 4. There seems to be nothing to write except what I have already written. There seems to be but a slight prospect of our getting away. Still I trust in God and when the right time comes I shall either leave here for some other part of earth or else for a home safe in Heaven.

Thursday, November 5. To day General Dow came and gave out some clothing to the boys that were the most needy. It was very pleasant and warm.

Friday, November 6. In camp on Belle Isle yet with very little to eat and very anxious to be off.

Saturday, November 7. To-day makes two weeks on this little miserable Island. There is a great deal of sickness and suffering and quite a good many deaths.

Sunday, November 8. This is the third Sabbath of our Captivity and although we look a little pale we are very healthy considering the place & food we have. There was a little disturbance last evening and the rumor is that several made their escape, but one was shot dead and three wounded. Rumors that we will get sent away in two or three days.

Monday, November 9. This is a cold day and it snows a little at times. We have had a quarter of a loaf of corn & wheat bread mixed & one mouthful of meat for all day.

Tuesday, November 10. This morning we got our breakfast, or what we ought to have had for supper last night, at 8 o'clock—the earliest we have had it since being on the Island. We draw corn bread, and it is nothing but corn meal and water with a little salt.

Wednesday, November 11. Was a cold and windy day and we stood up and shivered nearly all the time in our tent. Thayer is sick & George Hood & Fred Harris. There is more suffering here in one week among 5,000 than there is in our own Army in a month.

Thursday, November 12. Was a very pleasant day and it was quite a relief to the naked fellows. There were over 700 more poor fellows bro't in to-day from Burnside's army.

Friday, November 13. Once more the morning has dawned pleasantly upon 6,000 miserable sufferers. There were 7 reported dead this morning and I know there were 4 by a man that saw them.

Saturday, November 14. There are some 50 more prisoners that just came in. Twelve men were carried out dead this morning. It has been quite pleasant till evening when it began to rain and rained by spells all night. It is three weeks this morning since we were bro't to this Island.

Sunday, November 15. Once more the holy Sabbath finds us in Richmond a prisoner of war suffering, but yet hopeful, and I for one, not once wishing our Government to give one iota to the one mule Confederacy. I drew a good blanket from Uncle Sam's stock. It was much needed and thankfully received. It is quite warm and pleasant.

Wednesday, November 18. On the Island and all about the same—only Thayer was taken out to-day with the sick.

Thursday, November 19. Nothing new. It is the one cry all the time for something more to eat yet we get enough to keep us alive. We have very little wood.

Friday, November 20. It is just about one dining every day. All the talk is for more to eat and when will we be exchanged or paroled. We have only bread issued to us and 2/3 of a loaf of corn meal baked in small lo[a]ves.

Saturday, November 21. Every day is about the same. Some of Uncle Sam's pork and salt beef but none issued to-day. Four weeks of misery is passed.

Sunday, November 22. One more Sabbath we are obliged to spend on this miserable secesh Island. I received a letter from George and wrote one back on the same 1/2 sheet of paper.

Monday, November 23. They say that we shall have our pork cooked or else not at all. We will get only about 1/2 of what we ought by such a smouge [smudge?] game. It is cold and rainy.

Tuesday, November 24. No news more than we have every day.

Wednesday, November 25. Always the same cry "for more food and when shall we get away."

Thursday, November 26. This I expect is a day appointed for Thanksgiving. We have a great deal to be thankful for and yet we are too apt to feel differently while under adverse circumstances I am thankful that our health is so good and we are preserved for some more usefulness hereafter.

Friday, November 27. To-day is about like all the rest. We have rumors of Braggs' defeat by Grant & the capture of a large part of his Artillery.

Saturday, November 28. It is now five weeks this day chat we were brot to this miserable hole. We see but little prospect of getting away yet we have hope and hear good news from Grant.

Sunday, November 29. Another Sabbath finds us yet on Belle Isle, making five Sundays spent here under a Rebel guard. We Squadded off to-day, and Co. B changed their places and got with the 24th squad. It is a miserable disagreeable day, raining all the time.

Monday, November 30. There seems to be no news to write here. One day is about the same as another.

DECEMBER

Tuesday, December 1. Another month is begun and yet no prospect of our being taken off of this miserable Island.

Wednesday, December 2. Nothing new only we hear a little about the defeat of Bragg & a rumor of an engagement between Mead & Lee. We all went out and counted off again.

Thursday, December 3. All the business we have to keep ourselves busy with is to pick lice & talk about what we will get to eat.

Friday, December 4. Another day has passed and we are yet among the living and suffering.

Saturday, December 5. This day I received a letter from George and I answered it immediately. He sent a box the same day.

Sunday, December 6. This is the sixth Sabbath we have spent on Belle Isle. I never tho't so much of the advantages of being where I could attend Divine Services as since my confinement here. We hear very much profane language used and have no chance of getting out of hearing. I still have faith that it will all result in some good.

Monday, December 7. It is now seven weeks this evening since our capture and although we all have suffered much yet we are willing to continue serving our country to the best of our ability during the time of enlistment but are very anxious to get out of the hands of the inhuman enemy. Congress meets to-day at Richmond and in Washington.

Tuesday, December 8. Nothing new so there is little use of writing anything.

Wednesday, December 9. To day is my Twenty-Fifth birthday & it is truly the most lonely and miserable one I ever spent and hope it will be the last I may be obliged to spend in the miserable rotten Confederacy.

Thursday, December 10. One more day is gone and one less to spend on "Belle Isle." There were four dead men carried out—three were chilled through this night [and] one was killed, by an axe, trying to steal a blanket.

Friday, December 11. Nothing new.

Saturday, December 12. Seven weeks ago to day we were brot to this poor miserable camp.

Sunday, December 13. This is the 7th sabbath we have spent on Belle Isle.

Monday, December 14. Eight weeks to-day since we were taken prisoners and they have been the longest I ever knew.

Tuesday, December 15. This month is now half gone and yet we wait for the happy day to come when we are to be sent home.

Wednesday, December 16. Nothing new every day is long and we all rejoice at its close.

Thursday, December 17. One day more we have lived on this Isle & I think about the song we have "lived & suffered." Truly it is a hard life yet I cannot, like some, find fault with our Government. There have been a good many shoemakers gone to the city to work.

Friday, December 18. To-day the river is very high and it is growing colder.

Saturday, December 19. The river is so high that the Officers tents are flooded and they have to sleep in in [sic] the bread house. We have only one meal and that is meat & bread at 3 o'clock. It has been a very cold

& dreary day. It is just two months to-day that we were captured.

Tuesday, December 22. It is pretty cold & there is more suffering from that reason than most any other cause.

Wednesday, December 23. Every day brings the same daily duty, that of hunting lice.

Thursday, December 24. This day makes nine weeks of suffering on Belle Isle. We all are in hopes to get off soon but for all that it looks dark.

Friday, December 25. Well to day is surely a melancholy instead of a merry Christmas. Truly we will know how to appreciate our comforts when we are once more comfortably situated. It has been cold and disagreeable and we were obliged to stand out nearly all day and then did not squad off. I did not hunt lice to-day as usual. I am thankful that my health is yet good while so many others are suffering from disease.

Saturday, December 26. Another week is gone and none of us have gone from the Island except those who have rec'd their *final* discharge. I think there were two frozen to death during the week.

Sunday, December 27. One more Sabbath we have been obliged to remain here, yet I feel thankful that a part of our number have been taken away although it was not my privilege to go. There were 500 either Paroled or Exchanged. The report is that they are to take us all away as fast as possible. I am thankful that a part can go if the rest are obliged to remain. I received a letter from George.

Monday, December 28. This has been a somewhat anxious day as we expected some more would be sent away but were all disappointed. Yet were told that 1000 would be sent to-morrow. I drew a new overcoat and was much pleased to get it.

Tuesday, December 29. This has been a day of anxiety by the whole camp as they promised to take either 1000 or 1500 away but none went. The Rebels refuse to recognize Genl. Butler as one of our Commissioners; therefore the exchange was stop[p]ed. We think it will soon go on again but are very anxious.

Wednesday, December 30. Well this month is nearly gone and we are yet prisoners of war. I think there is no doubt but we will have to spend our New Year's here.

Thursday, December 31. This is the last day of the year and we are still on this miserable Island with pretty poor prospects of being released.

JANUARY 1864

Wednesday, January 6, 1864. The boys are all giving up the hope of getting away this month.

Thursday, January 7. To day I got a Box from home. It came in the care of Lieut. Boyd. I was very happily surprised at its receipt I wrote a letter home.

Friday, January 8. To day there were several men carried out dead, and, to the everlasting disgrace of the Surgeon, were laid out back of the Hosptl and the *Hogs* eat the face off of one of them.

Saturday, January 9. I received a note from Geo. Barse [now a fellow prisoner] & Twenty Dollars in Confederate. Also a bundle of papers from Detroit. I received two letters from George & ans[wered] the same.

Sunday, January 10. Nothing of interest has transpired to-day.

Monday, January 11. To day we have heard that we were to be sent away instantly. I got a letter from Geo.

Tuesday, January 12. A pleasant day but nothing of interest transpiring.

Wednesday, January 13. All quiet to-day.

Thursday, January 14. I wrote a letter home and one to Mrs. Thayer [mother of fellow prisoner Eli Thayer].

Friday, January 15. We were confident that we would all be inside of our own lines but here we are yet and no prospect of getting off very soon.

Saturday, January 16. The usual occupation that of hunting lice. We hear that the flag of truce boat is up and expect to hear the news about Monday.

Sunday, January 17. Sunday and yet not where we can enjoy its advantages.

Monday, January 18. Nothing new although the "Flag of Truce" was up. I wrote a letter to George.

Tuesday, January 19. Every day seems to be just about the same.

Wednesday, January 20. All quiet.

Thursday, January 21. To-day I heard from my Box. It was drawn by a man in Co. C. who ans[wered] to my name. As he was sent onto the Island a couple of days afterward I got part of the things.

Friday, January 22. This day I was called out and had a good visit with Col. Lefavor [Heber LeFavour] of the 22nd Inft. I also received and wrote a letter to George.

Saturday, January 23. All quiet to-day & nothing new.

Sunday, January 24. This sabbath has been spent about the same as all the rest while here. I received a fine present from Col. Lefavour. It was a large paper of rice—I think about ten pounds. It was gratefully received & will be long remembered.

Monday, January 25. To-day I wrote a letter home and to Col. Lefavour. Also to W[illiam] H. Pepper. We are having splendid weather.

Tuesday, January 26. The weather is very pleasant

and just such as one could enjoy were he at liberty. Still I feel thankful we are so kindly favored.

Wednesday, January 27. Still we have such fine weather yet no news about our getting away from the Island.

Thursday, January 28. Pleasant weather yet, but no news.

Friday, January 29. Pleasant. No news.

Sunday, January 31. Well this month has gone and yet we are not released from our prison. I hope our captivity may result in good yet it seems hard to be so long a prisoner.

Saturday, February 6. One day during the week one of our men was carried out dead or supposed to be and as they put him into the box he moved but was simply taken out & laid on a board with a piece of tent over him and left to die.

Sunday, February 7. This being the first Sabbath of the month I will write a little although every day is about alike here for which reason I will only write once a week. We have about 9000 prisoners on the Island and many are without tents and *suffer*, suffer SUFFER.

Saturday, February 13. Nothing of interest has passed during the past week except the recognizing of Genrl. Butler as Commissioner. We hope some terms of exchange will be arrived at soon.

Sunday, February 14. Still another week commenced and we are yet confined on the Island. I am blessed with good health and try to keep up good spirits yet it is very hard sometimes. I live in the hope of getting away before the hot weather commences.

This unidentified member of the **Fifth Michigan Cavalry** displays his Spencer repeating rifle, a weapon that gave the regiment unmatched firepower on the battlefield.

Saturday, February 20. One more week has gone and I have been blessed with good health with the exception of one fit of the ague. There have several hundred been taken away from the Island and we suppose they go to our lines.

Sunday, February 21. Another week is begun but the prospect is that we will soon be away from the Island as several squads go every day.

Saturday, February 27. One more week has gone and we are yet a prisoner. I received a letter from Geo. and also answered it. He started a Box for me the 25th of Jan. I wrote a note to Lieut. Barse about it. Thank God my health is good yet.

Sunday, February 28. Well another week has commenced and still no news of a parole or Exchange. It looks very dark yet as it is always the darkest just before day. I will continue to hope for the best and pray God to guard us against all evil.

MARCH

Saturday, March 5. We expected to be sent away this week but did not come it. [William B.] Finch, [Charles J.] Schultz, [Frederick] Harris & A. Simmons went.

Sunday, March 6. One more week has commenced and although a few have been paroled they are sending the most of the men to G[eorgi]a.

Saturday, March 12. Last Monday we, Beckwith & I, left the I[slan]d and was taken with a lot of others over to the city. Wednesday we left for Georgia on the 4 o'clock train. We remained at Charlotte all night Saturday.

Sunday, March 13. This morning we tho't we had gone as far South as we cared about and so about 11 o'clock jumped out of the car and took a little walk of about five miles nearly west where we put up till evening. We have one cracker and a small piece of meat.

Monday, March 14. Last night we traveled about 12 miles. Stop[p]ed at a Nigger Cabin & got our supper and three days rations for which we gave ten dollars Confed. & a little tin pail. Went West.

Tuesday, March 15. Last night we traveled about 14 miles. Just at dusk we went up to a large house and got our supper, but they mistrusted us and we were very glad to get away. The old Gent had gone off and not got back or I guess we would have got in a trap. As it was we had to tell some big lies.

Wednesday, March 16. Last night we got a good supper of some Darkies and then traveled 16 miles N[orth] W[est] and camped in the woods.

Thursday, March 17. Last night we took supper at a widow's house—had fried pork, eggs, peaches, corn-cake molasses, coffee & greens. We then went North west passing through the village of Shelbyville and traveled 20 miles when we again put up in the woods for the day. We did not stop once to rest.

Friday, March 18. Last evening we got some corn bread and milk, butter & an egg a piece at a young man's house who had been a soldier—17 months. Of course, we told him some pretty big stories after which we went on our journey and got about 20 miles nearer the end. Just at day break where we camped on a mountain. We did not stop once to rest. Traveled N.W.

Saturday, March 19. Last night we traveled about 18 miles in a westerly direction passing through a little villaige. We had supper at a Widow's house who had three sons in the army. The man who worked her place lived with her. We got a good deal of information from him.

Sunday, March 20. Last night we had supper with a secesh family who had two sons in the army. After which we went about 22 miles passing through Howard's Gap. We camped about 16 miles from Ash[e]-ville. There were two men where we got supper. We traveled about N. W .

Monday, March 21. Last night we had supper at a house where there were no men but the ladies [sic] husband was in the army. We then went about 22 miles passing through the village of Ash[e]ville, and left the main road about five miles from the villiage. Went N W nearly all night.

Tuesday, March 22. Last night we got our supper with a man who belonged to the militia of Bunkman Co.

[Buncombe County, North Carolina]. We then went about 13 miles and it snowed so we were obliged to stop. We went to a house and staid nearly all day and got our dinner. The man of the house was a runaway from the C[onfederate] S[tates of] A[merica]. He was not at home.

Wednesday, March 23. Last night we went about 6 miles and stayed in a mill all night. In the morning we went to a house and went to bed and stayed till moust [sic] sun down. Had breakfast & dinner. Snow about 8 in. deep & very little travel.

Thursday, March 24. Last night we went about 4 miles and was captured by a Lieut. Cook where we staid all night and the next day. We were very well treated.

Friday, March 25. Last night we were taken back about one mile and guarded all night by 4 boys at a ladies house. We were treated first rate. In the morning we were started toward Ash[e]ville with 2 men, one without any arms and the other with an old musket. We went about 5 miles & then ran down a steep place in the mountain and got away.

Saturday, March 26. Last night we were recaptured and taken down to the Sandy Mush and kept all night at a Mr. Reeves. This morning we started for Ash[e]ville & arrived there in the P.M. all right. We were taken to an old Colledge [sic] about 2 miles from the town and kept. We were put in with one man said to be a deserter from Indiana. We were treated very kindly.

Sunday, March 27. Well we are prisoners this beautiful Sabbath after having our liberty very nearly 2 weeks. I believe all will turn out for the best, yet it does seem very hard to be kept so long. We hear that they are exchanging prisoners again and we may not be detained very long. We cook our own rations.

Monday, March 28. Were in the old Colledge all day. Nothing of any importance transpired.

Tuesday, March 29. All quiet. We are in prison yet and likely to be there for some time to come.

Wednesday, March 30. All quiet and the same old story.

Thursday, March 31. Last night a fellow who claimed to be from Indiana tried to run away from the Guards and was killed instantly.

APRIL

Friday, April 1. This is the first of the new month and we are yet prisoners with a not very promising prospect of a release. Yet they tell us it is certain there is being a general exchange of prisoners. We are to start for Camp Vance on Monday I expect.

Saturday, April 2. Another week has gone and we are yet in the hands of our enemies. We are guarded with the conscripts who would all be glad to see our armies gain every battle and force the South to live under the old constitution, which, they say, is good enough.

Sunday, April 3. Sunday again finds us prisoners and will soon be sent back to Richmond, there to suffer or else to be exchanged. Are treated very well by both Officers and men while at Ash[e]ville.

Monday, April 4. It was too stormy to go to Camp Vance to day besides last night the Guards were all taken away except just enough to guard the prisoners. (Conscripts).

Tuesday, April 5. The men came back to-day and we are to go away to-morrow. It has been a cold and disagreeable day.

Wednesday, April 6. This morning we left the old Colledge near Ash[e]ville and marched about 25 miles and the men are very much used up.

Thursday, April 7. This day we marched about 20 miles and camped for the night. All pretty sore and lame.

Friday, April 8. This day we marched 18 miles and arrived at Camp Vance near Morganton about 2 o'clock and there we met two Captains, one from Maine & one from Ohio. They had escaped from Salsberry [Salisbury, a Southern prison camp] and got recaptured.

Saturday, April 9. Remained all day at Camp Vance. Nothing new.

Sunday, April 10. Still at Camp Vance. Capt. Reed is a lively fellow and pretty talkative. Capt. Litchfield is a pleasant fellow and we all keep up good spirits.

Monday, April 11. This day has passed off very quietly.

Tuesday, April 12. This day we started about noon for Salsbury and arrived about 5 o'clock. We found pretty good quarters at least—a great deal better than any other place we have found.

Wednesday, April 13. I beg[g]ed an envelope and wrote a letter to George. Called to see the Officers and found them all a fine cleaver [sic] lot of men and of good educations.

Thursday, April 14. All has passed off very quietly to-day. Capt. Chase has gone to Richmond and expects to be exchanged. The prospect is good for a speedy deliverance from bondage.

Friday, April 15. Every day being so very much alike it is of little use to write.

Saturday, April 16. All quiet. It seems as if the prospect of being exchanged is no better than it was a month or so ago. Some have gone of course, yet so few go at a time it amounts to very little.

Sunday, April 17. Another Sabbath and I am in prison at Salisbury and likely to remain there for some time to come. I trust that the time is not so very far off as it now seems.

Monday, April 18. Nothing new to-day. The all-absorbing topic is, when will we be exchanged?

Tuesday, April 19. Everything is quiet and nothing new to talk or write about.

Wednesday, April 20. To-day we have the news that City Point will cease to be a Neutral point after the 25th of this month.

Saturday, April 23. This week has gone & the prospect is about the same for an exchange.

Sunday, April 24. To-day is the holy Sabbath, yet by the actions of the prisoners a person would not mistrust its being the day it is. I still have hopes of an exchange in a month or two but a great many have given it up.

Saturday, April 30. The week and also the month is gone with this day but no news of any consequence have we received.

MAY

Sunday, May 1. This Sabbath morning was ushered in by a hard rain storm. We have hopes that this month will see us safe in our own lines.

Saturday, May 7. This week has passed very quickly considering all things. We receive various news from Richmond about the fighting between Grant's and Lee's Armys but nothing discourageing. I busy myself by studying a latin Grammar.

Sunday, May 8. This week will be one of great anziety [sic] in regard to the fighting to be done.

Friday, May 13. Had news that Longstreet was wounded.

Saturday, May 14. This week has passed off as usual, except that Friday Capt. Alexander took command of the prison and we were called out twice to muster. In the P.M. we were forced to witness the whipping of two deserters and then threatened with the same if we were not very careful. One of the men got 25 & the other 51 blows. We have good news from Grant.

Sunday, May 15. Well one more week has commenced and we are prisoners with very little prospect of getting away very soon. Last night an officer was bro't here who tried to make his way to Tenn. but only got about 25 miles. He jumped from the cars. News that Stewart [Stuart] was killed.

Saturday, May 21. During the past week we have very meager news from the Armies, yet so *far* all looks very favorable for our cause. It seems that Sherman has been successful in the north of Georgia. The body of [Brigadier] Genl. [James B.] Gordon was brought to this villiage today.

Sunday, May 22. This day passed till about 4 o'clock before I knew it was the Sabbath. I played two games of chess which I would not have done had I known or tho't of the day. I went down into the yard and heard a very good sermon by a Pres[byteri]an Minister. The text "Come unto me all ye that labor & are heavy laden & I will give you rest." This was the first tim[e] I have heard a sermon for about 14 months. I hope we will have the opportunity often.

Friday, May 27. This P.M. we left Salisbury enroute once more for Americus, Ga. The ladies on [sic] Concord having prepared some "snacks" for their wounded, and as there were none on the train they gave to our men & we gave then 3 cheers. About 8 o'clock I jumped out of the car window followed by [William C.] Beckwith & [George A.] Hudson. We traveled all night and went about 15 miles, calculated to have made about 10 miles on our right course for Tenn. This Sat. maorning [sic] finds us within about 40 rods of the Atlantic, Tenn. & Ohio R. R.

Saturday, May 28. This day we tried to sleep but the mosquitos troubled us so we slept but little. In the P.M. we went about 3 miles west when it commenced to rain hard and we staid all night in an old house. We had a good sleep except Beckwith who was sick. We had the opportunity, and of course improved, to take a leaf out of an Atlas containing N[orth] C[arolina] G[eorgi]A & Tenn.

Sunday, May 29. To day we have kept going pretty nearly all the time but sticking closely to the woods. Hudson went to two houses & got a good supply of bread, the people having all gone to Church. Just at dark we crossed the Catawba River in a Canoe. We traveled in all, *I should think*, thirty miles nearly west. During the night we got a good bunch of onions. We have been highly favored thus far.

Monday, May 30. We traveled but little to-day thinking it unsafe to do so. After dark we went on our journey but made little headway, only going to within about one mile of Lincolnton. Beckwith got separated from us near some iron works and we spent a long time in getting together again. We went about 14 miles.

Tuesday, May 31. We all went to a house & got a good supper just before dark. We had quite a good deal of difficulty in keeping roads running the right way, yet we traveled till day-light and went about 20 miles on nearly the right direction. The lady at whose house we

had supper charged us nothing except to be good soldiers and of course we promised to be.

JUNE

Wednesday, June 1. This day we traveled but little. We got our supper at a poor man's house and then went to the Rutherford road which we got on about 9 o'clock, and traveled till nearly daybreak going about 15 miles.

Thursday, June 2. This day we kept the woods till nearly dark when we went to a free Bl[ac]kman's house and got our supper. We told him who we were and he treated us very kindly but being a poor man could not give us anything to take along. We went only about 9 miles it being very dark, and somewhat rainy.

Friday, June 3. It rained nearly all day and we stayed in an old house till nearly night, when Hudson went up to a house and got us some supper. As soon as it was dark we were on our road to-ward Rutherford, which place we passed all right. It rained nearly all night and we were wet through. Traveled 18 miles.

Saturday, June 4. To day we have remained in the woods till about 3 o'clock when we went to a house and got our supper. We then went to a Widow Geeze [Guise or Geese?] house and told her who we were and remained all night as it still kept raining.

Sunday, June 5. To-day we traveled 4 miles in the right direction & got on the Hickory Nut road. We got supper about 10 o'clock at Widow Whitesides. She got up and gave us a very good supper, she is a Union Lady but has a son in the C.S.A. We traveled over 20 miles in all before morning in the right course.

Monday, June 6. This day we remained in the woods near C. L. Harris a member of the Legislature. At evening we went to him and told him who we were and he gave us some bread and said they were to picket the road for us that night and we better get on as fast as possible. He is a Union man but has to keep quiet. We came 17 miles—six miles from Ash[e]ville.

Tuesday, June 7. We remained in the woods pretty close to a house till just at dark when we went there and got our supper and quite a good supply of bread and meat. We found the lady to be Union all over. There was a young man who had been in the service two years but he was Union too. We flanked Ash[e]ville and as the bridge near town was guarded we had to go five miles below to another. We crossed just at day light and were seen by a Wench and a man but could not see whether he was white or black.

Wednesday, June 8. We took supper at a Militia man's house and he was a rabid secesh but we pulled the wool over his eyes pretty easily. We only traveled about 13 miles on account of losing the road. We flanked Leceister on the right.

Thursday, June 9. To day we got on the right road again and as soon as it was dark started on our journey. We traveled hard in the rain till just before day break when we stop[p]ed at Capt C[oo]k's and warmed and got some breakfast when we took to the woods.

Friday, June 10. To day we remained all day in the woods near Lieut. Cook's and about 6 o'clock his boy piloted us over the mountain to Mr. Sexton's where we stayed all night. He treated us very well.

Saturday, June 11. This morning we left Mr. Sexton's bright and early and went on our journey traveling only about 13 miles. We got our supper at Mr. A. Jones' on the bank of the French Broad. We went about five miles in the evening and slept beside the road. We found plenty of Union people along the road to day. We felt like free men.

Sunday, June 12. Had breakfast with a good Union man by the name of John Maloy and he kept us in his woods all day and bro't us our dinner. At night we crossed the river about 2 miles above Newport and got a Secesh canoe and went down the river. We ran over a mill dam and upset. Floated down the river all night and got our breakfast with a Mr. Davis.

Monday, June 13. We paddled our canoe down the river till about 10 o'clock when we stop[p]ed at a Mr. Elliott's and got our dinner and slept a couple of hours. We were treated *very* kindly indeed. Mrs. Elliott gave us each a pair of socks. We gave our canoe to Mr. E. and borrowed an old one from him & left at Dandridge.

Tuesday, June 14. We arrived at Strawberry Plains about 11 o'clock this A.M. We met with the most friendly reception by the 10th Mich. Cav. I then met with Brother Lyman I could not express the joy of that meeting had I the eloquence of a Demosthenes or Cicero. I never *was so happy* to see any individual before. Separated from my friend and companion *Beckwith*, for whom I entertain the hi[gh]est regard and the love of a brother.

● ● ● ● ●

On June 15, 1864, Edwin Bigelow was sent north to a military hospital where he recuperated from malnutrition and other prison ailments. He was honorably discharged on August 9, 1864, but that did not end his participation in the war. On October 20, 1864, he was commissioned as a captain in the First U.S. Colored Artillery and later served as inspector general for the First Brigade, Department of the Tennessee. He mustered out of service on March 31, 1866, and later moved to Jackson where he ran a successful drugstore.

Uneasy Neighbors

By Martin J. Havran

The Civil War created stresses on the international border separating Michigan and Canada. However, with a few isolated exceptions, Americans and Canadians lived and worked harmoniously during the early 1860s.

Canadian-American relations during the Civil War has been the subject of numerous research projects, but local aspects of the problem have been largely ignored. Thus, in studying the activities of Confederate agents in Canada, the presence of Jacob Thompson in Niagara or Clement C. Clay in Montreal is mentioned, but their activities in local Canadian communities have received little attention because of two pertinent factors: the study is chronologically too broad to warrant attention and local incidents are immaterial to the general overall scene. Nevertheless, the local community remains in most cases the sounding board and foundation for the national policy, and it is here that the former becomes meaningful.

The relations between Windsor and Detroit between 1861 and 1865 were typical of the many border communities where Canadians and Americans lived sometimes peacefully but oftentimes with considerable animosity. Here, a small Canadian community, bound by the strict neutrality proclamation of Great Britain lay just across the river from Detroit, a vital part of the Union, which was at war with the seceded Southern states, termed the Confederate States of America. That there would be conflict under these circumstances seemed certain. It is the purpose of this study to examine some aspects of this relation. The incidents recounted had no great influence upon the national scene and only temporarily affected the thinking in the Windsor-Detroit area. The more important issues of the day, such as the Underground Railroad, the slavery controversy and reciprocal trade or annexation, have been omitted from this discussion; and the residence and activities of Clement L. Vallandigham in Windsor, desertions from the Union army to Canada West and attempts by both the Confederate and Union governments to enlist Canadians have been emphasized.

In order to understand the atmosphere of friendship that prevailed between the United States and Canada at the time of the opening of the Civil War, an examination of precedents is necessary. To be sure, there developed as early as 1842, following the Webster-Ashburton treaty, a tradition of arbitration that developed into a permanent *modus vivendi* yet strong in 1860. Canadians generally had come to believe that with a degree of self-government and commercial *laissez faire* they could develop into a nation free from both the dominance of Great Britain and the designs of American jingoists, who had been pressing for the annexation of their lucrative, undeveloped northern neighbor. The break from Great Britain in commercial affairs had come only with the abrogation of the Navigation Acts, while the movement for the annexation of British North America became meaningless with the signing of the Reciprocity Treaty of June 5, 1854. Since the Navigation Acts did not allow British North America to trade with the United States, the interests of Canada turned to annexation. Numerous attempts to bring about annexation failed since, although many favored the movement, the great majority of both Americans and Canadians remained opposed to it. By 1857 the operation of the Reciprocity Treaty had brought Canadians commercial prosperity. Their political endeavors had turned to confederation and with the strengthening of feeling within British North America the Canadians developed a national self-interest that eventually conflicted with both the United States and the Confederate States of America during the Civil War. With these considerations in mind, then, the question of conflicts and opinions in Windsor and Detroit may be examined.

Attempts by members of the Union and Confederate armies to recruit soldiers in Essex and Kent Counties proved a serious point of conflict. In this regard, two considerations must be kept in mind. First, attempts to recruit in any portion of British North

America was a violation of the neutrality of that dominion as laid down in the proclamation of neutrality by Queen Victoria on May 13, 1861. Second, and more precisely, recruiting involved a violation of the Foreign Enlistment Act of 1818, which carried with it a penalty that could be imposed on anyone who undertook the enlistment of British subjects for foreign service. This act, which also applied to her dominions, specifically prohibited, in the event of British neutrality, "the enlistment by a British subject in the military or naval service of either belligerent."

Detroit newspapers recorded several attempts by Americans to enlist Windsorites. The editor of the *Detroit Advertiser and Tribune* wrote that the extraordinary bounties offered by the United States government for army recruits had the effect of inducing numerous desertions from the British regulars stationed at Windsor. This tendency by Canadians, indirectly influenced by the Union army, became so pronounced in Windsor that the Canadian government stationed a squad of soldiers, the "Lookout Party," at Windsor to prevent desertions from their ranks. An estimate made by a local army official placed the number of enlistees at sixteen out of a total of twenty deserters. Edmund Newman was arrested at Windsor while trying to cross the river and was confined to the jail at Sandwich, pending trial.

Several cases of direct attempts to canvass troops in Windsor were made. In one instance the *Detroit Advertiser and Tribune* noted that during the two or three weeks prior to July 1864, several Confederate agents had visited Windsor and had succeeded in obtaining fifty or sixty recruits. It was noted rather vehemently that the majority of them were "truant rebels, who have escaped from union prisons." Again, Thomas Brown, a black man, was apprehended and placed on two hundred-dollar bail in Windsor for attempting to entice John Cash and Peter Clark to enlist in the First Michigan Colored Regiment. The editor of the Chatham *Planet* protested loudly when, on a visit to Detroit, he was approached by a recruiting agent who attempted to bribe him into enlisting. The Canadian writer remarked that there were numerous American recruiting officers in Canada West looking for men to fill Union muster rolls. Here were recorded three instances of American violations of the Foreign Enlistment Act. When it is remembered that all the activity was carried on surreptitiously, one can well imagine how many more actual attempts in enlisting occurred. Unfortunately, there remains no way to determine the actual number of

Canadians who accepted the bribes and bounties of enlisting agents. No records are extant for the number of Canadian-border inhabitants who joined. Professor Fred Landon, who has done considerable research upon Western Ontario's relations with the American Midwest, writes that of all the families of Western Ontario interviewed by him, almost everyone counted a member who had served either in the Union or Confederate armies. Dr. Marcus L. Hansen, citing a standard authority on the numbers of Canadians in the Federal armies, lists 53,532 as being born in the British-American provinces. This, of course, takes into account those Canadians who were residents in the United States at the beginning of the Civil War.

The Canadian authorities declared alarm at the enlisting agents' activity in British North America. In a dispatch, Lord Lyons, British minister to the United States, informed Sir Edmund Head of attempts by Americans to recruit in Canada for the U.S. Army and informed Head that he had notified the American government of this activity. The U.S. War Department, replied Secretary of War Simon Cameron, had not given authority to any officer of the government or any other person to raise recruits for military service in Canada. Thus, in effect, the secretary of war repudiated the activities of recruiting agents in Windsor or anywhere else in British North America.

The great number of desertions from the U.S. Army proved more pregnant in stirring up animosity between residents of Windsor and Detroit than did the recruiting problem. The mighty United States, speculated Detroiters, need not pay heed to the exhortations of Canadian officials interested in curbing violations of Canadian neutrality. In this instance the process was reversed, with the American authorities criticizing and even denouncing Canadians for their failure to stop deserters from entering and for allowing them to remain without taking action. The shoe was on the other foot, a painful foot, to be sure.

Before the passage of the severe and direct Conscription Act of March 1863 the number of desertions from the Union armies into Western Ontario was not extraordinary, but with the enactment of this law, desertions increased alarmingly. At first the presence of deserters in Windsor caused little concern among Detroiters. But when deserters spread out by 1864 to all parts of Western Ontario, attention was aroused. The number of these men there became so numerous that local workers found difficulty in obtaining work on the farms because "farmers could obtain all the helpers

Ohioan Clement Vallandingham (center), a hardened Southern sympathizer, lost his seat in Congress and was forced by the United States govern-ment to leave the country in 1863. He settled in Windsor, Ontario, where he continued correspondence with the Confederacy and aided rebel agents.

they wanted by promising nothing but shelter and board." Moreover, Detroiters, as well as most Northerners, came to believe that the Canadians were decidedly pro-Confederate. Detroiters could watch with anxious eyes the activities of Confederate agents and sympathizers comfortably ensconced just across the river at Windsor. To them, Windsorites became Confederate sympathizers if they would allow Clement L. Vallandigham to live unmolested for several months among them.

Mrs. John (Amelia) Harris, a resident of London, noted in her diary under date of August 6, 1862, that the daily arrival of American deserters in that town was so great that "the stationmaster has been requested to send as many empty cars as he can to Windsor to bring the Americans and their families who are escaping from conscription. They are seeking a home in Canada until the war is over."

On August 6 alone over 100 Americans reached London. In yet another case quite a number of black troops of Barnes' Regiment deserted to Windsor shortly after they enrolled. The editor of the *Detroit Free Press* showed great consternation when he wrote that the war was being conducted partly for the elevation of the "blackman" to a position of social equality with his white brethren and that the desertions showed the basest ingratitude. The same paper, during 1863, mentioned several instances of desertion and draft evasion. The editor noted on February 20 that 1,942 "skedaddlers from the draft" escaped into Canada, while on March 5 there appeared a notice that "there is a hegira of people to Canada to avoid the draft." Again on June 13 it was recorded that one Sergeant John Morey, a deserter from the Sharpshooters who was on trial before a court-martial, had escaped to Windsor. Animosity increased when the editor noted on December 1 that a man named MacAllister crossed the river at Windsor, enlisted in Detroit, collected his bounty and resumed to Hamilton.

The *Detroit Advertiser and Tribune* found articles concerning desertion a fine means of increasing circulation, especially if they followed the pattern of that concerning John Dronian. Two women, apparently enamored of this recruit, yet unaware of the criminality of their offense, concealed him in their home, furnished him with women's apparel and conveyed him to Windsor in a small boat. After having stayed in Windsor for a few days, Dronian decided to visit his benefactors and was captured while hiding under their bed in the young ladies' home. Later, the same journal reported that on a Saturday evening a recruit, who had received his full bounty for enlisting, was captured while in a boat on the Detroit River on his way to Windsor. Also captured was a member of the black regiment waiting to be ferried across. The editor frowned upon the few men who had built up an extensive trade in transporting deserters across the river.

It has been noted earlier that the residents of Detroit felt considerable animosity against Windsor's authorities for their lack of action in apprehending deserters. In fact, the *Detroit Advertiser and Tribune* considered many of the inhabitants of Windsor "a collection of renegades and cutthroats." A later article deplored the flagrancy of Windsor's authorities in not seizing deserters who made a regular practice of congregating upon the ferry dock to insult commuters. "Several young ladies," wrote the editor, "have been subject to the taunts of these miserable curs." The *Detroit Advertiser and Tribune* assailed Windsorites for allowing bounty-jumpers and deserters to "go and come at pleasure." To all appearances no one molested them. Each day, the writer noted, six or seven crossed the river to swindle the American government by accepting bounties and deserting. Nor did authorities at Windsor

stop attempts by Americans to capture these persons. In one instance, United States detectives succeeded in entrapping two men in Windsor who had been extensively engaged in aiding desertions. If these accounts be true, then the streets of Windsor did swarm "with these temporary and in many cases undesirable residents."

Contrary to whatever editors thought about the negligence of Windsor law enforcement, the Canadians had set up the machinery both for preventing recruiting in British North America and for curtailing the activities of undesirable persons. Late in the war Denis Donohoe, a Canadian official, informed Lord Lyons, who had apparently been plagued with pleas to curtail the harboring of these men, that the Canadian Frontier Police had been duly vigilant in trying to stop the activities of agents who made a business of supplying substitutes for conscriptees. Even though it was difficult to bring about a conviction in many instances, the imprisonment of some, Donohoe remarked, served to deter others from attempting the same activities. On the local scene Windsor did show a willingness to cooperate when the law clearly showed need of enforcement. Sheriff John McEwan of Essex County was not negligent in duty. Warner, a Cleveland counterfeiter, had escaped to Windsor. While there he was captured and placed under arrest on the complaint of the U.S. marshal from Cleveland. Since the Webster-Ashburton treaty included an extradition clause, a formal request was made for Warner's surrender to the Cleveland authorities. He was subsequently delivered. Had not this been a clear case of Canadian cooperation? Had the Detroit officials exercised their right of extradition there is all the reason to believe that Windsor would have complied with their pleas. But, it must be remembered, most of the bounty jumpers, deserters and even Confederate agents in Windsor had committed no crime. As long as they did not violate Canada's neutrality, break its laws or disturb the peace, they were entitled to asylum. Obviously, however, Detroiters, as part of the Union engaged in a war, did not think in terms of law but rather in terms of emotion. Often inactivity, even though it was justifiable, proved more harmful to public opinion than did action.

Minor conflicts developed from national pride and served to arouse enmity. In one instance a number of British soldiers, en route to Fort Malden, Amherstburg, attempted to forcibly haul down the American flag on the steamer *Heather Bell*, docked at Windsor. When Sergeants Kelly and Brown ordered some of their troops to remove the flag, American passengers on board sprang to defend it. A fight was expected but cooler heads prevailed. The editor of the *Detroit Advertiser and Tribune* deplored the rowdy incident since he could find no reason for the attempted insult. Americans, he said, felt proud to see foreigners on their soil and to extend the homage due to strangers. Although he believed that the better portion of the Canadian people disapproved of this insult, he declared that it did little to cement good feeling. A similar incident took place in Sarnia on August 26, 1863. When the American consul in that town raised the Stars and Stripes over his office, the Canadian residents grew excited. Crowds gathered, swearing that the flag must come down. Several times over several hours new flags were raised when one after another was stolen. Possibly this feeling against the American, as symbolized in the flag, stemmed from the policy of the Huron *Signal*. How could Canadians of that area favor the Union when this journal advocated a Southern policy? It frankly announced its sympathy with the South and felt that Southerners were valiantly fighting for their freedom. If the American flag had been raised in a similar incident in Port Huron, perhaps its residents, too, would have lowered it.

One Britain, whose home was in Windsor, phrased the feeling of animosity between Canadians and Americans aptly when he ascribed it to constant haranguing by both newspapermen and readers of the Windsor-Detroit area. The editor of the *Tribune* took another view. He blamed Canadians for the prevalence of ill will in the community. Canadians, he believed, would have liked to see the ruin of the United States' commercial, industrial and financial interests. Only a fanatical patriot could have espoused such wild cause for criticism.

Of tremendous importance to the rising emotional strain between Canadians and Americans were the activities of commissioned Confederate agents. This, thought Americans, showed the real tenor of Canada's feeling against the Union. To be sure, this was an erroneous assumption since it has already been shown on a local level that Canada met its responsibilities whenever the law demanded it. In analyzing the problem it should be remembered that the activities of these agents were conducted secretly and that therefore in most cases the Canadian government was unaware of them. Confederate agents operated in Windsor, as well as in London, Niagara and Toronto. In fact, Windsor, proximate to the Midwest, was one of the closest Canadian communities to the centrally located Confederate state of Tennessee. Moreover, Windsor proved to be a welcome haven for the numerous "doughfaces" that left states like Ohio and Illinois because of conflict with Union authorities.

The commission of Jacob Thompson, former secretary of the interior in President Buchanan's cabinet, was typical of those who came to Canadian soil. Having professed a special trust in the zeal, discretion and patriotism of Thompson, President Jefferson Davis directed him to proceed to Canada, where he would conduct himself in a manner conducive to the furtherance of the interests of the Confederate States of America. The Canadian provost marshal general, Colonel Hill, reported to the Union government that he had received disclosures from several sources that a rebel agent had just arrived at Windsor with certificates of specie, deposited in places in the rebel states, amounting to over one hundred thousand dollars. Hill noted that these certificates bore the signature of Christopher G. Memminger, were drawn in favor of one Henry Marvin and would be readily negotiated at Windsor.

As early as November 1863, the Windsor-Detroit area became alarmed over rumors of a rebel plot that was to originate at Windsor. A dispatch by Secretary of War Stanton to the mayor of Detroit, William C. Duncan, served as the basis for the anxiety. Stanton communicated that he had been officially notified by the governor general of Canada that there was a plot afoot to invade the United States, destroy the city of Buffalo, take possession of some of the steamboats on Lake Erie and with them surprise Johnson's Island (off Sandusky Bay) and liberate the Confederate prisoners of war confined there. The editor of the *Detroit Free Press* in a feature article wrote that he had learned from persons who had visited Windsor the day before that Southern refugees there frankly confessed their plan to be very similar to that reported by the dispatch, and that it was to have been carried out on the following Sunday. In this instance Detroiters found assurance in Windsor's sincerity. The same editor informed his readers that the Windsor authorities would use every means to prevent a breach of neutrality. A strong patrol was stationed at Windsor and three miles downstream at Sandwich, which included artillery that was put on the riverbank to repel any possible naval attack.

Perhaps the most memorable affair involving Confederate agents in the Windsor-Detroit area was the *Philo Parsons* incident. This event has been thoroughly investigated elsewhere and all that needs to be done here is to relate its reaction in this area. In effect, it was an identical plan to that which had been discovered in

November 1863. The statement of the pilot, Michael Campbell, may be taken as reasonably accurate. On a Monday morning the *Parsons* was moored at the dock of the Detroit firm of Trowbridge, Wilcox and Company, where it took on two passengers. Four or five additional men boarded at Sandwich and at Amherstburg about twelve others boarded, making the total about eighteen. When the steamer was well out into Lake Erie, the passengers seized control of the vessel. While the *Parsons* was taking on wood another little lake steamer, the *Island Queen*, came alongside, was boarded, the passengers and crew driven off and scuttled in the lake. The ultimate object of the raid on the *Parsons* was to launch an attack upon the USS *Michigan*. The men under Bennett G. Burleigh, the Confederate agent in command, refused to attack but returned to the Detroit

River, where they put into shore at Sandwich Point.

On learning that Burleigh's men had disembarked at Sandwich, American authorities journeyed to Windsor on Wednesday, September 21, to arrest them. Unfortunately, all but three had left Windsor early that day, but that trio remained all day without being captured. During the night they left for Belle River, a community about twenty miles up from Windsor on Lake St. Clair. As usual, the Detroit newspapers harangued their neighbors for allowing these men to escape. The editor of the *Detroit Advertiser and Tribune* remarked that it was generally understood, if not certain, that the Canadians connived at their escape and warned them that their stay in Windsor would be dangerous. Although his loving neighbors, the Canadians, entertained strong prejudices against Americans, he wrote, there was no rea-

Detroit's City Hall, shown here in 1862, was a prime location for army recruiting agents, political speeches and patriotic rallies during the Civil War. The building also housed Federal officials who kept a cautious eye on Detroit's Canadian neighbors.

son for their aid to "every brow-branded scoundrel and vagabond who can unite himself to them by the bond of common hatred" of the United States. Moreover, he continued, if Canadians in Windsor were animated by one spark of generous honor and common decency, they would feel the gross insult they had made to Americans.

The documents concerning Canadian authorities and the activities of Confederate agents in Canada show conclusively that the Canadians realized that there had been movements in and around Windsor that warranted watching. Lord Lyons communicated to Viscount Monck that he had received word from Secretary of State Seward advising caution over the centralization of Confederates at Windsor. Obviously, the authorities at Windsor had no way of determining the exact time or even the persons who would engage in raiding the United States. It can be well imagined how confused the situation had become in Windsor with enlisting agents, deserters, additional British troops, Confederate agents and residents intermingled in the small community. Furthermore, no proof for arrest could possibly have been gained against Confederates as their activities were closely guarded secrets.

With the perpetration of the *Philo Parsons* affair, Canadian authorities both in the national administration at Toronto and in Windsor set up the necessary machinery to capture the rebels who were allegedly violating their asylum in Windsor. Instructions were forwarded to the local Canadian Officers of Justice to use every exertion under their power for the detection and arrest of persons concerned in the incident. Also, the solicitor-general for Canada West was authorized to render United States authorities any assistance they might request. In Windsor itself active measures were adopted for guarding the frontier against further attempts by Confederates to raid the United States. Gilbert McMichen of Windsor agreed to serve as a stipendiary magistrate for that part of Canada lying west of Toronto and Penetanguishene, and he had the power to appoint others to maintain the peace and neutrality in that area. Moreover, at a meeting of the Windsor town council, a resolution was adopted requesting Mayor Samuel S. Macdonnell to communicate with the Governor-general on the advisability of having a detachment of troops stationed there to prevent further raids. A small squad of men was sent and housed in Windsor's town hall. William Scott, magistrate in Essex County, and approximately forty others requested that the mayor call a town meeting so that action could be taken to ascertain the "best and proper means of

defence against the unlawful and unjust proceedings of parties said to be from the Confederate States." At the meeting, which took place on Tuesday afternoon, December 20, 1863, William Scott declared that under Canadian law, persons were entitled to asylum as long as they respected the law. He deplored those who fought for the Confederacy but did not wear a uniform, for no one could be a true soldier, he continued, unless he wore a uniform. Scott proposed resolutions calling for the establishment of a large police force and a bell to sound out an emergency. James Dougall, prominent Windsor merchant and public figure, proposed a resolution that all rebel raiders be treated as criminals rather than as belligerents, and these resolutions were adopted. After more than two and a half years of war, Detroiters finally approved of Windsor's precautionary measures.

In December 1864 the residents of Windsor and Detroit became alarmed over further alleged activities of rebels in Windsor. Major General Joseph Hooker informed Brigadier General Edward D. Townsend that he had learned from Detroit of the manufacture of "Greek Fire" by refugees and deserters from the Confederacy at Windsor. The new weapon was to be used in burning American frontier communities. Little could be found by this writer about "Greek Fire," other than its manufacture. What it was, or what its effect could have been, has not been learned. Since nothing came of this weird production, it can be discounted either as rumor or as abortive propaganda, but some activity produced a raid scare in Windsor about that time since military headquarters ordered two companies of regulars from London to Windsor. The Windsor town council was directed to prepare a reception for them. The editor of the *Tribune* analyzed the movement of troops as one calculated to aid in cementing the friendship between the two countries inasmuch as the presence of the troops tended to arrest activity by "desperate and abandoned characters."

The bulk of the difficulties already referred to, with the possible exception of the *Philo Parsons* incident, had no significant influence either in Canada or in the United States. However, the residence of Clement L. Vallandigham, alleged to be a rebel conspirator, in Windsor created more tension in the United States than his stay of August 24, 1863, to June 14, 1864, warranted. Vallandigham did not violate, with one possible exception, Canada's neutrality or directly aid the Confederate states in any material way while in Windsor. Moreover, the evidence seems to indicate that Vallandigham's asylum remained as peaceful and harmonious as would that of any other exile who was forced to escape from dangerous circumstances. It is well known that while in the United States, Vallandigham spoke bitter words against the Lincoln administration, but his reasons for attacking the Republican Party need not concern us here.

It will be recalled that after a bitter trial and sentence of close confinement, Vallandigham was banished to Confederate territory. Almost immediately he escaped to begin a tour up the St. Lawrence and Lakes Ontario and Erie. He selected Windsor, just across the river from Detroit, as an asylum because, as he says in his writings:

> It was easy of access and convenient for communication with Ohio and the Northwest; while the beautiful Detroit River and Lakes Erie and St.Clair, full of fish and fowl and the thick forests around abounding in game, could afford healthful exercise for the body and pleasure to the mind.

The *Detroit Advertiser and Tribune*'s editor found small satisfaction in Vallandigham's arrival. The paper spoke sarcastically of him as a "poor persecuted martyr" whose "arrival was delayed for several days in order to allow full time for preparations," albeit by a host of rebels. After a short speech of welcome by the host of Hirons House, Vallandigham responded with "sighs, tears and groans." The height of the editor's disfavor was shown by the printing of what he considered the order of procession accompanying the visitor:

1. A Porter's head
2. A pair of stout shoulders supporting a valise
3. A porter's coat tail
4. Vallandigham's cane, acting as honorary escort
5. Vallandigham's nose
6. Vallandigham
7. Vallandigham's coat tail
8. A pair of bushy whiskers
9. Owner of do-do
10. Coat tail, with white handkerchief, exposed, of owner of bushy whiskers
11. Dog—(loquiteur, "bow-wow"!)

The next day, approximately thirty-five prominent citizens of Detroit crossed the river to pay their respects to Vallandigham. Among the visitors were Cornelius O'Flynn, Alexander Frazer, acting mayor Francis B. Phelps, Francis X. Cicotte, William Dyson, Bernard O'Grady, Alderman Joseph Hoek and James McGonegal, John L. Chipman and Deputy Sheriffs Sparling, Ven and Wilkinson. Judge Cornelius O'Flynn

expressed the feelings of a considerable number of Detroit residents "who deprecate the tyranny which exiled [Vallandigham], . . . guilty of no offence and in violation of the constitution and the law." Clement Vallandigham's reply was important as it showed the integrity of the man and pointed to the policy he was to follow while in Canada. Claiming the fullest right at home to criticize and condemn the men and acts of the administration and intending at the proper time to again exercise this right, he refused to speak a bitter word while on foreign soil, thus, in effect, refusing to violate his asylum.

In a letter to a friend in November 1863, Vallandigham described his daily life. He declared that he was in Windsor as calm, determined and busy as he was in the United States. He spent his time reviewing history and political philosophy, making notes and memoranda of the times, writing letters and "ready for any fortune." He also wrote that he enjoyed riding, walking, fishing and hunting. If one may judge from the exile's own words, no stretch of the imagination could construe them to include materially aiding the Confederacy.

If there were numerous people who disliked Vallandigham's activities, there were few who could have questioned his fine character and integrity. Among the many who visited him at the Hirons House, perhaps the one who most appreciated and best described the man was a writer of the Cleveland *Plain Dealer*, a Democratic paper. After having listened to Vallandigham in conversation, the writer could not help but disagree with those who labeled him as traitor, rebel, secesher or copperhead. A half hour's visit left the reporter "richly repaid [by his] visit to the great exile."

Throughout Vallandigham's voluntary exile in Windsor, the *Detroit Advertiser and Tribune* continued its vindictive verbal assault while the *Detroit Free Press* assumed a more conservative position. On August 28, 1863, the *Advertiser and Tribune* called the exile an "exhibition" and a "snaix," and on April 7, 1864, a "miserable exile from his native soil." The *Detroit Free Press* declined to comment upon the minute activities of Vallandigham, but it assumed a realistic attitude about these activities. The man was for peace, as he himself said, and although the *Press* did not agree with his policy, it recognized his right of free speech. Throughout May and June the paper championed his cause since he had become, to many, a symbol of President Lincoln's "despotism."

Although there was no conclusive proof, nor is there now, of Vallandigham's involvement in overt conspiracies while at Windsor, several accusations were made against him. His name was falsely linked with the *Philo Parsons* incident of November 13, 1863. The *New York Times*, for example, printed an article that accused him of having "fully arranged" the plot to arm and equip rebel veterans, make Buffalo a heap of ashes and consume Detroit. Others rejoiced in "producing evidence" to show that Vallandigham aided and abetted deserters who fled into Windsor. In this instance, it was asserted that the exile, upon arriving at Windsor after a trip to Ohio, was heard in conversation with a refugee, a deserter from the Thirteenth Michigan Volunteers. Vallandigham, upon hearing that the deserter and his companion were about to return, advised them, it was alleged, not to go and promised them financial aid if they remained. The deserters later were assured by another of their group that everything was arranged, that Vallandigham would advance them money to pay their hotel bills and that he would even furnish them with funds to go to any part of Canada they wished to go. "In this way," the source reported, "two recruits were lost to the Federal service."

In another connection Vallandigham was accused of indirectly swindling money from the U.S. Army. It was reported that the exile often gave letters of credit and introduction to deserters in Windsor on parties resident in Cincinnati without their permission. These deserters would cross the river at Wyandotte, a few miles west of Detroit, proceed safely to Cincinnati, enlist, collect their bounties, desert and return to Windsor. It is impossible to ascertain absolutely whether Vallandigham was actually implicated in these activities. If they are true, then those who contend that he was physically involved

in Confederate conspiracy while in Windsor would have a strong case for his condemnation. It remains a matter of pure conjecture since the obviously biased policy of the *Detroit Advertiser and Tribune* could have concocted any number of spurious stories. As Professor Lester B. Shippee has so aptly noted, these writings were part of popular Northern opinion which "grossly maligned this gentleman, who at no time sought to aid the South or to wage war against the union."

It goes without saying that the relations between Windsor and Detroit from 1861 to 1865, herein discussed, involved no issues which produced even a threat of war between the United States and British North America. Earlier questions involving Great Britain, its Dominions and the United States had precipitated talk and even preparations for war, but by the time of the Civil War, there was no serious consideration of war between the two countries. Controversial issues such as desertion, recruiting and Confederate conspiracy engendered no substantial hostility in public opinion. Radical persons poured out vindicative phrases against Windsor's laxity in not enforcing what Detroiters thought Canadian law should contain. It is the contention of this writer that Canadian authorities remained correct in their interpretation. Clement L. Vallandigham's sojourn in Windsor received more attention than was warranted. It is probable that he was not physically implicated in anti-Union activity nor did he violate his asylum there. Had not emotion raised the harsh voices of a few radical Unionists, Windsor-Detroit relations during the Civil War would have been as normal and peaceful as would have any two communities in a similar state, one a belligerent, the other a neutral.

Return to Spotsylvania

By Bob Korroch

*Described as the best skirmish regiment in the Union army's Second Corps,
the Twenty-sixth Michigan saw its share of heated fighting during the
Battle of Spotsylvania. Lieutenant Leonard Hunt of Lowell,
who served with the Twenty-sixth, vividly recorded the events
in his diary. More than 130 years later, his great-great-grandson
retraced Hunt's steps on the now peaceful battlefield.*

Leonard Hunt's pocket-sized diary is bound in black leather with an envelope-like flap that neatly tucks under a narrow leather strap across the cover. On the flap, the phrase "DIARY 1864" is stamped in gold. Inside the front cover is written in pencil: "Leonard H. Hunt, 1st Lieut. 26th Mich Vols." On its pages twenty-three-year-old Lieutenant Hunt chronicled the Twenty-sixth Michigan's engagements during the 1864 Virginia campaign.

My grandmother left the diary to me when she passed away in 1984. Leonard Hunt was her grandfather and my great-great-grandfather. Although I did not fully appreciate the meaning of her gift at the time, I believe Grandma knew my love of history would eventually lead me to open the diary and explore its bounty.

From the diary, I learned that Leonard Hunt was involved in the Battle of Spotsylvania Court House, Virginia, on May 12, 1864. Eight years after receiving the diary, my own military career brought me to Virginia, where I could explore the Civil War battlefields and trace Leonard Hunt's steps.

The National Park Service operates the Fredericksburg and Spotsylvania National Military Park, which commemorates four major actions of the Civil War: Fredericksburg (December 1862), Chancellorsville (May 1863), the Wilderness (May 1864) and Spotsylvania. I started my visit at the Spotsylvania battlefield exhibit shelter. Murals on the walls depicted different aspects of the battle, but I wanted specific information about the Twenty-sixth Michigan.

"I'm looking for my great-great-grandfather," I stammered. "The Michigan Twenty-sixth. Where was he on May twelfth?" I asked my interpreter.

Apparently, she was used to being spoken to in excited fragments. She leafed through the worn books. As she focused her search, she paused to answer other visitors' questions about drinking fountains, fast-food restaurants and walking tours. Trying to hide my anxiety, I returned to the murals. I began studying a depiction of a battle at a place called the Bloody Angle. It showed an assault by Union troops on May 12.

"They were with either Burnside or Hancock," the interpreter said, answering my request. Early in my visit, I learned that when referring to troop movements, Civil War historians often speak of generals who led armies and corps—the two largest groupings of soldiers during the war.

"Hancock," she said after more leafing.

"Which corps?" I asked, wanting her to tell me of the soldiers.

"The Second."

"And, they were here on the twelfth?" I asked, pointing to the Bloody Angle mural.

"Yes," she said, "Hancock was there."

Enough of Hancock, I thought to myself. Where was Leonard Hunt? I thanked her and went to see where Leonard Hunt had been. I drove a short distance along a road to the Bloody Angle.

The winter of 1863-64 was an anxious time for the North's Army of the Potomac. The war against the South was entering its third year. The men of the Twenty-sixth Michigan spent the winter camped with the Army of the Potomac along the north bank of Virginia's Rapidan River, anxious to return to the towns, farms and families they had left behind.

During that time, Leonard Hunt focused on Lowell, Michigan. He wrote letters and hungered for replies in the mail. He sought newspapers from home and devoured every piece of information he received. He kept close track of other men who departed and returned from furlough in Michigan and asked them for news of home.

Leonard was commissioned a second lieutenant in August 1862 to fill a vacancy when the Twenty-sixth Michigan was formed in Jackson, Michigan. After leaving Jackson in December, the regiment was assigned to provost duty near Washington, DC. Its first contact with the enemy came during the seige of Suffolk, Virginia, in April 1863 . Later that year the Twenty-sixth was sent to New York City to help preserve order during the draft riots. In October 1863 the Michiganians returned to Virginia, where they became part of the Army of the Potomac's First Brigade, First Division, Second Corps.

One unusually bright and warm morning, Leonard heard the noise of a gathering crowd. Bare-chested with fists upright, Captain Nathan Church, the regimental adjutant, was in the center of a crowd, circling his worthy opponent, Captain Franklin Johnson. The men engaged in an exchange of blows that Leonard described as an "exhibition of skill in the way of boxing." Leonard found the display entertaining and ruled that "the Adjt appeared to have the best end."

Later that day, Leonard attended the funeral of a friend, Chad Dewey, who had become one of many victims of disease in the Union camp that winter. "Chad Dewey's body was carried to the Grave this afternoon funeral sermon was preached by the Chaplain of the 81st Penn." After the burial, Leonard wandered over to the adjutant's quarters and waited for the mail to arrive. The mail came, but there was none for him.

Leonard spent the last winter months in camp at musters, parades, officer's school and picket duty. He read voraciously, especially a number of popular novels that he borrowed or purchased from the sutler.

In April 1864 Leonard spent a fifteen-day furlough in Lowell. On his return to the Army of the Potomac, Leonard wrote in his journal that the army looked "as natural as ever." But the army was changing. General Ulysses S. Grant had been appointed commander in chief of all of the Union armies.

In the late evening of May third and early morning of the fourth, the Army of the Potomac crossed the Rapidan River, beginning a campaign that Grant soon declared as one he planned to conduct even "if it takes all summer."

Within a few hours, Leonard found himself entering the Chancellorsville battlefield, where one year earlier the Army of the Potomac had suffered a humiliating defeat. There, the soldiers of the Second Corps found a field strewn with human bones and the skeletons of horses. The Twenty-sixth camped on a part of the old battlefield. Leonard felt sick.

The restless night in the gloomy fields at Chancellorsville was Leonard Hunt's last bit of calm before the beginning of a thirty-nine-day campaign that pitted the Army of the Potomac against General Robert E. Lee's Army of Northern Virginia. One of the most dreadful encounters of the campaign happened at the Bloody Angle during the Battle of Spotsylvania.

As the Army of the Potomac advanced toward Spotsylvania, the Twenty-sixth, renowned in previous campaigns as the best skirmish regiment of the Second Corps, served as fingers serve a person without sight— touching and probing, extending and retracting, constantly assessing the lay of the land and the position of the enemy.

Early in the afternoon of May 5, the forces engaged in a fierce battle in the thick underbrush and bogs of the Wilderness. In two days of fighting, the Union army suffered over 17,500 casualties.

The Twenty-sixth was spared the horrors of the Wilderness, but found itself holding the Union army's left flank on the morning of May 7. At about 7:45 A.M. Leonard watched two companies from the Twenty-sixth's right deploy west and south as skirmishers to relocate the enemy. While the skirmishers worked their way toward the rebel line, the regiment watched in anticipation. Movement on a hilltop across from their position caught the regiment's attention. It was an enemy horse artillery piece. Like a band of big brothers, fearful that their skirmishers had wandered into danger, the remaining eight companies of the Twenty-sixth Michigan double-timed down a slope, across a railroad embankment and up the opposing hill in an attempt to capture the Confederate gun.

Concerned for the eager volunteers' safety, Colonel Nelson A. Miles, commander of the First Brigade, sent his aide-de-camp, First Lieutenant Robert S. Robertson, to bring the Michiganians back. Before they could be recalled, the Twenty-sixth engaged dismounted enemy cavalry, taking several prisoners and a dispatch from General Lee. Leonard counted some four or five men wounded.

On May 8 the Twenty-sixth marched south, extending the Union flank to Todd's Tavern. There, Leonard supervised Company I's hasty effort to construct breastworks and establish a defensible position. As the remaining three divisions of the Second Corps arrived at the tavern and took over the breastwork construction, the First Division broke to the west to test the enemy's position at Corbin's Bridge over the Po River.

The division formed in line of battle. Leonard fell in with the Twenty-sixth, taking a position in the front line in the march toward the unknown rebel position at the Po. As the Union force advanced, their skirmishers engaged rebel cavalry that took a few shots and then turned back toward the river. Suddenly, reinforcements joined the rebel cavalry. Firing commenced on both sides and in this brief exchange, Leonard was injured. In his diary he noted, "Got hit in the thigh with a shot bullet." Apparently the injury was only a flesh wound since Leonard remained with his company.

Around 6:00 P.M. the Union division fell back to the earthworks around Todd's Tavern. The rebel pursuers broke off after determining that they were approaching the entire Second Corps. Leonard was the Twenty-sixth's only reported casualty at the Battle of Todd's Tavern.

During the next three days, May 9-11, the Twenty-sixth stayed in nearly constant contact with the enemy as the Second Corps moved south and east from Todd's Tavern toward Spotsylvania Court House.

On May 9 the Twenty-sixth deployed as skirmishers and guided the First Division's advance across the Po River. On the morning of May 10 the Twenty-sixth Michigan and the Eighty-first Pennsylvania were positioned near the Block House Bridge, again with the Michiganians deployed as skirmishers to sound the alarm in case the enemy attempted to cross the Po. Leonard noted that the rebel sharpshooters were "very troublesome."

At about 2:00 P.M. the alarm sounded from the rear, where General George Meade, commanding general of the Army of the Potomac, learned of the approach of rebel infantry from the southwest. Meade sent Second Corps commander General Winfield S. Hancock to supervise the withdrawal of his First Division. The withdrawal back across the river was hectic, at best, and nearly desperate. The exchange of artillery fire was heavy. Two or three regiments never received the order to retire and suffered heavy losses as the enemy force engulfed the abandoned Union positions. The Twenty-sixth took position to cover the division's withdrawal across the river, recrossed following the rest of the division and then deployed on picket. The regiment suffered three wounded and one missing. At the end of the day, Leonard noted in his diary that the Twenty-sixth had become divided and "had a rough time in general" in the Battle of Po River.

That same afternoon five thousand Union troops attacked a salient in the enemy line that was a mile deep and a half-mile across. Grant recognized that the prominence—dubbed the "mule shoe" because of its shape—was a weak point in the rebel line.

Twenty-four-year-old Leonard Hunt joined the Twenty-sixth Michigan Infantry in August 1862. While in command of Company I, Hunt was wounded on May 8, 1864, but he managed to stay with his command. Four days later, he saw action at the Battle of Spotsylvania.

The first Northern attack on the mule shoe was successful but eventually failed for lack of support. Grant then ordered the mule shoe attacked with even greater numbers of men.

In preparation for the attack, the Second Corps was ordered to reconnoiter as far back as Todd's Tavern and south of the Po River. This scouting mission was to be a final check for any significant rebel force threatening the right flank of the Union army before its Second Corps left that section of the line after dark. The First Brigade, which included the Twenty-sixth Michigan, was selected for the assignment.

Colonel Nelson A. Miles divided his brigade into two parts. The 26th Michigan, 81st Pennsylvania and 163rd Pennsylvania were deployed across the Po; the 61st New York and 140th Pennsylvania were deployed to Todd's Tavern. The 26th moved about two miles up the north bank of the Po and then crossed at Tinder's Mill. Again deployed as skirmishers, seeking out enemy positions, the men advanced down the river to find the enemy's left and assess its force. They met the rebel pickets, drove them in and then charged the skirmish line sent to oppose them. Fire was exchanged for half an hour at this position, within three hundred yards of the enemy entrenchments.

Having accomplished their objective, the Union skirmishers retired to their former position north of the river. During this mission the Twenty-sixth suffered three killed and fifteen wounded.

That evening Leonard sought the company of friend and brother-in-law, Arvine Hunter. Not much was said. Leonard simply noted in his diary that "Arvine and myself are together under a big tree."

Just two months older than Leonard, Arvine, son of Robert Hunter Jr. and Caroline Peck, had enlisted in Company I with Leonard in 1862. Entering the service as a sergeant, he ended the war as a second lieutenant.

When their relief arrived on the picket line at about eleven o'clock that night, the men of the Twenty-sixth were ordered to assemble and prepare for a march.

According to a National Park Service pamphlet, the Spotsylvania battlefield looks today much as it did in 1864. Low mounds remind visitors of the rebel works that once stood shoulder high, reinforced with timber. The lush wooded area behind the works may have provided rebel troops cover from the rear. The rebel position was a formidable stronghold.

Because of the lack of cover in the open field that separated the opposing positions, the attackers planned to make their advance just before dawn. Any advantage gained, however, was lost due to the steady rains and uncompromising mud.

In command of Company I, Leonard passed word to the adjutant that the company was ready to march. Rain had been soaking the rolling Virginia landscape since nightfall. The men were drenched and weary and had less than five hours to join the division.

The regiment lurched forward and stumbled ahead. For the first few steps, they became a struggling throng as each man tentatively searched for sure footing. Some sloshed through puddles; others struggled to free their boots from thick, red mud or strode through patches of tall grass.

After four hours, the regiment's progress slowed while the men slogged into deep mud churned by the thousands of men gathering for the assault against the rebel works. The regiment stumbled as the men anticipated an end to their march. The darkness receded and gray clouds appeared on the horizon.

In the rising daylight the Yankees formed for the charge. The ranks closed together, regimental colors were raised and the mass of troops began moving ahead.

The Twenty-sixth assumed a position at the head of the advancing Second Corps. They led the column across an open field and up a rise, where they met scattered gunfire. Expecting to meet the enemy's works on this rush, some of the soldiers began yelling.

Instead, rushing up to the top of the rise, the Union troops found little opposition. Discolored ground off in the distance indicated that the rebel works were still about two hundred yards ahead. Pressing forward, the infantrymen crashed through the abatis constructed from small pine trees. The Union troops aligned themselves and then charged up the final slope.

The Michiganians were among the first Union troops to reach the rebel works. After a brief hand-to-hand encounter, the Twenty-sixth's colors were the first planted on the rebel works. Brigadier General Francis Barlow, commander of the Second Corps' First Division, later recorded: "I remember the thin picket line of the enemy with their bewildered look. There was a little patter of bullets, and I saw a few of our men on the ground: one discharge of artillery . . . and we were up on the works with our hands full of guns, prisoners and colors."

Major Robert Hunter, a rebel staff officer, recorded his view of the Union attack: "The storm had burst upon us. I could see General [Edward] Johnson with his cane striking at the enemy as they leaped over the works, and a sputtering fire swept up and down our line, many guns being damp. I found myself . . . in the midst of foes, who were rushing around me, with confusion and a general melee in full blast."

Leading the Twenty-sixth Michigan, Major Lemuel Saviers became the object of concentrated enemy fire. A musket ball penetrated his chest and entered his left lung. Another musket ball cut left to right passing through both his shoulders. A shell explosion broke three ribs on his left side and bared his lower spine.

The Twenty-sixth became mingled with other regiments and charged along the rebel line at a run, capturing a large number of prisoners, guns and colors. General Winfield S. Hancock reported to General Meade: "My troops are in great disorder, but I am working hard and will soon have them under organization." After advancing about a mile the Union force met rebel works nearly perpendicular to the line they had been rolling through. At this unexpected juncture, the Twenty-sixth, as well as the entire First Brigade, fell back and re-formed.

After 9:00 A.M. the Twenty-sixth, along with the First and Second Divisions of the Second Corps, were essentially out of the action, spending the late morning hours re-forming and constructing works east of the mule shoe's apex. Miraculously alive, Major Saviers was removed from the battlefield. In the meantime, the battle began to concentrate around an angle in the Confederate line west of the apex.

Around noon Captain Nathan Church, acting commander of the Twenty-sixth, led a collection of about one hundred Michiganians and additional troops from the Sixty-first New York to the vicinity of the west angle, where the rebels had returned to their works.

The Yankees crept along the outside of the works they earlier had taken, passing in front of the Second Corps' Second and Third Divisions and some men of the Sixth Corps, to a point nearly opposite a large oak tree that eventually was felled by musket fire. There, the small column overlapped the Confederate line about half the length of the regiment, its right resting near the oak.

Church's band suddenly leaped to their feet and fired a volley over the top of the enemy works. Some lifted themselves over the works and dropped into the entrenchments, wildly swinging their muskets with bayonets fixed. Rebel reinforcements joined the fight, which ensued at point-blank range.

Despite suffering four wounds, Major Lemuel Saviers of Franklin stayed at his post during the Battle of Spotsylvania. He fully recovered from his injures and was promoted to colonel on September 12,

Through the afternoon, the Federal troops maintained firing lines for extended periods of time within ten to twenty yards of the breastworks. Men from both sides fired at each other point-blank through the logs of the works. Soldiers reached over the top of the works with their muskets, blindly firing down the other side. Others engaged in hand-to-hand combat.

The Twenty-sixth fought for more than an hour over the enemy works before the rebels began waving white handkerchiefs on their rammers. Firing ceased and the rebels surrendered. For about eighty yards the Confederate line rose up and approached the captors. At the same moment, they were joined by reinforcements. Most of the rebels quickly returned to their works, except about twenty who were taken prisoner. The Twenty-sixth resumed its fight with the newly arrived rebels until relieved and moved off the line.

In fourteen hours of battle, the Twenty-sixth suffered twenty-seven killed, ninety-seven men wounded and fourteen missing. Most of those missing were determined later to have been killed. Seven out of nine color guards for the regiment were killed or wounded. Leonard survived Spotsylvania unscathed. Army of the Potomac casualties totaled approximately eleven thousand killed, wounded or captured; rebel losses were comparable.

While Leonard survived the horrors of Grant's spring offensive, his wife was losing a battle at home. On August 9, 1864, near Petersburg, Virginia, Leonard learned that Annie's health was failing. He requested a pass home, noting, "I have just received news of the severe illness of my wife who is not expected to survive. The doctor in attendance has given up her case as hopeless."

On August 10 Leonard was granted a fifteen-day leave. The next morning he attempted to walk from camp near Petersburg to City Point on the James River. Stricken by colic, he was forced to return to camp. Before day's end, he left camp again but once more returned to camp. The next morning brother-in-law Arvine accompanied Leonard to City Point in an ambulance. At City Point Leonard boarded the steamer *John*

Brooks, which carried him along the James River up to Fortress Monroe at Hampton Roads and then up the Chesapeake Bay by moonlight to Washington.

In Washington Leonard boarded a train bound for New York and proceeded home to Lowell, carrying his small black diary and hoping to find his Annie alive. Leonard opened the diary and then made the last entry in his 1864 diary on August 13:

> Arrived in Washington at 8 o'clock this A.M. Went up and received pay bought some clothing. Saw Col Farrar on the Street. Also met one of my boys on the street. J. R. Bormund. Left Washington for NY at 6:30 P.M. this is my 24th birthday.

Twenty-year-old Annie died in Lowell that same day.

Despite efforts to extend his leave because of his own failing health, Leonard returned to the field and resumed his post in command of Company I. In March 1865, just a month before the war's end, Leonard was discharged due to disability from chronic illness.

After visiting the Spotsylvania battlefield, I began searching for more information about Leonard Hunt. Files I obtained from the National Archives allowed me to piece together Hunt's military career, but the response from the State Archives of Michigan brought richness of another order. I learned there existed a photograph of Leonard. The inscription—in Leonard's own writing—read, "L. H. Hunt, 1st Lt. Co. I, 26th Mich. Lowell Mich." I presume that the photograph was taken in 1864, after he had been promoted in December 1863.

Through his diary, books and government records, the story of Leonard Hunt has begun to unfold before me. With Leonard's photograph on my desk, I am continuing my research with inspiration. Now, when I ask myself about my great-great-grandfather's thoughts and emotions in 1864, I can look at his photograph while I piece my image of him together in my mind.

The Trial and Execution of the Lincoln Conspirators

By Judge R. A. Watts

*At the end of the Civil War Lieutenant Colonel Richard A. Watts of Adrian
found himself caught up in the nation's greatest conspiracy trial.
Watts, a participant in the Lincoln conspirators' trial proceedings,
gives an eyewitness account of their trial and execution.*

One of the most interesting contributions to wartime history made in recent years is this story of the trial and execution of the Lincoln conspirators as told by the late Judge R. A. Watts of Adrian, Michigan, and published serially in the Adrian *Telegram*, in April 1914. Its inclusion of material not previously been made public warrants its preservation in permanent form; it is here reproduced substantially as published in the *Telegram*. Of the narrator the *Telegram* says in its issue of April 17: "Judge Watts, whose military service extended throughout the war writes from the standpoint of not only an eye-witness, but of an active participant, At the time he was attached to the staff of General Hartranft and was on duty at the federal prison at Washington throughout that tense and exciting period, as acting assistant adjutant general. His duties included the carrying of all dispatches between Secretary Stanton and the prison, and the handling of many official orders, and he was in constant personal touch with every detail of the momentous proceedings, from the reception of the prisoners to their death and burial." In his eighty-third year, Judge Watts died on June 25, 1920, at his home in Adrian.

• • • • •

At the time of the assassination of President Lincoln I was at home, recovering from a wound received during the final assault upon the Confederate lines in front of Petersburg, April 2, 1865.

When I returned about April 25 I found our old division in camp near Alexandria, eight or ten miles from Washington, and at once reported to General Hartranft in command on whose staff I had served during the last year.

Within a day or two after my return an order from the war department was delivered to the general, directing him to report at once at the Washington arsenal, in the city of Washington, for special duty. Accompanying this order was a private note from Major General Hancock, commanding the middle military division, saying that the special duty, for which the general had been detached, might continue for several months and that he was at liberty to take with him such of his personal staff as he might choose.

The general handed me the order of the secretary of war and the note of General Hancock, with instructions to be ready to accompany him.

Within an hour the command of the division had been transferred to General Griffin, the next officer in rank, and we were mounted and on our way to Washington. Neither of us had the remotest guess what the special duty might be, and it may be imagined that our curiosity was at high tension during that ride.

As we rode upon the Long Bridge, spanning the Potomac, I was most forcibly reminded of the last time I had passed over it and the marvelous contrast between then and now. That was on Wednesday following the first battle of Bull Run. I was then a private soldier stretched out in an ambulance by the side of Captain Will Graves, my company commander, who like myself, was suffering from a fierce attack of the measles. My wound had not been dressed, and my clothes were stiff with blood and dirt; each jolt of the ambulance caused severe pain.

The first battle had resulted in an utter rout and shameful retreat. To me, weak from the loss of blood and most fearfully sick, everything looked awfully dark. On the seat by the side of the driver sat the late Captain J. H. Fee, then Corporal Fee, my chum in college and comrade in arms. He was the quartermaster, commissary, surgeon and nurse for this squad of two.

At this crossing four years later the war was over, the Union preserved no more battles, no more wounds, home not far away. I was well-mounted, wearing the uniform and sword of a staff officer, riding by the side of the major general I loved so well, and in excellent health. All the world looked happy and my own heart sang with joy.

On reaching the entrance to the arsenal grounds we were met by Major Benton of the ordnance department, who seemed to be expecting the general, as he at once escorted us to the residence part of the old District of Columbia prison but unused as a prison for a number of years. We there found quarters provided for us, consisting of pleasant rooms with desks, tables, chairs, beds and stationery, all ready for use and needful for comfort.

Very soon General Hancock and several of his staff drove up and the general at once explained that this place had been designated as a military prison for the confinement during the trial, of the parties charged with the conspiracy to assassinate the president and others, and told General Hartranft that he had been selected as special provost marshal general to be in command, and that he would at once be furnished an official order from President Johnson defining his duties.

We then passed back into the prison proper and there found a number of cells, constructed in the usual manner of early days, with walls, ceiling and floors of heavy stone masonry, opening into corridors. These cells had lately been cleaned and prepared ready for use.

After returning to the office provided, General Hancock earnestly impressed upon General Hartranft that the secretary of war and others were in possession of facts, indicating that the conspiracy to assassinate was widespread, and that there was apprehension lest there might be an organized attempt to rescue these assassins. He then added, "You have been selected for this command because of the confidence Secretary Stanton has in your fidelity and courage."

I, who had served at his side from the Wilderness until the final close throughout all those trying days during which every soldier showed the mettle of which he was made, felt that I knew the general as well as any other man and was made very proud that he had been thus distinguished.

But, notwithstanding the honor thus bestowed upon the general and my appreciation of his kindness in keeping me with him, I was free to admit to myself that the situation was not to my taste. I had but little liking for cells and bars and the mystery and things whispered but not seen. As the situation developed from day to day, I liked it much less.

It grew to be extremely gruesome.

The next morning a brigade of infantry, a battery of artillery and a battalion of cavalry reported to General Hartranft and went into camp just outside the arsenal grounds and during the day one of the regiments marched inside the enclosure and stacked arms.

The Washington arsenal is situated on a point of land at the foot of Four and One Half street, near the navy yard; on the west and south it is touched by the Potomac River, on the east by a deep channel for the use of vessels. My memory is that in 1865 it was surrounded by a high board fence, with a high gate at the entrance.

The prison building was an old-fashioned brick structure sixty to eighty feet wide, three stories high, about two hundred feet long. It stood in the center of a large area, surrounded except at the entrance by a thick brick wall twenty or thirty feet high, after the usual manner of state prison enclosures.

On the afternoon of this day a heavy guard was stationed all around the main enclosure, and from that time until the prison was closed in July neither egress nor exit to or from these grounds was permitted, except on a written pass. The only exception was the coming in and passing out of a regiment of infantry each morning as the guard was relieved. The same regiment never returned nor did the same soldier ever stand guard twice on the same spot. When all the regiments of the brigade had once been used as guards, another brigade took its place, and thus many regiments were used during the two months' time we occupied this place.

On the second morning General Hancock visited us again. At that time it was considered necessary that we have more assistance in the main prison building, and Colonel McCall of the 200th Pennsylvania, Colonel Frederick of the 209th, Colonel Dodd of the 211th, and Lieutenant Geisinger of the 208th, all of our old division and all exceptionally trusted officers, were ordered to report at once, and all remained until after the execution in July following. Assistant Surgeon George L. Porter of the regular army, a nephew of Admiral Porter, also reported and was added to the staff and remained with us until after the prison was closed.

A week or two later my old comrade Captain Rath, with whom I had served for two years in the Seventeenth Michigan Infantry, was also ordered to report for such special duty as might be required.

Soon after dark of the second day Colonel L. C. Baker, chief of the government secret service, came to the prison, accompanied by four secret service officers, who were assigned quarters and remained on duty continuously until after the execution in July.

Near midnight General Hartranft, Colonel Baker, the four detective officers and Colonels Dodd, Frederick and McCall, with a company of infantry, moved down to the wharf in the rear of the prison, and on a signal from Colonel Baker a gunboat lying at anchor in the Potomac steamed alongside and the commandant of the vessel delivered to General Hartranft the prisoners Lewis Payne, G.A. Atzerodt, David Herold, Spangler, O'Laughlin, Samuel Arnold and Dr. [Samuel] Mudd, all heavily ironed. They were at once placed between two lines of armed soldiers, marched to the prison and placed in separate cells.

An evening or so after, Colonel Baker and another officer brought Mrs. Surratt in a closed carriage. She was for the time being also placed in a cell but subsequently removed to a room on the third floor.

From the time the prisoners entered these cells until their execution on July 7, two armed soldiers stood guard, night and day, at the door of each cell, while at the main door leading into the prison apartment either Colonel Dodd, Colonel McCall, or Colonel Frederick, with a company of infantry, were at all times on duty. The company of soldiers was relieved each morning, others always taking their place, and, as in the case of the outside guard, the same men never returned a second time and no soldier ever stood guard at the same post twice, nor more than two hours.

To avoid self-destruction, each of the prisoners, except Mrs. Surratt, was compelled to wear a thickly padded hood upon his head, with only holes for his eyes and a slit at the mouth, through which he was fed.

The handcuffs consisted of heavy bands of iron about each wrist, connected by a bar ten inches in length; upon the ankles an iron band was riveted, connected by a chain of only sufficient length to permit short steps, and to this chain was attached an iron weight. These manacles upon wrists and ankles were worn continuously, all during imprisonment, night and day.

Mrs. Surratt was never manacled and, although always under strict guard, was furnished suitable wholesome food, and at all times and in all ways was treated with the courtesy, lenity and kindness due to her sex. During much of the time she occupied a large airy room on the third floor, and her daughter Anna was frequently permitted to be with her.

As the summer advanced the heat became so intense that danger of insanity or death, caused by the fearful

A veteran corps commander of Gettysburg and the 1864 Virginia Campaign, General Winfield Scott Hancock had the task of overseeing the prisoners charged with conspiring to assassinate President Abraham Lincoln.

heat of these hoods, seemed greater than the possibility of self-destruction and the hoods were removed.

While the health and safety of these men were guarded with the utmost vigilance, to make certain that the gallows should not be robbed, it must be confessed but little care was taken for their comfort. Indeed, it is beyond question that no prison of modern times was ever guarded with such rigid rules and severe discipline.

I held the official position of acting assistant adjutant general. My duties never brought me into personal contact with any of the prisoners, and I rarely saw any of them, except as they were seated in the courtroom during the trial. However, all orders, communications, reports and official papers pertaining to the management of the prison came within my department and I was familiar with all that transpired.

Assistant Surgeon Porter made personal examination of each prisoner twice each day, and his report was incorporated into the general report each day made of all conditions about the prison and a copy furnished the War Department.

General Hancock visited the prison at least once a day during the time of our occupancy, and General Thomas Eckhert, then one of the assistant secretaries of war, also spent much time each day in and about the prison. He was afterwards for many years president and general manager of the Western Union Telegraph company.

By means of the daily reports of Generals Hancock, Eckhert and Hartranft, the great secretary of war was kept in constant touch with every detail, and it was well understood that it was his iron hand that controlled and specified every precaution for the safe keeping of the prisoners here confined.

A room in the third story of the building was fitted up for the use of the military commission during the trial. This room was about thirty by fifty feet in area, situated in the northeast corner.

Across the west end was a raised platform used as a dock for the prisoners. At the south end of the dock a door opened from the prison, so that they never passed near any spectator, as they were brought in and taken from the courtroom.

A large table was placed near the north side, for the use of the commission, around which they were seated during the trial. Near the west end of this table was an elevated seat for the use of the witnesses while being examined.

Near the south side was a long table for the use of the official shorthand reporters, Samuel Pitman and the Murphys, father and two sons. Close to the prisoners' dock were two tables for the use of the counsel for defendants. At the east end an elevated seat was occupied by General Hartranft, provost marshal general.

About the first of May President Johnson issued an order convening a military commission for the trial and directed the secretary of war to detail nine competent military officers to serve as such commission. He further directed the judge advocate general to prefer charges against the eight conspirators under arrest and all others alleged to have been associated with them in the conspiracy and to proceed with the trial as speedily as the ends of justice would permit.

The secretary selected Major General David Hunter, General Lew Wallace (author of *Ben Hur* and *The Prince of India*), General A. V. Kautz, General F. M. Harris, General A. P. Howe, General James A. Ekin, General Robert S. Foster, Colonel D. R. Clendenin and Colonel C. H.

Thomkins. General David Hunter was designated as president of the commission.

Judge Advocate General Joseph Holt, Colonel H. L. Burnett and John A. Bingham, a member of Congress from Ohio and appointed special assistant judge advocate for this trial, represented the government.

Within a few days the members of the commission and the prosecuting officers assembled in the room provided. As soon as they were organized ready to proceed, the eight prisoners were brought into the room. Each was seated in the dock by the side of an armed soldier, and at all times thereafter each prisoner was seated between two soldiers while in the courtroom.

Reverdy Johnson, U.S. senator from Maryland, one of the leading constitutional lawyers of the country, appeared as counsel for Mrs. Surratt; associated with him were Messrs. Clampit and Aiken of Washington.

General Thomas Ewing Jr., a son of former Senator Ewing, was retained by Dr. Mudd and Edward Spangler. Frederick Stone of Maryland appeared for Samuel Arnold and young Herold. Walter S. Cox, an able attorney of Charles County, Maryland, was employed by Michael O'Laughlin. Payne and Atzerodt were represented by Doster, a bright young attorney from Baltimore.

The charge and specifications against defendants were then read by Colonel Burnett, assistant judge advocate. The substance of the charge against each was: "maliciously, unlawfully and traitorously, and in aid of the existing armed rebellion against the United States, on or before the 5th day of March, 1865, and on divers other days between that day and the 14th day of April, 1865, combining, confederating and conspiring together, with [naming each defendant] John H. Surratt, John Wilkes Booth, Jefferson Davis, George N. Sanders, Beverly Tucker, Clement C. Clay, Jacob Thompson, and others unknown, to kill and murder Abraham Lincoln, late President, Andrew Johnson, Vice-president, William H. Seward, Secretary of State, and Ulysses S. Grant, then in command of the army of the United States," and so on, closing with the formal parts of the charge.

The specifications varied as to each defendant. Surratt was specifically charged with harboring, concealing, counseling, aiding and abetting all the defendants.

The specifications against Herold was aiding and assisting Booth to escape, knowing he had assassinated the president. Dr. Mudd was alleged to have aided and assisted in the escape of Booth.

The specifications against Payne was assaulting, cutting and wounding Secretary Seward with intent to murder him. Atzerodt was charged with lying in wait with intent to murder Andrew Johnson. That against O'Laughlin was lying in wait with intent to murder Ulysses S. Grant.

Spangler was alleged to have aided Booth in reaching the president's box in the theater and guarding the approach to prevent interference with Booth's attack. Samuel Arnold was charged with counseling, combining, and confederating with each and all of the other defendants.

After the charge and specifications had been read, Senator Reverdy Johnson handed to General Hunter a plea to the jurisdiction of the military commission.

After the plea had been received, General Harris, one of the commissioners, objected to the appearance of Senator Johnson as counsel, claiming that he had written and published a letter advising the citizens of Maryland that the test oath of allegiance was not binding. The voice of General Harris indicated much feeling, when he said that he for one would not permit any man entertaining such sentiments to challenge his right to sit in this trial.

These two, both Southern men, one from West Virginia, the other from Maryland, were typical illustrations of the fierce bitterness entertained between those of the South who were in opposition during the Civil War. Both were large men, and both became excited and aggressive during this controversy.

Senator Johnson seemed to be in a towering rage when replying to this imputation of disloyalty. He said he was licensed to practice his profession before every court in the state of Maryland and before every federal court in the country, including the Supreme Court of the United States and that he had taken the oath of a U.S. senator and occupied his seat unchallenged as to his loyalty. The senator and General Harris glared at each other, with such threatening looks that it seemed as if there might be immediate trouble.

At this point General Wallace suggested that in view of the broad terms of oath of a U.S. senator, it seemed wiser to withdraw the objection. General Harris complied with the suggestion and the plea to the jurisdiction was filed and read.

Mr. Johnson then picked up his hat, bowed to the commission and retired. My memory is that he did not again return to take part in person during the trial.

A copy of the charge and specifications was then delivered to each of the counsel for defendants, and the court adjourned.

After the commission had reconvened on the next morning the prisoners were again brought in and seated in the dock. The taking of testimony was at once begun and continued from day to day, until all the evidence on behalf of the government and of the defendants had been produced, closing about the middle of June.

While I remember much of the general substance of the evidence, it would not seem profitable to attempt to summarize it, as lack of space would forbid.

Mrs. Surratt and Dr. Mudd were convicted chiefly upon the testimony of a Mr. Weichman, who at the time of the assassination and for some time previous had made his home with Mrs. Surratt. He was an intimate friend of the family and had been a college chum of John H. Surratt. If he had at anytime been in sympathy with the conspiracy to assassinate, it did not appear either in his own or any other evidence. He was seemingly not only a willing witness but a "swift witness." Counsel for the defendants did not attack him as severely as it seemed to me they might have done. It

Lewis Powell, an ex-Confederate soldier, stabbed Secretary of State William Seward, then wounded the secretary's son, before running out in the street screaming, "I'm mad! I'm mad!" Powell was sentenced to death for his actions.

may be, however, that they had in mind the legal maxim "Never prove too much."

The most notable witness was General U. S. Grant. His testimony was intended to establish the boundary lines of the military district, which included the city of Washington, and its purpose was to show that the assassination and conspiracy was within the authority of the military and thus born upon the jurisdiction of the military tribunal.

Our office, being on the ground floor of the building, was first entered by the general. He came in alone, his escort remaining outside. This was the first time I had ever met General Grant face to face, and naturally I observed him very closely. I had formed the impression that the general was slow and cautious in both his physical and mental movements and was much surprised to find just the opposite characteristics. When notified that the court was ready for him, he darted out into the corridor and swiftly went up the stairs.

His swift motions nearly caused him a serious, if not fatal, accident at that time. The corridors to each of the three stories of the building were alike, with a door at the end of each, but the outside balcony at the third and second floors had been removed. When the general came downstairs into the second-story corridor, seeing the door at the end, he started swiftly for it and barely saved himself from rushing out and falling fifteen to eighteen feet upon the stone steps at the entrance.

During the long trial, clashes between counsel were frequent and often most spirited.

Mr. Bingham was an able trial lawyer, and at every opening given by opposing counsel he would rake the whole Confederacy, from Jeff Davis all down the line to the prisoners at the bar. The Confederate chief, having been named in the charge, gave a wide range for his savage onslaughts. He always addressed himself directly to the counsel for defendants, and as all of them except General Ewing were Southern men and the loyalty of some of them not of the positive kind, it may be understood that they were often forced to exercise much self-restraint.

General Ewing, however, had a record for loyalty not open to attack. He had held the position of brigadier general in the federal army. His brother, Hugh Ewing, was also a general officer and still in the service. His sister was the wife of General W. T. Sherman, who in skill and great achievements was at least second, if not equal, to either Grant or Lee. More than that he was an able attorney, splendidly equipped and he never hesitated to strike back with vigorous blows.

The duty of preparing the evidence and presenting it in logical sequence largely fell to Colonel H. L. Burnett, assistant judge advocate, and was performed with much skill. No one connected with the trial had a more minute familiarity with all the details.

Judge Holt was an elderly man of even, conservative temperament. He had been at one time on the bench in Kentucky. During the trial he seemed to act as legal adviser to the commission and often intervened to quiet disputes between counsel. I remember him as the Nestor of the legal members present during the trial.

It has been asserted many times that the trial was behind closed doors. That is not true; yet it must be conceded that but few of the general public could gain admission to the courtroom.

The limited space would admit but few at a time, and the officials, attorneys and guards almost filled it. However, many military officers, judges, governors, senators, members of Congress and others of sufficient influence to secure a pass, were admitted. It is needless to say that, under no circumstances, could anyone gain entrance to the arsenal grounds, much less to the courtroom, without evidence of loyalty free from doubt.

After the testimony had closed, in order to give counsel time to prepare their arguments, the court adjourned until June 16.

When the commission reconvened, the first argument, having been prepared by Senator Johnson, counsel for Mrs. Surratt, was read by Mr. Clampit, associate counsel. The substance of the senator's argument was a very elaborate and able discussion of the plea to the jurisdiction of the military commission, which had been filed when the defendants were first arraigned.

The special points raised by counsel were:

1. The crime charged was not an offense against any military rule or law, but was a crime cognizable only by the common and statute law, and therefore not triable by a military tribunal.

2. That the civil courts in the District of Columbia were all open and exercising all their functions without hindrance or obstruction of any kind whatever.

3. That each of the defendants was a civilian and had at no time belonged to any branch of the military service of the United States, and therefore entitled to a trial before a jury of twelve men and in a civil court.

4. That at the time of the trial the war had closed by the surrender of all the insurgent armies and navies.

Attorneys Ewing and Cox following also made very able arguments along the same line, and in addition analyzed and discussed the evidence, so far as it applied to their respective clients. The argument of General Ewing was particularly emphatic and almost caustic, even going so far as to insist that the finding and sentences of the commission could not be justified under even the color of lawful authority.

The other attorneys made able arguments in behalf of their clients and, with the exception of Payne, Atzerodt and Herold, insisted with all the power at their command that the rule of reasonable doubt should apply and that if applied, it would acquit their clients.

To those who listened as spectators, however, this rule of reasonable doubt had but little if any place in this trial. It seemed to be only a question of probabilities. Neither the members of the commission nor the people of the North were in a frame of mind to entertain or even tolerate any technical rules.

These nine soldiers constituting the judges in this case had but little sympathy or patience with the sentimental saying that "It is better that ninety-nine guilty escape than one innocent should suffer." The suffering of the innocent during the last four years had filled the measure. There was no place for sympathy here, and every attempt to create favor by appeals of that nature met with frowns and disapproval.

The arguments of counsel lasted about two weeks, closing near the last of June. Mr. Bingham consumed several days in his closing address.

I recall Mr. Bingham with a clearer vision than any of the other attorneys or members of the commission. He was of small stature, a spare but most expressive face, and when excited his eyes fairly glowed. During his address he wore a long, black coat, after the fashion of that day. It reached almost to his shoe tops. When referring to the rebellion or any of its leaders, especially Mr. Davis, his invective burned and seared like hot iron, but when he touched upon the great and lovable qualities of the martyred Lincoln his lips would quiver with emotion and his voice become as tender and reverent as if he were repeating the Lord's Prayer.

On June 30 the commission convened to consider the verdict and fix the penalties.

It may be of interest at this place to state some of the powers and duties of a military commission, which are much greater than those of the ordinary jury in criminal cases.

This tribunal was law unto itself. It made its own rules of procedure. It was the sole judge of the law, as well as of the facts. It passed upon the admissibility of all evidence offered during the trial, and exceptions to its rulings were not entertained or recorded. It was empowered not only to decide the question of guilt, but it also had the power, and it was its duty, to fix the penalties.

The president of the United States, and he only, could review, change, modify, approve or disapprove of the findings or sentences.

The deliberations of the commission were behind closed doors, only the members of the commission and the judge advocate and his assistant were present.

The verdict and sentence were required to be assented to by only two-thirds of the members of the commission. Nothing in the records, so far as I ever knew, stated whether the verdict was unanimously agreed upon, or by only two-thirds, as the form of the verdict followed the form uniformly adopted. It was substantially as follows:

> After mature consideration of the evidence in the case of _____ the commission find the said _____ of the specification guilty, of the charge guilty, and the commission do therefore sentence him the said _____ to be hanged by the neck until he be dead, at such time and place as the president shall direct. Two-thirds of the commission concurring therein.

The same form was used in the cases of Payne, Herold, Atzerodt and Mrs. Surratt. In the case of O'Laughlin, Spangler, Arnold and Dr. Mudd the only variation was in the sentences. Spangler was sentenced to imprisonment at hard labor for the term of six years at such place as the president shall direct. Dr. Mudd, O'Laughlin and Arnold were sentenced to hard labor for life at such place as the president should direct.

On the 5th of July the president issued the following order:

> The foregoing sentences in the cases of David E. Herold, G. A. Atzerodt, Lewis Payne and Mary E. Surratt are hereby approved and it is ordered that the sentences in the cases of David E. Herold, G. A. Atzerodt, Lewis Payne and Mary E. Surratt be carried into execution by the proper military authority under the direction of the secretary of war on the 7th day of July, 1865, between the hours of 10 o'clock A.M. and 2 o'clock P.M. of that day.

On the same day the president made a further order directing that O'Laughlin, Arnold, Spangler and Dr. Mudd be confined in the military prison at Dry Tortugas in accordance with their sentences.

On the morning of the Seventh Messrs. Clampit and

Aiken, counsel for Mrs. Surratt, applied to Judge Wyle of the District of Columbia for a writ of habeas corpus for their client. The judge issued the writ and caused it to be served upon General Hancock, commanding him to produce the body of said Mary E. Surratt before him at 10 A.M. of that day at the criminal courtroom in the city of Washington.

General Hancock immediately sent a staff officer notifying General Hartranft of the situation and cautioned the general to instruct the guards not to admit the United States marshal to the grounds of the prison under any circumstances, as he understood a like writ had been issued directed to General Hartranft.

If such writ had been issued, it was never served and indeed could not be served for the reason that the marshal could not have gained entrance to the prison grounds.

As soon as President Johnson learned the writ had been issued, he promptly made an order suspending the writ and specifically directed General Hancock to state the fact of the suspension of the writ, as his return thereto, and to proceed with the execution in accordance with the previous order.

Between one and two o'clock of that day, July 7, Mrs. Surratt, Herold, Atzerodt and Payne were removed from their cells and escorted by a soldier on each side to the gallows standing in the open area inside of the high brick wall. Mrs. Surratt was accompanied by two Catholic priests, each carrying a crucifix and breviary and uttering a prayer that Mrs. Surratt seemed to be repeating. This scene was most solemn and affecting. Each of the others was also attended by a clergyman.

The four were assisted to ascend the steps leading up to the gallows platform and seated in chairs. Major General Hartranft and staff, in full dress uniform, passed up onto the platform, and the General at once in a low, quiet tone read the sentences. While reading, the general's hat was removed and, the sun being excessively hot, the writer of this narrative held an umbrella over him.

The ropes, fastened to a cross beam above, dangled in front of each. The noose was quickly adjusted upon each by a secret service officer and they were required to rise and step forward upon the traps, Mrs. Surratt and Payne upon one, Herold and Atzerodt upon the other. The traps were held in position by heavy braces beneath. Captain Rath gave a signal, the two braces were knocked from under by a heavy beam swung by two soldiers, and the four simultaneously dropped to death and eternity.

After thirty minutes each was examined by Surgeon Porter, pronounced dead, taken down and placed in separate boxes. To avoid any mistake in identification in the future, I wrote the name of each upon a slip of paper, sealed it up in a small bottle and placed it in each respective box.

A detail of soldiers at once closed the covers and buried them in separate graves just inside the prison wall.

Within a day or two the other four—Arnold, Spangler, O'Laughlin and Dr. Mudd—were placed upon a man-of-war and taken under charge of Colonel Dodd to the military prison at Dry Tortugas.

The remains of Booth had been buried underneath one of the prison cells the night before our occupying the prison.

Thus closed the long trial by the punishment of the active members of this most wicked conspiracy—a trial which, because of the worldwide fame of Abraham Lincoln and of the cowardly and execrable manner of his taking off and because of the love of a great people that will continue all down the ages, will be known as the most famous recorded in the history of America.

During the time of the execution, Major General Hancock and staff and a number of other military officers of rank, in full uniform with side arms, and many officials of the government, stood near the gallows; a battalion of infantry stood at attention inside the wall, and another battalion fully armed were stationed upon the high wall surrounding the prison.

The order of the president, that the sentences of these parties "be carried into execution by the proper military authorities under the direction of the secretary of war," was certainly obeyed with all the formality and dignity that would be expected of two such soldiers as General Hancock and General Hartranft. The whole was most solemn and impressive.

During our charge of the prison we also received for safe keeping Burton Harrison, who had served as private secretary to President Davis during the existence of the Confederacy; Prof. McCullough of North Carolina, reputed to be a skillful chemist; and General Harris, a congressman from Missouri before the war and afterwards a senator from the same state in the Confederate congress.

So far as I know, no specific charge was ever made against either of these parties.

Mr. Davis was at that time in prison at Fortress Monroe, in charge of General Miles. I suppose Mr. Harrison was held upon the presumption that, if Davis could be shown to have encouraged or approved of the assassination of President Lincoln, his private secretary would have knowledge of the fact.

I remember Mr. Harrison as having an unusually strong, intellectual face and understood that he was a young man of fine literary attainments. He was excessively dignified and haughty, but whether these characteristics were natural, or whether he had imbibed them from his great chief, I do not know. He subsequently married a Miss Cary of Virginia, who has written many charming reminiscences and stories of those tumultuous days. Mr. Harrison's son, Burton Harrison Jr., is now one of the most vigorous and able members of Congress from New York and a very influential leader and adviser of the Democratic party. (He is now governor of the Philippines.)

Professor McCullough was suspected to have assisted in preparing clothing infected with smallpox and yellow fever for distribution in New York, Philadelphia and other Northern cities, and in an attempt to place poison in the Croton Reservoir in New York. General Harris had written a letter, introducing McCullough to President Davis and commending him as an expert chemist.

After the execution and removal of the conspirators, Mr. Harrison was taken by Captain Rath to Fort Delaware. General Harris was taken to Fort McHenry by the writer. I do not recall the disposition of McCullough.

After the purposes of the military prison were fulfilled, the writer in compliance with the order of the War Department, at once caused all official reports, orders and documents pertaining to the prison, to be boxed up and in person delivered them to Judge Advocate General Holt.

While a receipt was being prepared, I was seated in Judge Holt's office when the execution was mentioned. I said that all the officers at the prison were much surprised that, because of her sex, the sentence of Mrs. Surratt had not been commuted.

The substance of the judge's reply was that the president believed that she had been as guilty as any of the others but added that he might not have insisted on her execution, but for the imprudent action of her attorneys in obtaining the writ of habeas corpus. Everyone, he said, who knew Mr. Johnson, understood that he would not tolerate an attempt to force him into any action, and when he learned of the writ of habeas corpus the president became very angry and promptly ordered the execution to be carried into effect.

I mention this statement of Judge Holt because of a subsequent bitter dispute between him and the president, wherein the president sought to charge Judge Holt with misleading him into ordering Mrs. Surratt to be hung. It is, at least, a part of the *res gestae* of that controversy.

One of the last official acts of President Johnson was granting pardons to Dr. Mudd, Samuel Arnold and Edward Spangler. For this he received bitter censure from many. Having heard the testimony against these men and observed them during the trial, I have always felt glad that they were released. Michael O'Laughlin died in prison.

The successful management of all the details of the military prison fully justified the confidence reposed in General Hartranft. When the prison was closed, he not only received the commendation of General Hancock and the secretary of war, but also the thanks of the members of the commission and the attorneys on each side for his uniform courtesy and assistance during the long trial. But I felt that the most touching compliment, and I believe the most appreciated by him, was the sincerely expressed kind wishes of all the prisoners as their last good-bye.

There has been much discussion as to the merits of the question of the jurisdiction of the military commission, as well as to the question whether the evidence was sufficient to warrant the conviction, at least of a part of the defendants.

Whatever may be the better construction of the constitution and the law on the question of jurisdiction, it cannot be fairly said that this commission should be criticised for maintaining their authority to try these defendants. It must be remembered that they were soldiers, wearing the uniform of the U.S. Army, still in the service, subject to the orders of the commander-in-chief, the president of the United States, and to the commands of the secretary of war; that this commission was ordered by the president, and that these officers had been detailed for this special duty, and had been directed to proceed with the trial of the persons.accused of the murder of Abraham Lincoln.

That these soldiers should be expected to refuse to obey and to desert their post is most absurd. Indeed, if they had disobeyed, they would have been subject to court-martial and dismissed from the service in disgrace. It is the soldier's duty to obey and not to ask the reason why.

It would seem that the learned counsel must have known in advance that their able arguments would fall upon deaf ears, and it must have been that their only purpose was maintaining their reputation as members of their profession when the history of the trial should be written.

In anticipation of this grave question, the charge and specifications had been drawn with skill and great foresight.

The charge was "maliciously, unlawfully, and traitorously, and in aid of the existing armed rebellion against the United States combining, confederating, and conspiring together to kill and murder Abraham Lincoln, president, Andrew Johnson, vice-president, William H. Seward, secretary of state, and Ulysses S. Grant, then in command of the armies of the United States."

Being "in aid of the existing rebellion" and against the heads of the government, made the crime of a higher and greater grade than the simple murder of an individual; it was also a crime against the life of the government itself.

It may be seriously questioned whether the framers of the Constitution intended to prohibit the trial of even citizens before a military tribunal under circumstances and conditions then existing.

The trial and swift punishment of these execrable assassins was of the utmost importance. The excitement throughout all the land, North and South, was intense. The very air in and about Washington was murky with suspicion; whispers and rumors of contemplated assassinations were everywhere. President Johnson, members of the cabinet, commanders of the armies and other leading men of the administration were surrounded with cordons of guards for their protection. It may be well said that the country at large might have suffered far greater by temporizing, quibblings and delays than by any technical infraction of the strict letter of the constitution. General Grant spoke wisely when he said, "The will of the people is the law of the land."

At that time it was patent to everyone that a trial of these people before a jury impaneled in the District of Columbia would have failed to convict. Why make a farce of a cause of such stupendous importance? The trial and failure to convict John H. Surratt for the same offense two years later, before a civil jury, verified the wisdom of the military tribunal in this case.

As to the actual guilt of Atzerodt, Herold and Payne, there was no room for doubt. In the cases of Arnold, O'Laughlin, Spangler, Dr. Mudd and Mrs. Surratt there was much contradictory testimony. If the government witnesses were entitled to credit, the verdict was justified. If the witnesses for the defendants told the truth, there was room for doubt and for reasonable doubt, particularly in the cases of Arnold and Spangler.

Four of the conspirators in the Lincoln assassination were sentenced to death for their crimes. On July 7, 1865, they were hanged at the arsenal grounds of Washington's Old Penitentiary Building.

But here entered the serious difficulty for these defendants. All or nearly all the witnesses for the defense were either active sympathizers with the rebellion, or at best of most doubtful loyalty to the government. More than all else however every one of the defendants were most bitter in their hatred of Mr. Lincoln and the United States Government. These facts were the terrible make-weights that condemned them, where otherwise there might have been hope. What a boon to Arnold, Spangler and Mudd would a fair reputation for loyalty have been!

It has been said that the conspiracy to assassinate the president, vice-president and other chief officers of the government was but the wild scheme of crazy men. The same was also said of John Brown and his fanatical followers in their raid at Harper's Ferry. But may it not also be said, with equal plausibility, that such insanity was but another form of the same disease that in the early days of 1861 dominated many of the best and brainiest men of the South, impelling them to organize the most gigantic conspiracy recorded in history, with intent to assassinate the best government in the world, solely because the wisest and most lovable of men had been elected president? Having thus referred to the leaders of the rebellion, I may be pardoned if I add a word, in recognition of the valor, and as I believe, the good intentions of the common people of the South in following their states into secession.

After the governors and legislatures of the eleven states had, under the forms of regularity, withdrawn their states from the union and ratified the organization of the confederacy, then the question arose as to which government should have their allegiance. Add to this the fact that our Northern armies were rapidly organizing, with the avowed purpose of marching into their states and forcing them to return to the union. It certainly is not surprising that such gallant men should take up arms, in what they felt to be in defense of their states, and, as many of them believed, of their homes and firesides.

Unfortunately the people of the South were rushed into a choice so swiftly that they were only given opportunity to remember the first half of the historical proverb, that, regardless of the merit of the question or the motive of the participants, "Successful revolution is always called patriotism, and unsuccessful rebellion is forever branded treason."

There's much more

from the editors of

Thank God for Michigan! Collector's Issue

The most comprehensive—and colorful—look at Michigan in the Civil War in more than 30 years! This double-sized issue features more than 20 articles by some of the most respected names in Civil War research, and is illustrated with more than 200 rare and never-before-published images. 120 pages. $7.00

Thank God for Michigan! T-Shirt

The flag of the First Michigan Infantry is the backdrop for the words and likeness of Abraham Lincoln. Black cotton/poly t-shirt, adult sizes: S, M, L, XL, XXL. $14.95

Michigan's Civil War Flags Note Card Set

This handsome note card set features flags from Michigan regiments— Sixth Cavalry (shown), First Light Artillery, Second Infantry and Fourteenth Infantry. The back of each card offers a brief flag history; inside, the cards are blank so you may write personal messages. Set contains eight full-color cards (approx. 4½" x 6½") and eight envelopes. $6.00

Call 1-800-366-3703 or visit our web site:

on the Civil War

Michigan History Magazine

Michigan Soldiers in the Civil War

Updated and expanded fourth edition features new photographs, a new preface and more exciting information. A must-have for every Civil War enthusiast. By Frederick D. Williams. Illustrated. 88 pages. $6.95

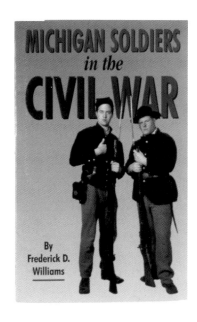

Thank God for Michigan! Coffee Mug

The mug tells the story of Abraham Lincoln saying "Thank God for Michigan!" when he saw the First Michigan Infantry march into Washington, DC. Mug also features the flag of the First and a likeness of the Civil War president. Eleven-ounce black ceramic mug. $7.95

Michigan's Civil War Soldiers Note Card Set

These images reach through the years to give you a glimpse of a few of Michigan's 90,000 Union soldiers. Featured are officers of the Michigan Cavalry Brigade (shown); an unidentified Fourth Michigan Infantry corporal; men of the Fourth's Company D; and congressional Medal of Honor winner Smith Hastings. Cards have a historical note on the back and are blank inside. Set contains eight cards (approx. 4½" x 6½") and eight envelopes. $6.00

www.sos.state.mi.us/history/mag/mag.html

ACKNOWLEDGEMENTS

Michigan and the Civil War: An Anthology was produced by the staff of *Michigan History Magazine*: **Dr. Roger L. Rosentreter**, editor; **Diana Paiz Engle**, associate editor; and **Paul D. Mehney** and **Sharon E. McHaney**, assistant editors. Additional editorial assistance provided by **Services for Publishers/Holland**. Text file production: **Mary Jo Remensnyder**, secretary. Order fulfillment: **Joni Russell White**, circulation clerk. Electronic book production: **Salt River Graphics/Shepherd**; and **TypeAlign, Inc./Lansing**.

Michigan History Magazine is one of the nation's leading state history magazines. First published in 1917, the award-winning bimonthly offers a contemporary and colorful perspective on Michigan heritage. Look for "Thank God for Michigan!" the 120-page Civil War collector's issue, and *Michigan Soldiers in the Civil War*, one of the magazine's best-selling Heritage Publications, now in its fourth edition. For order and subscription information telephone 1-800-366-3703.

PHOTO CREDITS

BIBLIOGRAPHY

"For the Glory of the Peninsular State," by Roger L. Rosentreter, appeared originally as "Michigan, My Michigan" in the May/June 1998 issue of *Michigan History Magazine* (vol. 82, no. 3). **"Profane, Hard Drinking and Eternally Grim,"** by Maria Quinlan Leiby, appeared in January/February 1994 (vol. 78, no. 1). **"Bound to See the President,"** edited by Frank L. Byrne, appeared in July/August 1979 (vol. 63, no. 4). **"Captured At Shiloh!,"** by Larry Houghton, appeared in March/April 1993 (vol. 77, no. 2). **"The Worst Colonel I Ever Saw,"** by Robert C. Myers, appeared in January/February 1996 (vol. 80, no. 1). **"Skirmishing At Shiloh,"** by Joseph Ruff, appeared originally as "Civil War Experiences of Joseph Ruff" in 1943 (vol. 27, no. 2). **"Captured At Bull Run,"** by Tony L. Trimble, appeared originally as "Michigan Profiles: William Herbert Withington" in July/August 1994 (vol. 78, no. 4). **"The Second Michigan Joins the Army of the Potomac,"** edited by Chester M. Destler, appeared originally as "The Second Michigan Volunteer Infantry Regiment Joins the Army of the Potomac" in 1957 (vol. 41). **"Alias Franklin Thompson,"** by Betty Fladeland, appeared originally as "New Light on Sarah Emma Edmonds, Alias Franklin Thompson" in 1963 (vol. 47). **"A China Doll for Abbie,"** by Larry Wakefield, appeared in September/October 1996 (vol. 80, no. 5). **"A Michigan Soldier Views Slavery,"** edited by George Blackburn, appeared originally as "The Negro as Viewed by a Michigan Civil War Soldier" in 1963 (vol. 47). **"From Allegan to Andersonville,"** by Albert Castel, appeared in July/August 1992 (vol. 74, no. 4). **"Guns, Grain and Iron Ore,"** by Albert Blum, appeared in May/June 1985 (vol. 69, no. 3). **"Rendering Invaluable Service,"** by Steven Dunker, appeared in January/February 1992 (vol. 76, no. 1). **"Fighting Is Not Very Funny Business,"** by Roger L. Rosentreter, appeared originally as "Samuel Hodgman's Civil War" in November/December 1980 (vol. 64, no. 6). **"Their Greatest Battle War Getting Into the Fight,"** by Hondon Hargrove, appeared in January/February 1991 (vol. 75, no. 1). **"Those Damned Black Hats,"** by Roger L. Rosentreter, appeared in July/August 1991 (vol. 75, no. 4). **"I Am An American,"** by Jessie Moore Loveridge, appeared originally as "Historical Notes: Colonel Orlando Moore" in 1931 (vol. 15, no. 2). **"Dearest Ben,"** by Albert Castel, appeared in May/June 1987 (vol. 71, no. 3). **"The Capture and Escape of Edwin Bigelow,"** edited by Frank L. Klement, appeared originally as "Edwin Bigelow: A Michigan Sergeant in the Civil War" in 1954 (vol. 38). **"Uneasy Neighbors,"** by Martin J. Havran, appeared originally as "Windsor and Detroit Relations During the Civil War" in 1954 (vol. 38). **"Return to Spotsylvania,"** by Bob Korroch, appeared in March/April 1994 (vol. 78, no. 2). **"The Trial and Execution of the Lincoln Conspirators,"** by Richard A. Watts, appeared in 1922 (vol. 6, no. 1).